Learning Technologies and User Interaction

Learning Technologies and User Interaction explores the complex interplay between educational technologies and those who rely on them to construct knowledge and develop skills. As learning and training continue to move onto digital platforms, tools such as artificial intelligence, predictive analytics, video games, virtual reality, and more hold considerable potential to foster advanced forms of synergy across contexts. Showcasing a variety of contributors who are attuned to today's networked technologies, environments, and learning dynamics, this book is ideal for students and scholars of educational technology, instructional design, professional development, and research methods.

Kay K. Seo is Professor of Instructional Design and Technology at the University of Cincinnati, USA.

Scott Gibbons is Adjunct Professor and Student Teacher Supervisor at the University of Cincinnati, USA.

Learning Technologies and User Interaction

Diversifying Implementation in Curriculum, Instruction, and Professional Development

Edited by Kay K. Seo and Scott Gibbons

Routledge
Taylor & Francis Group
NEW YORK AND LONDON

First published 2022
by Routledge
605 Third Avenue, New York, NY 10158

and by Routledge
2 Park Square, Milton Park, Abingdon, Oxon, OX14 4RN

Routledge is an imprint of the Taylor & Francis Group, an informa business

Library of Congress Cataloging-in-Publication Data
Names: Seo, Kay Kyeong-Ju editor. | Gibbons, Scott (Professor) editor.
Title: Learning technologies and user interaction : diversifying implementation in curriculum, instruction, and professional development/edited by Kay K. Seo, Scott Gibbons.
Description: New York, NY : Routledge, 2022. | Includes bibliographical references.
Identifiers: LCCN 2021012792 (print) | LCCN 2021012793 (ebook) | ISBN 9780367536336 (hardback) | ISBN 9780367545635 (paperback) | ISBN 9781003089704 (ebook)
Subjects: LCSH: Educational technology. | Computer-assisted instruction—Design. | Computer-assisted instruction—Curricula—Planning. | Career development.
Classification: LCC LB1028.3 .L37834 2022 (print) | LCC LB1028.3 (ebook) | DDC 371.33—dc23
LC record available at https://lccn.loc.gov/2021012792
LC ebook record available at https://lccn.loc.gov/2021012793

ISBN: 978-0-367-53633-6 (hbk)
ISBN: 978-0-367-54563-5 (pbk)
ISBN: 978-1-003-08970-4 (ebk)

DOI: 10.4324/9781003089704

Typeset in Bembo
by Apex CoVantage, LLC

Contents

Contributor Biographies

Mahir Akgun received his PhD in learning, design, and technology with a graduate minor in educational psychology from the Pennsylvania State University. He earned a BS in instructional technology and an MS in cognitive science from Middle East Technical University. He currently teaches statistics and data visualization courses in the College of Information Sciences and Technology at Penn State. His current research broadly focuses on human-centered learning analytics, search as learning, and epistemic agency. He uses both qualitative and quantitative research methods in his research.

Corey Duzan has worked in K–12 and postsecondary education for over 16 years in the disciplines of technology and engineering education. He has created and helped grow Project Lead The Way (PLTW) and TEE programs in multiple school districts and has worked with the College of DuPage to establish a TEE pipeline that attracts new people interested in teaching TEE and STEM. In addition, he is a master teacher for PLTW, where he facilitates core training for future PLTW teachers. Corey is a board member with the Technology Education Association of Illinois, a PLTW coach with MASS STEM Hub, and an adjunct professor at Joliet Junior College. He is currently a PLTW teacher at Lockport Township High School in Lockport, IL.

Sherman Finch is a visiting professor at Sam Houston State University. He received a BFA from the Rhode Island School of Design and two master's degrees from the Maryland Institute, College of Art: a multidisciplinary MFA at Mount Royal and a MA in digital arts and media. He is also a UX/UI designer who investigates user experience through traditional and digital media. As a designer, he works with brands and design systems to find technical and creative solutions for digital interactive-based environments, including projects focused on user-centered approaches.

Wendy Fox-Turnbull is an associate professor at the University of Waikato who is Deputy Head of School for Te Kura Toi Tangata School of Education. Wendy was chair of the Technology Education New Zealand (TENZ Council) from 2006 to 2018 and has convened two TENZ conferences, TENZ 2005 and TENZ/ICTE2017, and one International Technology Research conference (PATT) in 2013. She previously taught at the University of Canterbury's College of Education, in technology education, primary and secondary, professional inquiry studies and inquiry learning from 1997 to 2017. Research special interests include authentic learning in technology education, the place of women in technology-related careers, the role and nature of effective conversations in learning and teaching, and learning approaches for the 21st century. Wendy has presented regularly at PATT and other international conferences and published in a range of journals and books in the field of technology education. Wendy is a registered and certified primary teacher.

Scott Gibbons has worked in K–12 education for over ten years, teaching English language arts in both Kentucky and Pennsylvania. He is currently a PhD candidate at the University of Cincinnati, focusing on curriculum and instruction and teacher education. Scott has worked with many student teachers to improve their planning, implementation, and assessment. Scott's research interests include online teacher professional development and methods in teacher education.

Kim A. Hosler is the Director of Instructional Design at the United States Air Force Academy (USAFA) in Colorado Springs, CO. She also teaches part-time for University College at the University of Denver. Her doctorate is in educational technology from the University of Northern Colorado. Her academic areas of expertise and research include online teaching and learning and learner-centered instructional design. At USAFA, she facilitates and leads the biannual course director's workshop, consults with faculty individually on course design, and facilitates other workshops related to the design of effective and efficient instruction.

Hui-Ching Kayla Hsu is a research assistant professor and instructional designer at NYU Tandon School of Engineering. Her research focuses on engineering education, online learning development, and motivation to learn. She received her doctoral degree in learning design and technology from Purdue University. Because of her previous career as a journalist and internship at the United Nations, she is highly aware of her responsibility as a global citizen. She is committed to making online learning in STEM fields more engaging, more diverse, and more accessible for all by leveraging research-proven pedagogy and innovative technologies.

Qiyuan Li received her PhD in learning, design, and technology with a minor in statistics from the Pennsylvania State University. She is currently working as a data modeler and developer at Boston University. Her research focuses on the use of natural language processing and machine-learning algorithms to classify discourse. She has expertise in data architecture and programming using various tools.

Yun Li received her PhD from Texas A&M University, specializing in learning design and technology. She is currently a researcher at Texas A&M University, where she continues her research on interactive learning environment design, technology integration, and instructional design. She has collaborated with researchers and practitioners from various disciplines, such as engineering, medicine, and visualization. In addition to her experience in academia, she is an instructional designer with ten years of experience in design in both higher education and industry settings.

Emrah Emre Ozkeskin is a lecturer in Open Education Faculty, Anadolu University, Turkey. His research interests are adaptive learning environments, learning analytics, and instructional technologies. He has been published in several academic journals and international conferences.

Larissa Pahomov is a veteran teacher in the School District of Philadelphia. She has 13 years of experience teaching students English at Science Leadership Academy, a public high school with a focus on inquiry and project-based learning. She is the author of the teaching handbook *Authentic Learning in the Digital Age*, as well as chapters in the anthologies *Inside our Schools* and *Teachers Unions and Social Justice*. She received her master's degree in education from the University of Pennsylvania and is a National Board Certified Teacher.

Heather A. Robinson is an online learning consultant who has worked in the technology field since 1995. She teaches courses in the areas of computer science, information systems, and learning technologies. She holds a master's degree in information science and a PhD in learning technologies from the University of North Texas. Heather is currently researching critical pedagogy and care ethics in online learning.

Chastity Rohan has worked in K–12 public education for over 15 years in the disciplines of mathematics and engineering. She helped build the pre-engineering program at Grant County High School where she was the VEX robotics coach and Technology Student Association advisor. In addition, she is a master teacher for Project Lead The Way, where she facilitates core training for future engineering teachers. Chastity also has contributed to writing engineering state standards for Kentucky. She is currently a mathematics teacher at Larry A. Ryle High School in Union, KY.

Meranda M. Roy is the Online Learning Librarian at the University of North Texas, where she implements and promotes a variety of online tools, services, and initiatives for students, faculty, librarians, and staff. Her research interests include educational technology, training and development, academic development, program design, and evaluation.

Kay K. Seo is a professor of instructional design and technology at the University of Cincinnati. Her research focuses on learner engagement and interaction in virtual worlds and social networking spaces. She has published widely in top-tier academic journals and has presented numerous papers on instructional technology at nationally and internationally renowned conferences. She is the Founding President of the Learner Engagement SIG and the Learner Engagement Division for the Association for Educational Communications and Technology.

Priya Sharma received a PhD in instructional technology from the University of Georgia. She is currently an associate professor in the College of Education at the Pennsylvania State University. She teaches courses related to research methods, emerging technologies, and learning theory. She has more than 15 years of experience conducting research primarily focused on qualitative research, including discourse analyses and online ethnography, and more recently, research using social network analyses. Her research focuses on knowledge sharing and learning in informal and formal online environments, the role of emerging technologies in learning, and the use of data sciences in education.

Laura E. Sujo-Montes is a faculty member at Northern Arizona University, USA. Her work includes teaching and researching online learning environments, technology use in teaching ESL students, and online professional development.

Chih-Hsiung Tu is a professor at Northern Arizona University, USA. His research interests are distance education, socio-cognitive learning, socio-cultural learning, online learning community, social media, personal learning environments, and network learning environments.

Cong Wang received a BS in psychology from Sun Yat-sen University, an M.Ed in educational psychology from Beijing Normal University, an MS in statistics, and a PhD in educational psychology from Purdue University-West Lafayette. Her research focuses on college students' motivation and learning. She utilizes the framework of self-determination theory to study the impact of autonomy-supportive teaching approaches on learning. As a second line of research, she collaborates widely on studies where she employed complex statistical techniques to address educational research questions. Her primary tools are structural equation modeling, multilevel modeling, latent profile analysis, and meta-analysis.

Scott J. Warren is a professor of learning technologies in the College of Information at the University of North Texas. He has studied learning games and simulations in educational contexts for more than 20 years and is the author of the book *Learning Games: The Science and Art*. After completing additional doctoral research in logistics and operations management, his research practice now also includes how stakeholders may employ holistic systems analysis and evaluation approaches with business firms as part of their organizational learning and improvement.

Cherng-Jyh Yen is an associate professor of educational research and Statistics at Old Dominion University. He specializes in quantitative research design and data analysis. His primary research interest is in the prediction of online learning outcomes. His papers have appeared in peer-reviewed journals such as *Internet and Higher Education*, *Educational Technology and Society*, and *Computers and Education*.

Introduction

CHAPTER 1

Interactions and the Role of Technologies

Scott Gibbons and Kay K. Seo

INTRODUCTION

Interactions among users and learning agents such as peers, teachers, technology, and content are both diverse and complex, and gaining a better understanding of how users interact with those agents can provide clarity for educators in myriad fields when deciding on applicable learning plans and the appropriate vehicle to deliver engaging learning experiences. Because technology's role in education has recently expanded due to the coronavirus pandemic, this book aims to examine various forms of user interactions and the role learning technologies play in those interactions. Educators and researchers from fields such as engineering, technology education, military, and robotics have contributed their expertise on the many ways users interact and how those interactions can be perceived in providing professional development and innovative opportunities to those guiding interactions.

According to Kang and Im (2013), studying interaction is important because new knowledge is constructed through a variety of interactions, which speaks to the importance of interaction and the role new technologies can play in the learning process. In learning acquisition, researchers found that peer interaction is important for language learners because "learners can engage with L2 learning opportunities such as receiving modified input, noticing language errors, producing output, negotiating for meaning, and giving and obtaining interactional feedback" (Dao, 2020, p. 2). In another study, Hsieh (2019) discovered that the availability of online resources impacts students' collaborative mentality and ability to interact with peers, and Zipp and Craig (2019), through a study of learners' interaction with technology, found evidence to support the

DOI: 10.4324/9781003089704-2

claim that "individuals transfer their biases into virtual worlds" (p. 1399), impacting how designers view user interaction in virtual spaces. These important findings related to user interaction with a variety of agents can have a significant impact on future studies involving user interactions with technology, instructors, peers, and content. Understanding user interactions can impact course and program design, how educators interact with students, and how technology can be used to create meaningful interactions that lead to a better experience for learners.

In 1989, Michael G. Moore introduced three types of interaction: learner-to-learner, learner-to-teacher, learner-to-content (Moore, 1989). Later, Hillman, Willis, and Gunawardena (1994) added a fourth type of interaction: learner-to-interface. The *interface* refers to the type of technology being used to engage the learner. This book builds on Moore's and Hillman, Willis, and Gunawardena's four types of interaction, but most chapters focus on learner interaction through technology, because we think that given the current direction and role of technology in educational and research settings, that technology is on its way to becoming a critical component of all forms of interaction. For example, the emergence of videoconferencing as a result of the coronavirus pandemic has become mainstream worldwide, adding a layer of technology to interactions like learner-to-learner and teacher-to-learner. In addition to the four types of interactions, some chapters in this book narrow the interaction even further by specifying the type of learner. For example, Rohan and Duzan's chapter about K–12 educators' incorporation of technology into their curriculum views the teacher as the learner and discusses the teacher's interactions with technology in relation to how teachers use that new knowledge about technology to create more collaborative learning environments for students. Other chapters throughout this book do much of the same by addressing a specific field or subject area and explaining how different types of users interact with each other, their instructor, content, and technology, all while using a variety of learning technologies to meet users' complex needs.

TYPES OF INTERACTION

Many interaction researchers tend to focus on a single interaction within their research and explore how elements impact users regarding that key interaction. Chapters in this book take a different approach to interaction by focusing on the role learning technologies play in various forms of interaction. For example, in this book's "*Unit II: Diversifying Instruction*,"

Fox-Turnbull analyzes intercognitive talk among students in order to generate more meaningful lessons gauged to meet learners where they are in their use of learning technology. Like many other chapters in this book, Fox-Turnbull's chapter then reflects on a variety of user interactions such as user-to-user and user-to-teacher in order to highlight the many ways learning technologies play a role in different educational environments that use technology.

Learner-to-content interaction is not given its own subsection in this chapter, because individual chapters in the book do not specifically focus on a single type of subject matter. This is not meant to diminish the importance of learner-to-content interaction but to highlight the diversity among the chapters in the book. Moore (1989) states that learner-to-content interaction "is the process of intellectually interacting with content that results in changes in the learner's understanding, the learner's perspective, or the cognitive structures of the mind" (p. 1). Therefore, all chapter authors highlight aspects of learner-to-content interaction but do not focus on learner-to-content interaction within their discussion or analysis. Instead, authors acknowledge the subject matter in which their research took place and offer a variety of applications to many other subject areas. It is important to understand the interactions discussed in the following sections before proceeding to individual chapters that contain a more comprehensive look at how learning technologies impact interactions within a certain learning space. The remainder of this section provides a cursory view of the different forms of user interactions that are discussed throughout the book.

In the first subsection of this chapter, "Learner-to-Learner Interaction," the term "learner" is used in different ways. In the traditional sense, the term "learner" is often viewed as a K-18 student, and although that is the case in many chapters in this book, the term "learner" is also used in reference to an educator or researcher who is learning new technologies and experimenting with those technologies in different environments. In this book, each author clarifies how they are using the term "learner," but it is important to understand that anyone can be a learner, not just pupils sitting in a classroom. For example, Pahomov's chapter places the teacher as the learner and the student as the teacher regarding new technologies being implemented due to school closures during the coronavirus pandemic. Similarly, Hosler's chapter places instructional designers in the learner's seat as they assess the benefits of virtual reality and implement changes in military pilot training programs. The following subsections highlight the foundational components of learner interactions and position that discussion with existing research related to the different forms of interaction.

Learner-to-Learner Interaction

Learners often obtain just as much knowledge from each other as they do from instructors or technology programs (Dobao, 2012). Learner-to-learner interaction is when learners communicate or collaborate with one another in a physical or virtual environment where knowledge is exchanged and attained. In her research, Oyarzun (2016) discusses social presence in relation to learner-to-learner interactions. Oyarzun suggests that there are two important components to learner-to-learner interaction: intimacy and immediacy. Oyarzun explains, "Intimacy includes eye contact, physical proximity, and topic of conversation. Immediacy is the psychological distance between the communicator and recipient" (p. 3). With these components in mind, it is easy to assume that learner-to-learner interaction can only take place in person in a physical environment; however, with the sudden advancement of virtual learning platforms such as Zoom, Microsoft Teams, and Google Meet, to name a few, the limits of videoconferencing have been expanded and refined to where the learning environments are now geared toward learner-to-learner interaction. Many authors in this book discuss how virtual platforms promote learner-to-learner interactions by enabling users to see and hear each other, encourage learner-to-learner collaboration, and support a safe and comfortable learning environment.

Learner-to-learner interaction can and does take place in many subject areas, but it has been widely studied in language learning. Because learner-to-learner interaction is a key component in language learning, a language classroom is an ideal arena to establish and study a variety of learner-to-learner interactions. Although this book does not focus on language learning, previous language-learning studies can help to establish the foundation and importance of learner-to-learner interactions. Like many interaction studies, Peeters (2019) researched interaction in regards to language acquisition. In the study, Peeters explored how learners construct knowledge via social media outlets such as Facebook and how interactions with peers on Facebook affect knowledge development. Peeters found that "learners shape the online interaction process by sticking to a plan of action: engaging in cognitive and organizational processes while building social connections with others and exploring the concept of metacognition" (p. 3202). This research supports other researchers' findings (Haron, Natrah Aziz, & Harun, 2017; Shackelford & Maxwell, 2012) that learner-to-learner interactions are a powerful method for bolstering knowledge construction and reinforcing learning concepts. Haron et al. (2017) studied learner-to-learner interactions in e-learning and found that interaction among learners is critical to building a sustainable learning community. Learner interactions become part of the learning environment, particularly in virtual spaces.

In this book, authors discuss a variety of learner-to-learner interactions, and they position those discussions in terms of learner-to-learner interactions via learning technologies, whether those learning technologies are videoconferencing or learners collaborating with the aid of technology like social media, robotics, or virtual reality. Building a sense of community through learner-to-learner interactions is critical (Shackelford & Maxwell, 2012), and many chapters in this book speak to a sense of community through interaction.

Learner-to-Teacher Interaction

How learners and educators interact and the outcomes of those interactions are not concepts unique to this book, but learner-to-teacher interactions via learning technologies have recently taken center stage in K-18 education due to the ongoing coronavirus pandemic. The idea that teachers have knowledge, and through interactions with students, teachers bestow that knowledge onto their students is a dated view of learner-to-teacher interaction (Lane, 2018). There are many different theoretical views of how this knowledge transition takes place and which form of knowledge transfer is most effective, but authors in this book adhere more closely to Dewey's (1938) learner-centered understanding that teachers aid students in gaining and shaping knowledge by providing relevant experiences and guiding learning through experiences, as opposed to Hirsch's (1987) understanding of essentially bestowing knowledge onto students through direct instruction and designed memorization. In relation to a push for more learner-centered instruction, Naujokaitiene, Tamoliune, Volungeviciene, and Duart (2020) assert, "Teaching presence is important to facilitate students' cognitive presence also by shifting the responsibility of learning process to students themselves" (p. 240). Therefore, teachers need to understand that interactions with students matter because the teacher's physical or virtual presence plays an important role in student achievement.

With this existentialist view of interaction in mind, learner-to-teacher interactions can take different forms, and this type of interaction needs additional attention given the increased role technology is playing in classrooms around the world. It is important to consider learner-to-teacher interactions because doing so can help teachers "to provoke critical thinking easier, to induce focused discussions, to stimulate learners' personal interest and original understanding, and to raise learners' awareness of the learning process" (Naujokaitiene et al., 2020, p. 241).

Other researchers make similar claims about the importance of studying learner-to-teacher interaction. In Tu, Yen, Ozkeskin, and Sujo-Montes' chapter, they discuss how educators can build a stronger community of online learners through social learning analytics. In her chapter, Pohomov discusses how dialogue between students and teachers changes the type of authentic connections students have with their teachers. Hsu and Wang discuss on how presence impacts learning outcomes in immersive virtual reality. Learner-to-teacher interactions can have positive impacts on learner achievement and retention, but not all interactions are productive and with the implementation of more technology into classrooms and a push toward virtual learning, learner-to-teacher interactions have never been more essential.

Although technology can play an important role in creating more interactions between learners and teachers, learner-to-teacher interactions can be challenging. Tager-Flusberg (2015) discusses that teachers need to learn how to be flexible when interacting with students. Tager-Flusberg found that the teacher has control over the type of learning environment they create, and this environment plays a critical role in student achievement. A negative learning environment can stall learning, regardless of the instructional methods. Similarly, Li, Jee, and Sun (2018) found that the way technology is used with learner-to-teacher interactions is also important. In their study of 37 fourth and fifth grade English as a Foreign Language (EFL) students, Li, Jee, and Sun discovered that the way teachers use technology can actually create frustration and disengagement; the researchers state that "[t]he use of technology in these suburban/rural primary EFL classrooms was, unfortunately, restricting the communicative practices in the classroom" (p. 178). This is because teachers in Li, Jee, and Sun's study were using technology "as an alternative presentation tool to chalkboards and served a range of traditional pedagogical goals in teacher-centered classrooms" (p. 178). Teachers were using PowerPoint to display information without providing important explanations and creating a zone for learner-teacher communication. Li, Jee, and Sun go on to suggest that "the use of technology also limited teacher talk and minimized students' spontaneity and authenticity" (p. 178), which counters the intent for technology to create a more adaptable atmosphere for learner-teacher collaboration.

In various chapters in this book, authors identify and discuss opportunities for teachers to interact with learners, and authors discuss how teachers can create better opportunities for positive learner-to-teacher interactions. Naujokaitiene et al. (2020) indicate that "active learning through collaborative activities, communication, and discussions has come to be important for learners' engagement, the interest, and the overall success of the learning process while teaching and learning online" (p. 231). This form of learner-to-teacher interaction is highlighted throughout this book, and with the addition of learning technologies, readers will find ways to reach students regardless of time or space.

Learner-to-Technology Interaction

Technology has different functions in educational environments, and in those environments, learners interact with technology for different purposes. Technology can be used as a tool to teach concepts by which students interact with the technology to learn subject matter, technology can be a vehicle by which teachers deliver instruction to students, and technology can be an educational tool for learners to organize thoughts and collaborate. Collier-Reed, Case, and Linder (2009) assert that learner-to-technology interaction includes users interacting with technology to create a product or artifact, using technology as a process to progress to new knowledge, and using and making technology for different purposes. Nilsson, Gustafsson, and Sundqvist (2020) use the Collier-Reed et al. (2009) framework to study preschool children's interactions with technology. They discovered that there are two main ways students use technology in educational settings. The first way is students using technology to explore "the application of artifacts through instruction" and the second way is using technology to "build, create and construct using different techniques, materials and tools" (p. 17). The teachers in Nilsson, Gustafsson, and Sundqvist's study used learner-to-technology interaction to build students' "knowledge and skills and solutions to problems" (p. 17). Similarly, authors in this book view learner-to-technology interactions in much the same way. Li and Finch's chapter discusses how new technologies can play a role in learner-interface interaction. Hsu and Wang's chapter discusses how presence, immersion, and interactivity in immersive virtual reality environments impacts learning outcomes through learner-to-technology interactions.

Other ways learners interact with technology have a more direct impact on learner engagement. Learner engagement is when "students are physically, cognitively, and socially involved in the learning process" (Gibbons & Seo, 2019). For example, Purarjomandlangrudi and Chen (2020) studied online university students in Australia, and their findings revealed that in order for students to engage with online content, students first need to understand how to communicate via the online platforms, how to self-regulate their learning, and how to retain a positive attitude toward online programs. Therefore, teachers need to prepare students to interact with technology before students are placed in a situation where technology interaction is the main form of interaction. In this book, authors Warren, Roy, and Robinson provide much of the same ideas regarding their work with course designers in a transmedia learning experience. Engaging students using technology is not something that happens without teacher and peer collaboration. In fact, creating a positive learning experience using technology often works best "within a didactical system where teacher, students and content are understood as an undividable whole" (Svensson & Johansen, 2017, p. 161). In many situations, the teacher becomes the learner along with students, which can create a unique learning environment where students and teachers solve problems and interact with technology together. In this book, authors discuss the ways in which learner-to-technology interaction is being used in a variety of learning environments. Throughout the book authors offer ideas for teachers and researchers to use to explore and adapt different technologies to improving student efficacy and increasing learner engagement.

THEMES IN USER INTERACTION

This book is divided into three themes (three units): "Enriching Curriculum," "Diversifying Instruction," and "Revamping Professionalism." These units contain chapters that discuss various user interactions in more detail and in a range of environments. In Unit I, "Enriching Curriculum," authors examine analytic data that support online learning through discussion boards (Sharma, Akgun, and Li's chapter), virtual reality's impact on learner interactions (Hsu and Wang's chapter), and gaming's effect on users' critical thinking (Warren, Roy, and Robinson's chapter). In Unit II, "Diversifying Instruction," authors explore oral interactions in technology education (Fox-Turnbull's chapter), the role no-speech sound plays among users and user interfaces (Li and Finch's chapter), and enhancing community through the integration of interactivity and social network analysis (Tu, Yen, Ozkeskin, and Sujo-Montes' chapter). Finally, in Unit III, "Revamping Professionalism," authors discuss virtual reality's interaction with student learning in the United States Air Force Academy (Hosler's chapter), teacher and student interactions with learning technologies in K–12 education (Rohan and Duzan's chapter), the move from in-person student to teacher interaction to online student-to-teacher interaction during the coronavirus pandemic, and how a digital divide can impact learners' interaction with technology (Pahomov's chapter). The combination of the three units/themes along with their respective chapters provides a collection geared toward a wide audience of researchers and practitioners. Each chapter has two functions: It stands alone as a testament to how user interactions are unique to every learning space, and.it helps to paint a more cohesive picture of the role learning technologies play in various forms of user interactions.

User interactions can enrich curriculum by helping instructors and designers augment curriculum and implementation in order to create a collaborative experience for online and in-person learners. By viewing curriculum modification and development in new ways, with user interactions as a guiding principle, curriculum can move in innovative directions that encourage learner engagement. Pepin, Gueudet, and Trouche (2017) argue that interacting with technology can enhance teachers' *design capacity* and ability to develop engaging curriculum. Pepin, Gueudet, and Trouche define *design capacity* as "how teachers understand and transform existing curriculum resources (in this case digital resources) to (re-) design instruction" (p. 811). Chapters in Unit I, "Enriching Curriculum," challenge readers to rethink curriculum and think about curriculum from an interactive point of view with a mind toward technology integration.

Diversifying instruction through different forms of user interaction can impact how users relate to instructional delivery methods and content. Implementation of new learning technologies can drastically change instructional methods and the way teachers and learners view instruction. As mentioned earlier in this chapter, a learner-centered instructional approach is a common theme among chapters in this book. Effective instructional practices have been a topic of research and professional development for more than a century (National Education Association, 1893), and more recently, researchers Connor et al. (2011) use Child Characteristics x Instruction to help determine the type of instruction that works best in meeting students' learning needs. Although the research of Connor et al. focuses on reading achievement among young students, their findings are in line with arguments put forth by authors in Unit II, "Diversifying Instruction." Connor et al. maintain that student achievement is related to the design and implementation of an interactive learning approach. Chapter authors argue that in addition to interactive learning, the use of technology through oral interactions, nonspeech sounds, and community also play an important role in student achievement.

Using learning technologies to promote educator growth is another way interaction can play a role in professional development in different fields. Avalos (2011) argues that teachers need reinforcement and support in order to grow, and teacher growth can lead to improved student achievement. The coronavirus pandemic has forced teaching methods to evolve, and for that reason, teachers must adapt the way they view instruction and meet student needs. Through the use of learning technologies and a focus on user interactions, educational leaders can reinvigorate the profession to encourage current learning trends and increase learner engagement. Authors in Unit III, "Revamping Professionalism," discuss a range of topics in a multitude of environments, from K–12 education to Air Force pilots. Chapter authors build an overall argument that when educators put user interaction at the center of their planning and implementation, then they can grow professionally and positively impact student achievement. Because there are many different areas where teachers can develop their professional skills, chapters in this section address many different areas so that any practitioner or researcher can find useful information and ideas to address their own unique needs.

CONCLUSION

The design of this book aims to meet the needs of researchers, practitioners, and designers who plan to introduce or expand learning technologies in their curriculum. The chapters offer a fresh perspective on the role learning technologies play in learner interactions and learner engagement. Because interaction can take many forms, the intentional diversity among chapters targets many important areas where learner interactions take place. The goal of each chapter is to provide readers with an assortment of ideas and examples of how to think about interaction and how learning technologies can transform the educational environment in areas such as K–12, higher education, military training, and corporate training. Acknowledging the benefits of crossover from areas such as K–12 and corporate training reveals that different sectors can learn from each other (Gibbons & Seo, 2021), and this book provides a gateway for different fields to learn about, adapt, and implement learner interactions to benefit their own research and practices.

REFERENCES

Avalos, B. (2011). Teacher professional development in Teaching and Teacher Education over ten years. *Teaching and Teacher Education, 27*, 10–20. https://doi.org/10.1016/j.tate.2010.08.007

Collier-Reed, B. I., Case, J. M., & Linder, C. (2009). The experience of interacting with technological artefacts. *European Journal of Engineering Education, 34*(4), 295–303.

Connor, C. M. D., Morrison, F. J., Schatschneider, C., Toste, J. R., Lundblom, E., Crowe, E. C., & Fishman, B. (2011). Effective classroom instruction: Implications of child characteristics by reading instruction interactions on first graders' word reading achievement. *Journal of Research on Educational Effectiveness*, *4*(3), 173–207. https://doi.org/10.1080/19345747.2010.510179

Dao, P. (2020). Effect of interaction strategy instruction on learner engagement in peer interaction. *System*, *91*(102244), 1–13. https://doi.org/10.1016/j.system.2020.102244

Dewey, J. (1938). The need of a theory of experience. In *Experience and education: The 60th anniversary edition* (pp. 12–22). West Lafayette, IN: Kappa Delta Pi.

Dobao, A. F. (2012). Collaborative dialogue in learner-learner and learner-native speaker interaction. *Applied Linguistics*, *33*(3), 229–256. https://doi.org/10.1093/applin/ams002

Gibbons, S., & Seo, K. (2019). Learner engagement in teacher education. In J. Lampert (Ed.), *Oxford encyclopedia of global perspectives on teacher education*. New York: Oxford University Press.

Gibbons, S., & Seo, K. (2021). Technology's impact on interdisciplinary learner engagement: Bridging corporate training and K-12 education. In B. Hokanson, M. Exter, A. Grincewicz, M. Schmidt, & A. Tawfik (Eds.), *Intersections across disciplines: Interdisciplinarity and learning* (pp. 281–293). New York, NY: Springer.

Haron, H., Natrah Aziz, N. H., & Harun, A. (2017). A conceptual model participatory engagement within E-learning community. *Procedia Computer Science*, *116*, 242–250. https://doi.org/10.1016/j.procs.2017.10.046

Hillman, D. C., Willis, D. J., & Gunawardena, C. N. (1994). Learner-interface interaction in distance education: An extension of contemporary models and strategies for practitioners. *The American Journal of Distance Education*, *8*(2), 30–42.

Hirsch, E. D. (1987). Preface. In *Cultural literacy: What every American needs to know* (pp. xiii–xvii). Boston, MA: Houghton Mifflin.

Hsieh, Y. C. (2019). Learner interactions in face-to-face collaborative writing with the support of online resources. *ReCALL*, *32*(1), 85–105. https://doi.org/10.1017/S0958344019000120

Kang, M., & Im, T. (2013). Factors of learner-instructor interaction which predict perceived learning outcomes in online learning environment. *Journal of Computer Assisted Learning*, *29*(3), 292–301. https://doi.org/10.1111/jcal.12005

Lane, J. O. (2018). Lived experiences of new faculty: Nine stages of development toward learner-centered practice. *Journal of the Scholarship of Teaching and Learning*, *18*(3), 1–25. https://doi.org/10.14434/josotl.v18i3.23373

Li, G., Jee, Y., & Sun, Z. (2018). Technology as an educational equalizer for EFL learning in rural China? Evidence from the impact of technology-assisted practices on teacher-student interaction in primary classrooms. *Language and Literacy*, *20*(3), 159–184.

Moore, M. G. (1989). Three types of interaction. *The American Journal of Distance Education*, *3*(2), 1–7.

National Education Association. (1893). *Report of the committee of ten on secondary schools 1893*. Washington, DC: National Education Association.

Naujokaitiene, J., Tamoliune, G., Volungeviciene, A., & Duart, J. M. (2020). Using learning analytics to engage students: Improving teaching practices through informed interactions. *Journal of New Approaches in Educational Research*, *9*(2), 231–244. https://doi.org/10.7821/naer.2020.7.561

Nilsson, T., Gustafsson, P., & Sundqvist, P. (2020). Children's interactions with technology in teachers' self-reported activities in Sweden's preschools. *International Journal of Technology and Design Education*, 0123456789. https://doi.org/10.1007/s10798-020-09613-x

Oyarzun, S. E. A. (2016). *Effects of learner-to-learner interactions on social presence, achievement and satisfaction* (Publication No. 10.25777/6ya8-zk73) [Doctoral dissertation], Old Dominion University. ODU Digital Commons.

Peeters, W. (2019). The peer interaction process on Facebook: A social network analysis of learners' online conversations. *Education and Information Technologies, 24*(5), 3177–3204. https://doi.org/10.1007/s10639-019-09914-2

Pepin, B., Gueudet, G., & Trouche, L. (2017). Refining teacher design capacity: Mathematics teachers' interactions with digital curriculum resources. *ZDM – Mathematics Education, 49*(5), 799–812. https://doi.org/10.1007/s11858-017-0870-8

Purarjomandlangrudi, A., & Chen, D. (2020). Exploring the influence of learners' personal traits and perceived course characteristics on online interaction and engagement. *Educational Technology Research and Development, 68*(5), 2635–2657. https://doi.org/10.1007/s11423-020-09792-3

Shackelford, J. L., & Maxwell, M. (2012). Sense of community in graduate online education: Contribution of learner to learner interaction. *The International Review of Research in Open and Distributed Learning, 13*(4), 228–248.

Svensson, M., & Johansen, G. (2017). Teacher's didactical moves in the technology classroom. *International Journal of Technology and Design Education*, 1–16. https://doi.org/10.1007/s10798-017-9432-1

Tager-Flusberg, H. (2015). The development of English as a second language with and without specific language impairment: Clinical implications. *Journal of Speech, Language, and Hearing Research, 24*(2), 1–14. https://doi.org/10.1044/2015

Zipp, S. A., & Craig, S. D. (2019). The impact of a user's biases on interactions with virtual humans and learning during virtual emergency management training. *Educational Technology Research and Development, 67*(6), 1385–1404. https://doi.org/10.1007/s11423-019-09647-6

UNIT I

Enriching Curriculum

CHAPTER 2

Learning Analytics to Support Student Interaction and Learning Design

Initial Report on a Human-Centered Prototype Design

Priya Sharma, Mahir Akgun, and Qiyuan Li

INTRODUCTION

Interaction is an integral part of learning that occurs via interaction between individuals, artifacts, knowledge, and cultural practices. Interaction can be construed diversely: For example, Merriam-Webster's 11th Collegiate Dictionary defines interaction as "mutual or reciprocal action or influence" (www.merriam-webster.com/dictionary/interaction), while the Cambridge Dictionary defines interaction as "an occasion when two or more people or things communicate with or react to each other" (https://dictionary.cambridge.org/us/dictionary/english/interaction). Our perspective on interaction more closely maps onto the second definition, and in this chapter, we address interaction from a pedagogical and research perspective.

In face-to-face (f2f) learning contexts, interaction that occurs between students, their peers, and instructors is visible and can be used to inform pedagogy and design of activities. Interaction in online contexts is equally important and has been underscored in a variety of distance and online learning frameworks (Anderson & Garrison, 1998; Moore, 1997). Specifically in online contexts, bolstering interaction between students, peers, instructors, and content is key to reducing transactional distance (Moore, 1989), which is the sense of psychological distance felt by participants in the online space. Higher levels

DOI: 10.4324/9781003089704-4

of transactional distance correlate to fewer opportunities to interact and less persistence and learning online (Weidlich & Bastiaens, 2018). In contrast, increased interactions between student-student, student-instructor, and student-content are likely to provide more satisfactory learning experiences (Anderson & Garrison, 1998), although requiring higher time and cost investments.

In this chapter we report on the initial stages of a design research-informed project that mitigates the trade-offs of cost, effort, and interaction by using artificial intelligence, especially machine learning, to support instructors in quickly assessing student interaction in online environments.

Interaction and Learning in Online Contexts

As increasing numbers of students enroll in online courses, with an average 20% growth in enrollment each year (Lederman, 2018), it is imperative to design courses that support student engagement and interaction. The growth in online courses is accompanied by student and faculty preferences for blended learning (Brooks & Pomerantz, 2017), where some portion of the course content is delivered online. The increase in online and blended learning poses dual challenges for instructors and learning designers. First, the design of online experiences should closely attend to processes of learning, including interaction between student and peers, student and instructor, and student and content. Different learning theories emphasize different roles of interaction in the learning process, including the role of interaction in cognitive development (Vygotsky, 1978) and the role of social interaction in constructing shared knowledge (Roschelle & Teasley, 1995). Patterns of interaction between students have also been studied within computer-supported collaborative learning (CSCL) environments. Although the instructor's role in structuring learning activities is important for supporting interaction and collaboration, it is often overlooked in the literature (Kreijns, Kirschner, & Vermeulen, 2013). Growing evidence suggests that participants are unable to interact in CSCL environments without guidance or support (Kreijns et al., 2013) and that merely assigning students to groups in CSCL environments will not guarantee collaboration or interaction (Lipponen, Rahikainen, Lallimo, & Hakkarainen, 2003). Along with the design of various types of interaction, equally important is designing assessment and rapid feedback to students on their interactions. Assessing quality of engagement is an integral part of assessing the quality of each member's contribution to the group product, and instructor guidance for supporting students' participation in peer interaction is very important

(Hakkarainen, 1998). However, monitoring individual students' participation in online group discussions is a challenging and time-consuming task for most instructors. Analytics can be used to ease this burden, and analytic tools can be designed to support instructors in monitoring group discussions and detecting the quality of cognitive engagement demonstrated by group members.

Artificial Intelligence and Learning Analytics

Artificial intelligence (AI) applications in education are multiplying and could grow significantly in the coming years (Zeide, 2019). Machine learning, encompassed within the broader set of AI techniques, is a method of supervised/unsupervised classification and can produce software capable of recognizing patterns, making predictions, and applying newly discovered patterns to novel situations (Popenici & Kerr, 2017). Machine learning has been previously used in education to automate time-consuming tasks such as grading and provision of personalized feedback (Vie, Popineau, Bruillard, & Bourda, 2018) as well as provision of analytical or predictive information about student performance, dropout rate, and sentiment (Hu, Lo, & Shih, 2014; Li, Hoi, Chang, & Jain, 2010; Minaei-Bidgoli, Kortemeyer, & Punch, 2004). In this chapter we examine the design and use of a deep learning classifier that automatically analyzes online student discourse and generates visualizations to represent the data. The visualizations can be represented and manipulated via a learning analytics dashboard.

Learning analytics (LA) include the measurement, collection, and reporting of data to enhance student learning and design of the learning environment (SOLAR, n.d.). LA are well suited to analyze and represent big data generated via online learning; however, the challenge for educators is gathering and interpreting relevant data to form actionable insights into design and learning (Ferguson, 2012). Learning analytics dashboards (LAD) can address this need. Many LADs reported in literature gather and analyze data that are automatically generated by learning management systems. For example, data such as student access of resources, time spent, grades on quizzes, and so on can be used to identify students at risk of failure. In contrast, our prototype dashboard focuses on capturing, analyzing, and visualizing qualitative, discourse-oriented data to provide a more complete picture of student activities integral to interaction and learning to engender impact on user behavior change. Importantly, our project also closely links LAD design to theories of learning and design (Jivet, Scheffel, Specht, & Drachsler, 2018).

Designing Human-Centered Dashboards for Learning

A growing focus in the field of learning analytics (LA) is the use of human-centered design (HCD) to increase alignment between dashboard designs and their contextual use by stakeholders (Ahn, Campos, Hays, & Digiacomo, 2019). This move echoes a larger move by the Human Centered Interaction (HCI) discipline away from a system-centered approach to a human-centered approach that positions stakeholders' concerns and activities at the forefront of the design process (Bannon, 2011). Human-centered systems are designed and developed with the people who will eventually use the system. The HCD process uses methodologies and techniques that generate an understanding of the critical stakeholders, their needs, their activities, and the context in which those systems will operate (Giacomin, 2014). Learning analytic tools and dashboards have not always followed an HCD process, and the misalignment between their use and intent may result in a distrust of LA tools (De Quincey, Kyriacou, Briggs, & Waller, 2019), which in turn impacts real-world practices significantly. Thus, the success of LA tools depends on whether they were designed by considering users' needs and contexts (Shum, Ferguson, & Martinez-Maldonado, 2019). Involving stakeholders and users such as instructors, students, and administrators in the design process is important for better understanding how the users work with and act on LA tools in authentic teaching or learning contexts.

PROJECT CONTEXT: DEVELOPMENT OF AN INSTRUCTOR FACING DASHBOARD

In the subsequent sections of this chapter, we present a description of the design and development of an instructor-facing learning analytics dashboard that focuses on automatically analyzing and visualizing the quality and quantity of student interaction in online discussions. Despite an exhaustive web and citation search, we were unable to find a tool with the functionalities we expected, which led to our goal of tool development. Our design of the dashboard is guided by human-centered design guidelines, and in this first phase our design focused primarily on supporting instructor decision making and pedagogical intent. We used a participatory co-design process (Bratteteig, Bødker, Dittrich, Mogensen, & Simonsen, 2013) to refine and redesign the instructor-facing learning analytics dashboard, and we reported the process using a design-research informed approach. Our work began with a focus on solving a practical problem and identifying a suitable intervention; however, our work is also theoretically grounded. As we continued building our intervention, we saw opportunities for theory and design to inform each other, as is the general trend of design research (Easterday, Rees Lewis, & Gerber, 2018). As a first step, we focused on the instructor as stakeholder to design and refine an initial prototype of our learning analytics dashboard.

The context of this work is an undergraduate information sciences and technology course within a large northeastern university in the United States. The course enrolls about 6–8 sections with approximately 50 students per section every fall and spring semester. Sections are offered face-to-face as well as online, and our focus was to support instructors in managing the online sections. Our project team members' expertise spanned education, learning design, learning analytics, machine learning, and qualitative and quantitative research methodologies.

Initial Needs Analysis

Our first step was to explore the needs and challenges of one of the instructors of the information sciences class mentioned earlier. We conducted several interview-based, need-finding meetings to understand the challenges faced by the instructor in supporting and encouraging students to interact with each other and the course materials. The instructor assigned students to groups of 4–6 at the beginning of the course, and each group was tasked to complete 6 (six) group projects collaboratively during the semester. A sample activity may ask students to identify all the processes and interrelationships involved in the performance of a simple computing activity (such as printing or saving a file) and to create both a written description and a diagram of the process. Specific questions and prompts are also provided to guide the students through the different considerations (e.g., a more direct supportive prompt might read "How does the CPU communicate with the motherboard and the other parts of a system unit?"). Students then discuss their ideas and create the artifact. Through a process of reflection and guided prompting, we arrived at a list of key challenges encountered in the course as well as the types of technology that could help address the challenges. Key challenges identified by the instructor included assessing whether students were truly engaged in collaborative learning as well as the quality of the discussions and their focus on course content. The detailed list of challenges with their description is presented in Table 2.1.

Table 2.1 Listing of Key Challenges Faced by the Instructor

Key Instructor Challenges	*Description*
Know which students contribute to group discussions	The instructor wanted the ability to better understand who contributes or not to group work. The instructor also mentioned that having such an ability could help resolve conflicts that usually occur in groups when a group member does not contribute to group work.
Know the quality of student contributions within the group discussion	Apart from the quantity of interaction, the instructor also identified the importance of being able to assess students' performance based on the level/quality of contribution demonstrated in online group activities.
Know if students work collaboratively or cooperatively	The challenge was to ensure that students didn't divide activities into several tasks and then delegate tasks among group members. He noted that students tend to work cooperatively but that most of the online group activities designed for the course encourage students to collaborate.
Know if students missed any important course concepts when working on assigned group activities	The instructor noted that it is challenging to skim through discussions taking place within groups and identify if they use important course concepts/terms when completing group activities. He wanted this ability to detect any important concepts that students missed and to provide students with timely feedback.

Prototyping Learning Analytics Dashboard

Based on an initial needs analysis, we explored possible data and analytics that could assist the instructor. Interactions between students can be captured by using network analysis and sociograms and have been integrated in other learning analytic dashboards (Chen, Chang, Ouyang, & Zhou, 2018). The assessment of quality of student contributions was initially conceived and visualized as a table with student posts and the associated quality category.

Our approach to the project is embedded in sociocultural perspectives of learning (Lave & Wenger, 1991), and we view learning as an inherently social process (Vygotsky, 1978), where skills and knowledge are developed and advanced via collaboration and interaction (Stahl, 2005). For our project, we also focused on the concept of engagement, which broadly refers to "students' level of commitment and involvement with schooling" (Chi et al., 2018). Chi (2009) proposed the Interactive-Constructive-Active-Passive (ICAP), a cognitive engagement assessment framework that classifies learning activities into a taxonomy of *interactive*, *constructive*, *active*, and *passive*. Starting from the lowest level of cognitive engagement, *passive* activities are defined as "being oriented toward and receiving information from the instructional materials without overtly doing anything else" (Chi et al., 2018, p. 1786). *Active* activities are defined as overt learning activities that can be observed. *Constructive* activities require learners to produce additional outputs not contained in the explicitly presented information. Since learners would be active while producing outputs, constructive activities subsume active activities. The ICAP framework identifies "dialoguing' as key to *interactive* activities; activities are classified as *interactive* only with substantive dialoguing where students build on or respond to peer contributions. As the ICAP framework proposes, students become more cognitively engaged when they progress from *active* to *interactive*. In prior work (Li, 2019), a nascent machine-learning model was developed to classify discourse using the ICAP framework.

We designed a prototype learning analytics dashboard containing an instructor-facing component. The aim of the dashboard design was to provide comprehensible data-informed visualizations from multiple perspectives to assist the instructor in systematically evaluating students' learning engagement. This initial prototype used participatory co-design, where the theory-driven decisions of researchers and pragmatic goals of an instructor merged in the development of an instructional tool. For the dashboard and the learning analytics embedded therein to work effectively, we accounted for the instructor's pedagogical intent in planning and designing learning activities. We anticipated that the learning analytics could be used by the instructor to make informed decisions about how to adjust learning design when student behavior differed from expectations.

Design and Components of First Prototype Dashboard

The dashboard was designed to support the instructor in closely monitoring each group's weekly online activities, thereby allowing him to assess team member contributions to the group. Such assessments have been challenging and time-consuming for the instructor given the number of students in the course. To support the instructor's need to assess student engagement in group discussions, we developed a cognitive engagement visualizer module that displays an automatic classification of the student posts. Student cognitive engagement was analyzed via automated machine-learning algorithms using a Long-Short-Term-Memory (LSTM) neural network. For training the machine-learning model, we had to identify a suitable coding scheme that could analyze the quality of discourse and be adaptable and implementable for a machine-learning model. Based on prior work (Li, 2019), we identified Chi's Interactive-Constructive-Active-Passive framework as the most suitable. The ICAP framework (Chi & Wylie, 2014) has been used to evaluate the interaction level of MOOC discussion forum posts and comments and to automatically classify interactions via machine-learning algorithms (Wang, Yang, Wen, Koedinger, & Rosé, 2015). In our tool, we only used three levels (ACI, *Active-Constructive-Interactive*) of the framework, as *passive* activities are those in which students receive information from instructional materials and students cannot be observed doing anything overtly. Since activities in this study are online, the passive level cannot be observed and thus was not used for classification. Our tool used a machine-learning classifier to automatically code the posts into ACI levels.

To train the model, and with our university's Institutional Review Board approval, we collected and analyzed data from online group discussions in the introductory information sciences course. We retrieved approximately 4,650 discussion posts, and three human raters manually coded 500 discussion posts to reach an average of 0.75 inter-rater reliability. Coding was performed with an adapted version of the ICAP framework. The coders discussed discrepant discourse data, resolved conflicts, and agreed on codes for the 500 posts, which were subsequently used to train the machine-learning model. The trained LSTM classifier reached an 83% accuracy rate and a substantial level of agreement with human raters (cohen's kappa = 0.717) based on the collected data.

Another metric that helps assess interaction is social network analysis, in which network diagrams can be used to identify communication patterns between students (Dawson, 2010). Thus, we integrated an interaction visualizer module that displays the interaction between different students within the discussion groups. The sociograms aided the instructor in identifying social structures and individual positions within each team, as well as the communication patterns among students.

Implementation of First Prototype

In this section, we present our first implementation and evaluation of the learning analytics dashboard. The instructor used the dashboard to view data generated by 20 students in one section of the course. For this implementation, our main focus was understanding how to refine the analytic visualizations to help the instructor's assessment and learning design. Researchers met weekly with the instructor to discuss the output of analytics from each week of discussion and identify areas for further development or refinement of the dashboard. In the subsequent section

Table 2.2 Sample of Text Analysis in Cognitive Engagement Visualizer

Code	*Discourse*
A1	<@UKZB8V7FH> <@UKL81TX35> <@UKLDV2FEX> <@UKL990JDR> Sorry my phone refused to connect. Anyway I'll be out of econ at 2 ish so if we want to do on campus or online works for me.
A2	I fully don't understand microcode/ machine code apart from it's what the CPU's use and looks something along the lines of B 001002 C2 30
C	so the router is literally just the post office address of the digital world. It has an IP address and rejects any data packets that don't have "192.168.25.1" (specific IP address) to it. So ever new network needs 2 routers to talk to each other. One to send One to receive. And behind them is a server or station that distributes the packets accordingly
I	<@UKZB8V7FH> yes exactly except the CPU doesn't speak coding languages so it's on a whole different level in between what you and I normally think of as coding and binary code which is what RAM and ROM are. Stored series of ons and offs.

we present the iterative evaluation of and modifications made to the dashboard visualizations.

The first version of the dashboard provided two visualization modules displaying the different elements of engagement: The first of these was a cognitive engagement visualizer module (see Table 2.2), which was created to address the need to identify which students contributed to group discussions and to present an analysis of the discourse.

The visual displays students' messages and the discourse categories assigned to them. The categories presented in the ICAP framework were used to show students' level of cognitive engagement with course material and their peers during online group discussions. Category A corresponds to *Active*, category C corresponds to *Constructive*, and category I corresponds to *Interactive*. In the first iteration of the visualization, every student post was listed along with its ICAP category. When the instructor viewed this tabular listing of codes, he felt that the visualization did not provide a clear and quick evaluation of how and at what level students contributed to group discussions, since there was no sorting or categorization. A collaborative decision was made to visualize each group member's overall contribution to group activities by providing the total number of messages for each ACI category as well as at the group level. This resulted in a modified cognitive engagement visualizer (see Figure 2.1).

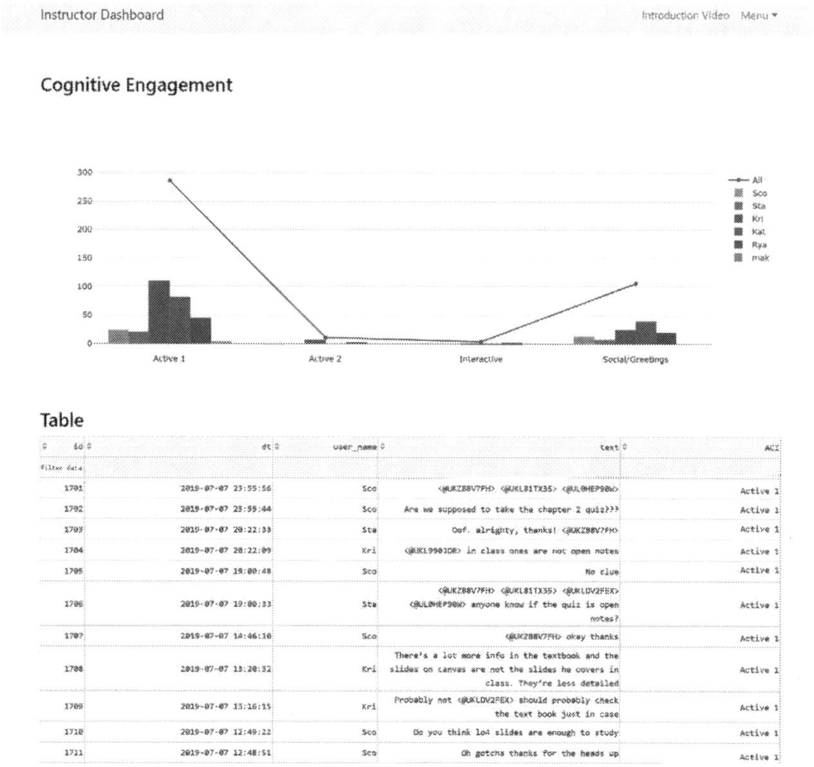

Figure 2.1 Redesigned Cognitive Engagement Visualizer

The second visualization was an interaction visualizer module (see Figure 2.2) that was created to address the instructor's focus on knowing whether students work cooperatively or collaboratively. For example, the visual presented to the instructor suggests that one student assumes a leadership role in the group and communicates with all other students in the network. Since other students do not seem to communicate with their peers, except the one at the center of the network, it can be concluded that students in the group engage in cooperation but not collaboration. The instructor noted that such a sociogram provides the opportunity to identify both the roles assumed by group members and how those roles could factor into students' level of contribution to group work. A redesigned version of the sociogram with in- and out-degree metrics that illustrate how many messages originated from and were sent to an individual was also added (see Figure 2.3).

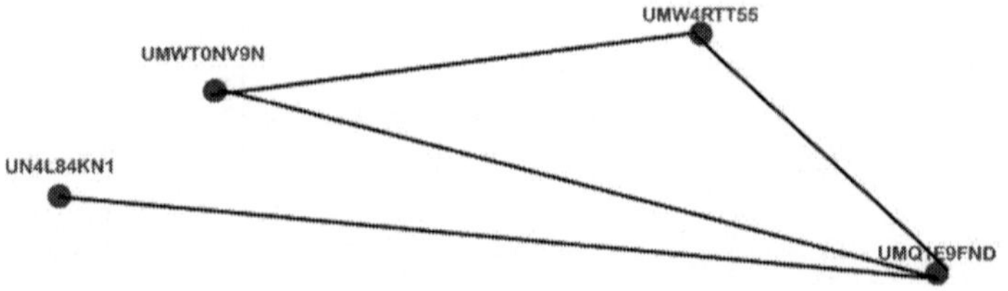

Figure 2.2 Initial Version of Interaction Visualizer Module

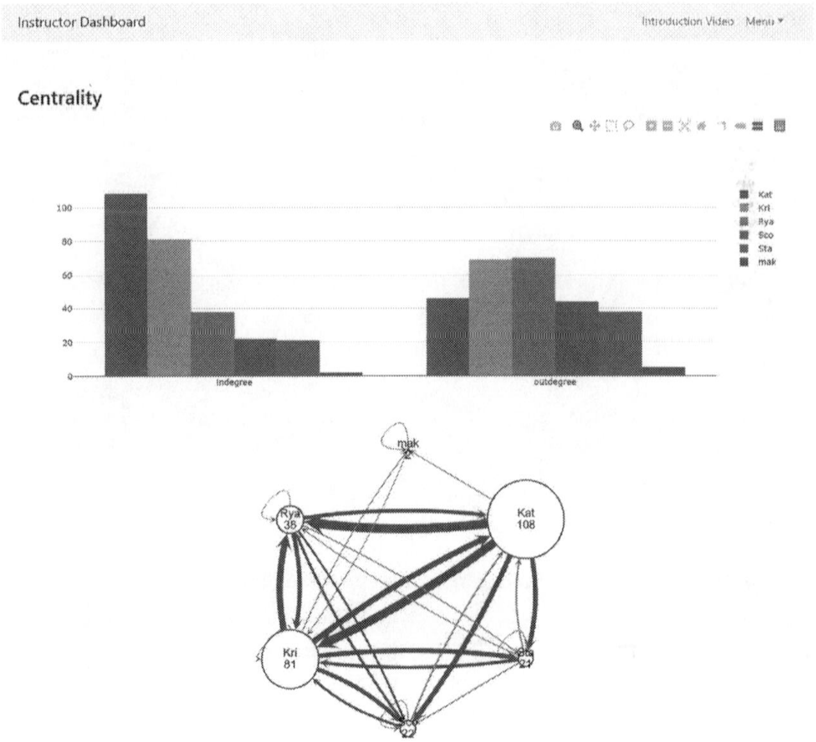

Figure 2.3 Redesigned Interaction Visualizer

Redesign and Iteration of Second Prototype

Our redesign of the dashboard for the second prototype focused on the two modules identified previously. For the cognitive engagement visualizer, we engaged in two types of modifications: First, we worked on generating visualizations that could better represent and aggregate the data for quick use by the instructor. A second modification was related to our coding scheme. In the initial round of coding, any on-task, content-related posts that did not display constructive features were classified within the *active* category. Drawing on insights gained through detailed discourse coding that preceded the machine training, and in consultation with the instructor, we decided to create two subcategories under the *active* category. If a student showed engagement with course materials in the post by paraphrasing, repeating, or identifying resources specifically related to the course content, then the post was coded as A2. On the other hand, peripheral course-related activities such as grading, discussions, and/or instructor-related comments that did not reference content but were clearly related to the course were coded as A1. Given these two new categories, the machine-learning model was retrained with new codes that represented the new categories.

Evaluation of Second Prototype

The second implementation of the ACI classifier within the dashboard indicated that students' posts were mostly classified as A1 or A2, meaning that the quality of students' engagement in group discussions was superficially course- or content-related. The revised sociogram helped to provide the instructor with a complete picture of the quality of students' engagement in group discussions as related to their communication patterns. For example, Group 2's network visualization (see Figure 2.4) was used to identify the effectiveness of the group's interaction process. The sociogram shows that *Kri* was very active in communicating with all other group members during the first week of the semester. However, the visualization does not provide any indication about collaborative learning taking place within the group, which was the pedagogical intent behind the learning activities implemented in the first week. Given that most of *Kri*'s posts were classified as A1, the instructor interpreted the diagram as follows: *Kri* showed mostly active behavior in group discussions and repeated the course concepts and shared assignment instructions in the group's discussion (based on the insight gained from the ACI classifier) because she appears to have assumed a leadership role in the group to encourage other members to work on the assignments (based on the insights gained from the sociogram).

A qualitative investigation of group conversations confirmed that *Kri* was trying to keep the group on task. The instructor decided to divide online class activities into two parts. Part 1 was designed to encourage each student to work on weekly tasks individually and then require them

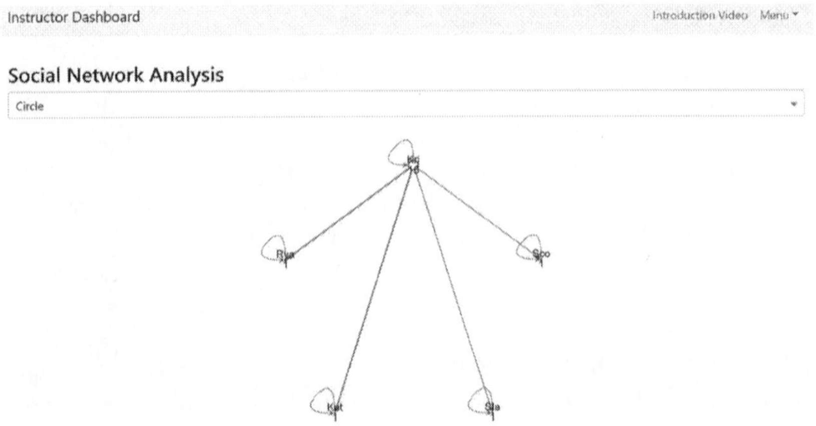

Figure 2.4 Early Network Visualization of Group 2

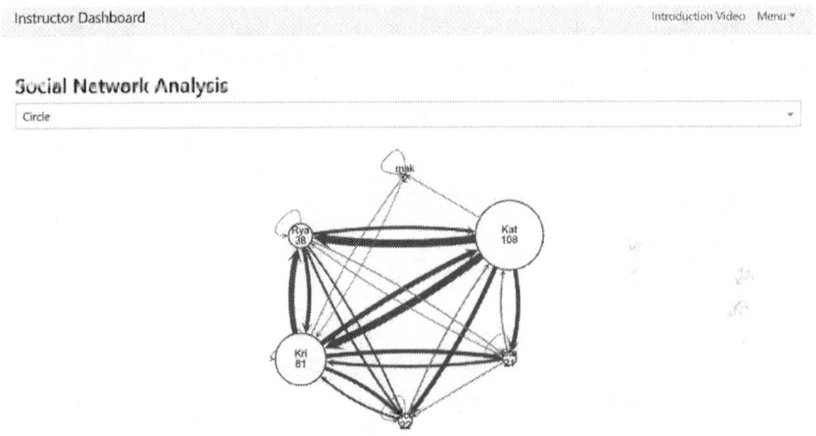

Figure 2.5 Network Visualization of Group 2 Later in the Semester

to seek consensus on the tasks within the group before moving to Part 2. In Part 2 students were asked to illustrate their group's thinking about the tasks via drawings. Figure 2.5 shows the communication pattern between the students during the last week of the semester. Although restructuring online group activities helped the group to become more collaborative when working on tasks, analysis of students' cognitive engagement still showed predominantly active behavior.

Emerging Need for a Content Visualizer Module

Adding two categories of *active* behavior within the cognitive engagement analysis helped the instructor assess whether a student was actively engaged with course materials. However, the categories lack detail about course concepts/terms discussed within groups. Thus, we decided to introduce a word-frequency visualization within the dashboard, which along with the ACI classification, allows the instructor to simultaneously monitor the course concepts as well as the level of cognitive engagement within student posts. For example, if all of a student's posts are classified as A2 or A1, and the posts only include terms like "CPU" and "RAM," the instructor can conclude that the student just paraphrased or repeated course materials referring to "CPU" and "RAM" without explaining how the CPU works with RAM in processing data. Such information can allow the instructor to construct personalized feedback that might recommend that the student strive to be more constructive in group discussions. If such a pattern is evident in most of the groups in the class, then the insights gained from the analytics can be used by the instructor to make decisions on the learning design (Bakharia et al., 2016). Such decisions could include adding activities designed to engage students in illustrating the process between the CPU and RAM or posing specific questions related to how the CPU and RAM function.

Third Dashboard Prototype

Apart from the cognitive engagement visualizer module and the interaction visualizer module, we also embedded a content visualizer module (see Figure 2.6) to the dashboard. This tool supports the instructor in monitoring the terminology mentioned in student discussions and deciding the level of engagement with course materials, concepts, and terms. We used text-mining techniques to undergird the content visualizer. Text mining has been used in other narrative/interpretive fields to identify patterns in the text (Garrison, Anderson, & Archer, 1999). These patterns can help to uncover relationships and latent themes within a body of text, and in the context of this study, the visualization allows the instructor to view group discussion text in the form of an easily grasped set of terms and frequencies. The chart allows the instructor to assess which technical and content-related terms are referenced by students in their discussions and which ones are missing. For example, the terms "multiprocessor" and "multi-core processor" are rarely mentioned by students; if, for example, these terms were integral to the project discussion for a specific week, the instructor could either probe student

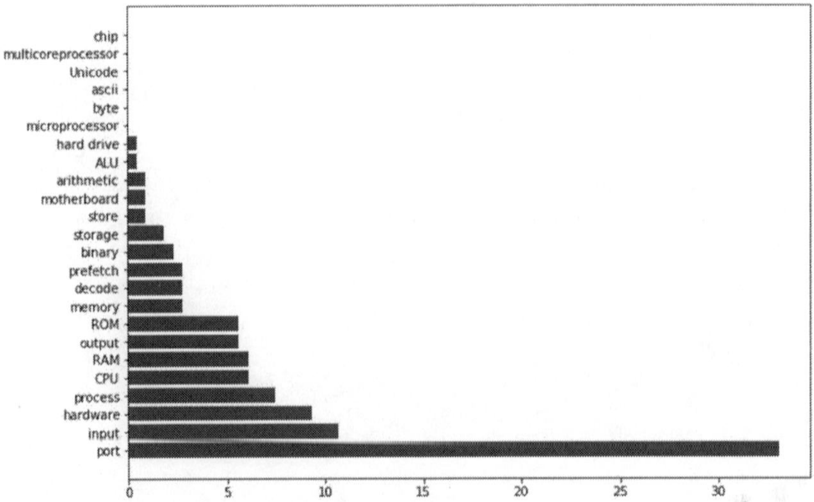

Figure 2.6 Content Visualizer Module With Word-Frequency Visualization

understanding of those terms or supply designed instruction to help students use and apply those terms in their discussion.

NEXT STEPS AND REFLECTIONS

We continue to work with the course instructor to refine the visualizations and to strengthen the machine-learning models and programs that undergird the learning analytics dashboard. However, based on the work we have accomplished so far, we have arrived at several reflections that may be of use to learning designers, researchers, and educators who intend to use learning analytics to examine interaction in online or blended settings.

Combine Learning Analytics and Learning Design Throughout the Design and Development Process

A crucial consideration in developing dashboards for learning analytics is balancing pedagogical, empirical, and technical expertise and using a pedagogically sound approach to data. As mentioned in previous sections, our work was primarily guided by empirical evidence of the value of interaction in online environments as well as the strong pedagogical focus on integrating mechanisms to support instructors in assessing and providing feedback on student interaction and engagement within online courses. At the same time, our team also consisted of members knowledgeable in the areas of machine learning, learning analytics, and programming, such that the pedagogy and empirical directions could be implemented in practice. The importance of creating interdisciplinary teams that represent multiple stakeholders is crucial to ensuring successful projects (Wright, McKay, Hershock, Miller, & Tritz, 2014).

By bringing to bear learning analytics (LA) and learning design (LD) on our conceptual design process, and identifying the pedagogical intent behind learning activities, we were able to focus on collecting appropriate data to inform learning design (Jivet et al., 2018). In our project iterations, LA provided insights on what students do (Nguyen, Huptych, & Rienties, 2018) in a pedagogical context, which in turn provided actionable insights to the instructor (Gašević, Dawson, Rogers, & Gasevic, 2016) and led to clearer contextualization of LA (Knight, Shibani, & Shum, 2018). Bakharia et al., (2016) proposed a conceptual framework aligning LD to LA that takes the teaching and learning context into account when interpreting learning analytics. In the framework, the instructor takes a central role in making decisions based on the analytics. Instructor involvement was key in our project as we depicted via the various phases of prototyping, and a significant portion of redesign and redevelopment was based on the instructor's use and evaluation of the tool for his pedagogic purposes. We plan to continue working with other instructors who teach the same information technology course so that we can solicit additional feedback from concerned stakeholders to contextualize and refine our design.

Focus on Iterative Design, Development, and Refinement

A key contributor to the development of the learning analytics dashboard was ongoing iteration and testing. From the perspective of learning design, this process maps closely on to rapid prototyping (Tripp & Bichelmeyer, 1990), and from a research perspective, we consider our process to be informed by design research where theory and intervention design work in tandem and mutually inform each other (Easterday et al., 2018). As we described earlier, our development of the tool was guided by the need for an emergent solution to a need, but our work is also grounded in theory that informs and contextualizes tool development. We had identified four main goals from the instructor's perspective: (1) *Know which students contribute to group discussions*; (2) *Know the quality of student contributions within the group discussion*; (3) *Know if students work collaboratively or cooperatively*; and (4) *Know if students missed any important course concepts*.

For the first goal, we created sociograms that allowed the instructor to quickly assess which students participate in the discussion. However, the sociograms only show presence or absence of activity, and in the next iteration we plan to integrate qualitative components of discussion within the sociogram. One possible contextualization is to change the width of lines to represent number of messages between pairs of students and different line colors to represent overall quality of communications so the instructor can gain quicker and more nuanced insights into student engagement. For the second goal, we identified an iterative process visible in the selection of an a priori coding framework for the machine-learning analyses, which was modified by the instructor's practical need and context to assess student learning – for example, the ICAP framework was modified to only use three categories (*Interactive*, *Constructive*, and *Active*), and further discussion with the instructor led to the development of two categories of *Active* (A1 and A2) to more clearly represent nuances in student discourse. These changes were then implemented in the design of the tool and the dashboard visualizations. While we don't anticipate changing the coding categories, we are in the process of adding further detail and nuances to the category definitions, including creating a future layer of machine-learning modeling where subcategories may be identified within the overall categories. As an example, within the A1 category – defined as *active* but peripheral to course content – we see lots of evidence of students taking on different group roles, such as facilitator, coordinator, and so on. These types of data and classifications can provide a substantial insight into types of roles that students adopt to further collaborative learning, which may inform instructor guidance to students on how engage in the activity. We anticipate similar refinements for visualizations for goals (3) and (4), with the goal to combine multiple visualizations for the same data, which may be helpful in making more contextualized design and pedagogical decisions (Bodily & Verbert, 2017).

CONCLUSION AND SUMMARY

In this chapter we reported on the iterative design of a prototype learning analytics dashboard informed by design-research. We worked with an instructor stakeholder to identify needs and develop a solution that integrated machine learning and learning analytics to explore student cognitive engagement and interaction in an online environment. We reported a series of design iterations guided by a human-centered design process and identified key implications that educators, learning designers, and researchers must consider for the design and development of contextual learning analytics.

Overall, as designers and instructors, we see learning analytics as having a significant role to play in teaching and learning. Based on the instructor's experiences with using the prototype, the process of focusing and addressing key pedagogical concerns using learning analytics was successful in assisting the instructor to examine students' quality and quantity of engagement and collaboration within the course. However, the process is time- and resource-intensive and requires a multidisciplinary team of data scientists, designers, instructors, and researchers, as well as a commitment to ongoing design, evaluation, and refinement.

The utility of data sciences, artificial intelligence (AI), and machine learning (ML) is apparent in many business and manufacturing contexts, and education is also poised to reap some of these benefits. However a significant challenge is the complex social structures within teaching and learning and whether and how learning analytics, AI, and ML can be appropriately and fairly applied (Cukurova, Kent, & Luckin, 2019) to support the multiple educational stakeholders, including instructors, students, and administrators. Here too, we underscore the importance of using human-centered design and development strategies that put the needs of stakeholders first and the use of technology second.

REFERENCES

Ahn, J., Campos, F., Hays, M., & Digiacomo, D. (2019). Designing in context: Reaching beyond usability in learning analytics dashboard design. *Journal of Learning Analytics*, *6*(2). https://doi.org/10.18608/jla.2019.62.5

Anderson, T., & Garrison, D. R. (1998). Learning in a networked world: New roles and responsibilities. In C. Gibson (Ed.), *Distance learners in higher education* (pp. 97–112). Madison, WI: Atwood.

Bakharia, A., Corrin, L., De Barba, P., Kennedy, G., Gašević, D., Mulder, R., . . . Lockyer, L. (2016, April 29). A conceptual framework linking learning design with learning analytics. In *ACM international conference proceeding series* (Vol. 25, pp. 329–338). New York, NY: Association for Computing Machinery. https://doi.org/10.1145/2883851.2883944

Bannon, L. J. (2011). Re-framing HCI: From human-computer interaction to human-centred interaction design. In *CHItaly: Proceedings of the 9th ACM SIGCHI Italian chapter international conference on computer-human interaction: Facing complexity*. Alghero, Italy: Association for Computing Machinery, New York, NY. https://doi.org/10.1145/2037296.2037304

Bodily, R., & Verbert, K. (2017). Review of research on student-facing learning analytics dashboards and educational recommender systems. *IEEE Transactions on Learning Technologies, 10*(4), 405–418. https://doi.org/10.1109/TLT.2017.2740172

Bratteteig, T., Bødker, K., Dittrich, Y., Mogensen, P. H., & Simonsen, J. (2013). Organising principles and general guidelines for Participatory design projects. In J. Simonsen & T. Robertson (Eds.), *Routledge international handbook of Participatory design* (pp. 117–144). Routledge. Retrieved from https://doi.org/www.routledgehandbooks.com/doi/10.4324/9780203108543.ch6

Brooks, D. C., & Pomerantz, J. (2017). *ECAR study of undergraduate students and information technology*. Louisville, CO: ECAR. Retrieved from https://library.educause.edu/resources/2017/10/ecar-study-of-undergraduate-students-and-information-technology-2017

Chen, B., Chang, Y. H., Ouyang, F., & Zhou, W. (2018). Fostering student engagement in online discussion through social learning analytics. *Internet and Higher Education, 37*, 21–30. https://doi.org/10.1016/j.iheduc.2017.12.002

Chi, M. T. H. (2009). Active-constructive-interactive: A conceptual framework for differentiating learning activities. *Topics in Cognitive Science, 1*(1), 73–105. https://doi.org/10.1111/j.1756-8765.2008.01005.x

Chi, M. T. H., Adams, J., Bogusch, E. B., Bruchok, C., Kang, S., Lancaster, M., . . . & Yaghmourian, D. L. (2018). Translating the ICAP theory of cognitive engagement into practice. *Cognitive Science, 42*(6), 1777–1832. https://doi.org/10.1111/cogs.12626

Chi, M. T. H., & Wylie, R. (2014). The ICAP framework: Linking cognitive engagement to active learning outcomes. *Educational Psychologist, 49*, 219–243. https://doi.org/10.1080/00461520.2014.965823

Cukurova, M., Kent, C., & Luckin, R. (2019). Artificial intelligence and multimodal data in the service of human decision-making: A case study in debate tutoring. *British Journal of Educational Technology, 50*(6), 3032–3046. https://doi.org/10.1111/bjet.12829

Dawson, S. (2010). "Seeing" the learning community: An exploration of the development of a resource for monitoring online student networking. *British Journal of Educational Technology, 41*(5), 736–752. https://doi.org/10.1111/j.1467-8535.2009.00970.x

De Quincey, E., Kyriacou, T., Briggs, C., & Waller, R. (2019). Student centred design of a learning analytics system. In *LAK19: The 9th international learning analytics & knowledge conference* (pp. 353–362). New York, NY: Association for Computing Machinery. https://doi.org/10.1145/3303772.3303793

Easterday, M. W., Rees Lewis, D. G., & Gerber, E. M. (2018). The logic of design research. *Learning: Research and Practice, 4*(2). https://doi.org/10.1080/23735082.2017.1286367

Ferguson, R. (2012). Learning analytics: Drivers, developments and challenges. *International Journal of Technology Enhanced Learning, 4*(5–6), 304. https://doi.org/https://doi.org/10.1504/IJTEL.2012.051816

Garrison, D. R., Anderson, T., & Archer, W. (1999). Critical inquiry in a text-based environment: Computer conferencing in higher education. *Internet and Higher Education, 2*(2–3), 87–105. https://doi.org/10.1016/S1096-7516(00)00016-6

Gašević, D., Dawson, S., Rogers, T., & Gasevic, D. (2016). Learning analytics should not promote one size fits all: The effects of instructional conditions in predicting academic success. *Internet and Higher Education, 28*. https://doi.org/10.1016/j.iheduc.2015.10.002

Giacomin, J. (2014). What is human centred design? *Design Journal, 17*(4). https://doi.org/10.2752/175630614X14056185480186

Hakkarainen, K. (1998). Cognitive value of peer interaction in computer-supported collaborative learning. *The American Educational Research Association (AERA) annual meeting*. San Diego, April 13–17, 1998.

Hu, Y. H., Lo, C. L., & Shih, S. P. (2014). Developing early warning systems to predict students' online learning performance. *Computers in Human Behavior, 36*. https://doi.org/10.1016/j.chb.2014.04.002

Jivet, I., Scheffel, M., Specht, M., & Drachsler, H. (2018). License to evaluate. In *Proceedings of LAK'18* (pp. 31–40). Sydney, Australia. https://doi.org/10.1145/3170358.3170421

Knight, S., Shibani, A., & Shum, S. B. (2018). Augmenting formative writing assessment with learning analytics: A design abstraction approach. In J. Kay & R. Luckin (Eds.), *Rethinking learning in the digital age: Making the learning sciences count, 13th international conference of the learning sciences (ICLS)* (Vol. 3). London, UK: International Society of the Learning Sciences.

Kreijns, K., Kirschner, P. A., & Vermeulen, M. (2013). Social aspects of CSCL environments: A research framework. *Educational Psychologist, 48*(4), 229–242. https://doi.org/10.1080/00461520.2012.750225

Lave, J., & Wenger, E. (1991). *Situated learning: Legitimate peripheral participation. Situated learning legitimate peripheral participation*. Cambridge: Cambridge University Press. Retrieved from http://books.google.com/books?hl=en&lr=&id=CAVIOrW3vYAC&oi=fnd&pg=PA11&dq=legitimate+peripheral+participation&ots=OzqBxp_Jzo&sig=Efl3AqUt83clKuRPGeX7pbrBOkc

Lederman, D. (2018). *Online education ascends*. Retrieved from www.insidehighered.com/digital-learning/article/2018/11/07/new-data-online-enrollments-grow-and-share-overall-enrollment

Li, G., Hoi, S. C. H., Chang, K., & Jain, R. (2010). Micro-blogging sentiment detection by collaborative online learning. In *Proceedings – IEEE international conference on data mining, ICDM*. New York, NY: IEEE Computer Society. https://doi.org/10.1109/ICDM.2010.139

Li, Qi. (2019). *Examining the effects of learners' background and social network position on content-related interaction via the MOOC platform*. Pennsylvania State University. Retrieved from https://etda.libraries.psu.edu/catalog/16907qxl127

Lipponen, L., Rahikainen, M., Lallimo, J., & Hakkarainen, K. (2003). Patterns of participation and discourse in elementary students' computer-supported collaborative learning. *Learning and Instruction, 13*(5), 487–509. https://doi.org/10.1016/S0959-4752(02)00042-7

Minaei-Bidgoli, B., Kortemeyer, G., & Punch, W. F. (2004). Optimizing classification ensembles via a genetic algorithm for a Web-based educational system. *Lecture Notes in Computer Science (Including Subseries Lecture Notes in Artificial Intelligence and Lecture Notes in Bioinformatics), 3138*, 397–406. https://doi.org/10.1007/978-3-540-27868-9_42

Moore, M. G. (1989). Editorial: Three types of interaction. *American Journal of Distance Education, 3*(2), 1–7. https://doi.org/10.1080/08923648909526659

Moore, M. G. (1997). Theory of transactional distance. In D. Keegan (Ed.), *Theoretical principles of distance education* (Vol. 2, pp. 22–38). Routledge. Retrieved from www.aged.tamu.edu/research/readings/Distance/1997MooreTransDistance.pdf

Nguyen, Q., Huptych, M., & Rienties, B. (2018). Linking students' timing of engagement to learning design and academic performance. In *LAK '18: Proceedings of the 8th international conference on learning analytics and knowledge* (pp. 141–150). New York, NY: ACM. https://doi.org/10.1145/3170358.3170398

Popenici, S. A. D., & Kerr, S. (2017). Exploring the impact of artificial intelligence on teaching and learning in higher education. *Research and Practice in Technology Enhanced Learning, 12.* https://doi.org/10.1186/s41039-017-0062-8

Roschelle, J., & Teasley, S. D. (1995). The construction of shared knowledge in collaborative problem solving. In *Computer supported collaborative learning* (pp. 69–197). Berlin: Springer-Verlag. https://doi.org/10.1007/978-3-642-85098-1_5

Shum, S. B., Ferguson, R., & Martinez-Maldonado, R. (2019). Human-centred learning analytics. *Journal of Learning Analytics, 6*(2). https://doi.org/10.18608/jla.2019.62.1

SOLAR. (n.d.). *What is learning analytics?* Retrieved September 29, 2020, from https://www.solaresearch.org/about/what-is-learning-analytics/

Stahl, G. (2005). Group cognition in computer-assisted collaborative learning. *Journal of Computer Assisted Learning, 21*(2), 79–90. https://doi.org/10.1111/j.1365-2729.2005.00115.x

Tripp, S. D., & Bichelmeyer, B. (1990). Rapid prototyping: An alternative instructional design strategy. *Educational Technology Research and Development, 38*(1). https://doi.org/10.1007/BF02298246

Vie, J. J., Popineau, F., Bruillard, É., & Bourda, Y. (2018). Automated test assembly for handling learner cold-start in large-scale assessments. *International Journal of Artificial Intelligence in Education, 28*(4), 616–631. https://doi.org/10.1007/s40593-017-0163-y

Vygotsky, L. S. (1978). *Mind in society: The development of higher psychological processes.* Boston, MA: Harvard University Press. https://doi.org/10.1007/978-3-540-92784-6

Wang, X., Yang, D., Wen, M., Koedinger, K., & Rosé, C. P. (2015). Investigating how student's cognitive behavior in MOOC discussion forums affect learning gains. In *Educational data mining.* Retrieved from https://eric.ed.gov/?id=ED560568

Weidlich, J., & Bastiaens, T. J. (2018). Technology matters – The impact of transactional distance on satisfaction in online distance learning. *International Review of Research in Open and Distance Learning, 19*(3). https://doi.org/10.19173/irrodl.v19i3.3417

Wright, M. C., McKay, T., Hershock, C., Miller, K., & Tritz, J. (2014). Better than expected: Using learning analytics to promote student success in gateway science. *Change: The Magazine of Higher Learning, 46*(1). https://doi.org/10.1080/00091383.2014.867209

Zeide, E. (2019). Artificial intelligence in higher education: Applications, promise and perils, and ethical questions. *Educause Review.* Retrieved from: https://er.educause.edu/articles/2019/8/artificial-intelligence-in-higher-education-applications-promise-and-perils-and-ethical-questions

CHAPTER 3

Assessing the Impact of Immersive Virtual Reality on Objective Learning Outcomes Based on Presence, Immersion, and Interactivity

A Thematic Review

Hui-Ching Kayla Hsu and Cong Wang

INTRODUCTION

Sweeping the digital realm in the past few decades, immersive virtual reality (IVR) has attracted much attention from industry and academia. Various IVR applications have been generated in business, education, engineering, medicine, and psychology, followed by studies documenting the development process or examining the effects of IVR applications. Simply put, the effect of IVR begins with a technology-induced illusion that alters users' perception, and then the perception drives reality. A promising tool for teaching and training, this powerful medium offers access to experiences and places otherwise inaccessible to learners for reasons including finance, time, and safety (Chua, Sridhar, Zhang, Dissanayake, & Nanayakkara, 2019).

In recent years, a growing body of IVR literature has reported many factors that influence user experience. Although these studies provided a broad context in which to frame an understanding of IVR, they tended to employ an integrated approach, combining technical aspects and individual user conditions, to evaluate IVR experience and performance outcomes. Close examination of these factors has shown that presence, immersion, and interactivity are directly related to users' cognitive and affective interactions

DOI: 10.4324/9781003089704-5

in their IVR experience. As the rapid development of technology continues to enhance presence, immersion, and interactivity in IVR, the mechanism by which these components promote learning remains underexplored (Cox, House, Lopez, & Pool, 2017; Schott & Marshall, 2018).

Researchers and practitioners of IVR have pointed out the lack of theoretical understanding of the manner in which the virtual world experience brings about learning (Fowler, 2015; Loke, 2015). In response, we believe we can fill the gap by building a theoretical foundation based on an understanding of three crucial elements of IVR that are relevant to learners' cognitive and affective states. Thus, our purpose in this chapter is to examine presence, immersion, and interactivity through a thematic literature review designed to identify their relations with targeted learning outcomes in the studies we reviewed. We address the following questions:

1. How are presence, immersion, and interactivity defined, measured, or contextualized in IVR studies?
2. How are presence, immersion, and interactivity related to performance outcomes in IVR?
3. How can findings inform researchers and practitioners about the design elements of IVR that enhance learning performance?

As the innovation in IVR technology continues to captivate people, and reasonably priced products become widely available for educational use, we hope the nuanced knowledge of presence, immersion, and interactivity that we provide in this chapter will move us from viewing IVR as a technology to building an IVR pedagogy.

HISTORY AND RELEVANT STUDIES

The concept of virtual reality was introduced in the 1960s by Sutherland (1964) in his doctoral dissertation, "SketchPad: A Man-Machine Graphical Communication System," in which he described the use of a light-pen that allowed users to point at and interact with graphical objects displayed on a computer screen. Sutherland later published "The Ultimate Display," in which he envisioned the potential of computers to simulate reality. He believed that "with appropriate programming such a display could literally be the Wonderland into which Alice walked" (Sutherland, 1965, p. 2). The term "virtual reality" (VR) had gained popularity by 1989, when Jaron Lanier established a company called Virtual Programming Languages Research (Lewis, 1994). During the following decades, the rapid development of VR software and hardware expanded VR applications. One such application that emerged was immersive virtual reality (IVR), the focus of this chapter. IVR deploys technologies like Head-Mounted Display (HMD) or multiple projections to completely immerse the user in the digitally generated world (Furht, 2008). Its multisensory stimuli and stereoscopic viewpoints, often combined with motion-tracking or manipulative gadgets, create a vivid presentation different from the VR produced for desktop computing environments (Freina & Ott, 2015; Robertson, Card, & Mackinlay, 1993). Then, in the late 20th century IVR's educational potential increased (Phillips, 1998).

This chapter aims to provide insights on how presence, immersion, and interactivity have been studied in the literature and how they are related to learning achievement in IVR. In recent years, several systematic reviews of studies in VR fields with various purposes have appeared. In the rest of this section, we highlight the findings of relevant studies to provide a knowledge foundation and then point out the research gap this chapter aims to fill.

Radianti, Majchrzak, Fromm, and Wohlgenannt (2020) reviewed studies related to IVR applications for higher education, focusing on learning content, IVR design elements, and learning theories. They reported that in the studies they reviewed from 2016 to 2018, learning theories that could have served as a design framework were often omitted. In addition, their efforts to map out the connection between IVR design elements and learning content provided a comprehensive overview of how these elements were incorporated in educational IVR applications.

Jensen and Konradsen (2018) reviewed the use of HMDs in education and training with a focus on measured learner experience and learning outcomes. Their report, based on studies from 2013 to 2017, highlighted factors that influence immersion and presence, such as graphic rendering speed, personality traits, and the external viewing environment. Overall, their study provided an observation of the usefulness of HMDs in various learning domains documented in previous studies.

Mikropoulos and Natsis (2011) examined VR studies to elaborate on how the technical characteristics of VR can contribute to learning. Their review identified first-order experiences, natural semantics, autonomy, presence, and intuitive interactivity among the affordances offered by educational VR applications. In particular, they reported that 12 of the 53 studies they reviewed from 1999 to 2009 positively connected presence with learning; however, they also pointed out that the picture of these VR affordances in the learning process is not always straightforward. In terms of intuitive interactivity, Mikropoulos and Natsis indicated that empirical studies have shown no clear positive results perhaps because only a few studies incorporated intuitive interaction in VR.

These reviews, conducted over a span of the past two decades, not only provided a wealth of information regarding the educational use of VR but also informed the future research agenda, prompting the inquiries of the current chapter. First, related terms and concepts in VR educational applications are still emerging and thus may lack consensus or clarity; therefore, more work is needed to create a common understanding of terms and concepts as relevant theories are established (Radianti et al., 2020). Second, the influence of VR on learning has been unclear (Mikropoulos & Natsis, 2011), and its association with learning achievement has yet to be confirmed with rigorous research methodology beyond the technical usability report (Jensen & Konradsen, 2018; Radianti et al., 2020). Third, the rapid advancement in VR reflected in this series of review studies confirms the need to fully understand the learning affordances of VR. In 2011 Mikropoulos and Natsis found few studies documenting the use of intuitive interactivity in VR, yet today people employ myriad gadgets that provide haptic, tactile, and force feedback as well as alternative ways to navigate a VR system. Because educators recognized the value of an immersive learning experience at the end of the 20th century (Phillips, 1998), we believe studies accumulated in the two decades that followed deserve examination under a refined lens that focuses on presence, immersion, and interactivity. In this chapter we illustrate how these terms and concepts have been defined and measured in IVR studies that probed their impact on objective learning outcomes.

DATA COLLECTION AND ANALYSIS

We employed a rigorous method to select samples, identify matching articles, code the contents, and analyze the findings. Training sessions were conducted at the beginning of each stage to enhance the intercoder reliability. Differences occurring during the process were noted and then discussed further to reach a consensus.

Because of the increased popularity of IVR in numerous disciplines, we selected five research databases to ensure a comprehensive search: Web of Science (interdisciplinary), PubMed (biomedicine and health), IEEE Xplore (computer science and engineering), ERIC (education), and PsycINFO (psychology). We searched each database in April 2020 with keywords using the following Boolean search string:

> (immersive virtual reality) AND (presence OR immersion OR interactivity)

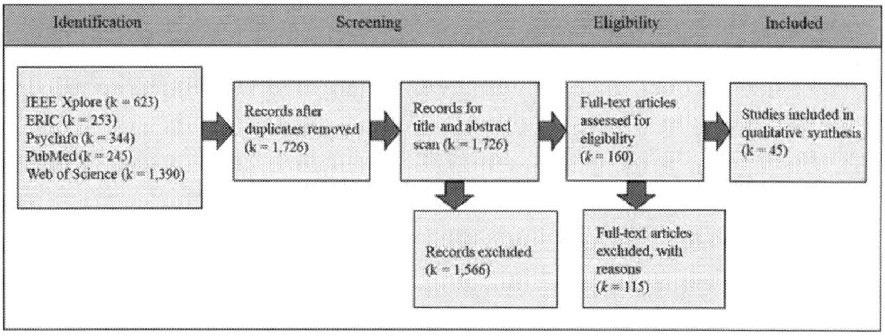

Figure 3.1 PRISMA Flow Chart for Reference Selection and Inclusion

The search, which included articles from peer-reviewed publications and conference proceedings from 2000 to March 2020, generated a total of 1,726 references, which were then filtered (see Figure 3.1) using the PRISMA flow diagram (Moher, Liberati, Tetzlaff, Altman, & PRISMA Group, 2009).

Following the inclusion and exclusion criteria shown in Table 3.1, 45 articles were included for the following coding stage in this qualitative synthesis.

After developing an initial coding scheme, we reviewed two samples from the identified studies and revised the scheme accordingly. The coded variables included Subject Field, Participants (primary, secondary, college, adult, special group), Focus (presence, immersion, interactivity), Definition, Measurement, Performed Tasks in IVR, Impacts on Learning Outcomes, Design Principles, and Pedagogical Implication. These coding

***Table 3.1* Inclusion and Exclusion Criteria**

Inclusion	*Exclusion*
• Articles that involved using immersive virtual reality in curriculum, instruction (training), and professional development. • Defined or measured presence, immersion, or interactivity in an immersive virtual environment. • With an experimental or quasi-experimental design that reported objective learning outcomes.	• Not about learning or teaching. • Not an immersive virtual reality. • No comparison (pre vs. post or control vs. treatment). • No objective learning outcomes reported. • Incomplete paper.

variables offered an in-depth view of the studies and helped answer our research questions.

RESULTS

Table 3.2 presents an overview of the characteristics of all 45 studies included in our study. Most of the studies related to the element of presence (k = 28; 62%), followed by immersion (k = 17; 38%), and then interactivity (k = 13; 29%). The subject fields included education, engineering, medical training, psychology, and specific cognitive or spatial tasks. The majority of study samples comprised college students and adults, but samples of elementary and secondary school students were also included. The sample sizes in these studies ranged from 10 to 1,138. A dagger mark next to the author's name indicates the study reported a positive impact of IVR on learning outcomes.

Presence

The majority of the reviewed studies examined the role of presence in educational IVR applications. These studies came from a wide range of subject domains with varying population groups.

Definition and Measurement

As shown in Table 3.2, most studies defined "presence" as a subjective perception of being in the virtual world (Heeter, 1992; Nichols et al., 2000; Slater & Steed, 2000; Witmer & Singer, 1998) that can reach a degree to which participants do not feel the facilitating medium (Lombard & Ditton, 1997). In some studies, presence was divided into two categories based on the focus of the IVR application. The first category was self-presence; that is, a psychological state in which virtual selves are experienced as actual selves (Passig, 2009). The second category was social presence; that is, the feeling of being present with another entity (Eynard et al., 2015).

In terms of measurement scales, the Witmer-Singer Presence Questionnaire (Witmer et al., 2005; Witmer & Singer, 1998) was the scale most frequently used in the studies reviewed, followed by the Igroup Presence Questionnaire (Schubert et al., 2001) and the SUS Presence Questionnaire (Slater et al., 1994). For measuring social presence, the Networked Minds Questionnaire (Biocca et al., 2001) was used in a study by Kim et al. (2015), and the Social Presence Questionnaire (Bailenson et al., 2001) was adopted by George et al. (2018).

Table 3.2 **Characteristics of Studies Analyzed**

Study Listed by First Author	*Subject*	*Focus*	*Definitions*	*Setup and Measurement*	*Results*
Alrehaili and Al Osman (2019)	Honeybee ecology.	Presence. Immersion.	Immersion/Presence – The sense of presence participants feel while interacting with the virtual environment.	Comparison: HMD VR, desktop VR, book. Immersion/presence – self-developed questionnaire.	No significant difference was found in presence/immersion between Immersive VR and Desktop VR. No significant difference was found in the knowledge tests across the three groups.
†Bailenson et al. (2008)	Physical Training (Taichi).	Interactivity.	Interactivity has been defined from three perspectives, including technology (Steuer, 1992), process (Rafaeli, 1988), and user (Kiousis, 2002; Wu, 1999).	Interactivity was assessed with three variables at two levels: Media (VR vs. video); Review (yes vs. no); and Separate views of themselves (yes vs. no).	Study 1: No difference in the objective learning assessment. Study 2: Participants in the VR condition outperformed participants in the video condition.
Barré et al. (2019)	Medical Training.	Presence.	Subjective experience of being in one place or environment, even when one is physically situated in another (Witmer & Singer, 1998).	Comparison: HMD VR vs. None. Presence questionnaire (PQ; Witmer & Singer, 1998).	Presence: No comparison. No significant difference was reported in performance between the two groups.

Bertrand, Bhargava, Madathil, Gramopadhye, and Babu (2017)	Precision Metrology.	Presence.	None.	Comparison: Large screen vs. HMD VR. Presence Questionnaire Ver. 3.0 (Witmer, Jerome, & Singer, 2005).	No significant difference in presence except for the simulation fidelity category. No significant difference was found on the cognitive domain and psychomotor domain of the performance test.
Buttussi and Chittaro (2018)	Engineering Training.	Presence. Immersion. Interactivity.	Presence – The sense of being in the virtual environment. Immersion – Immersion/display fidelity is about the realism of the output devices and the reproduction of sensory stimuli. Interactivity – None.	Presence – Igroup Presence Questionnaire (Schubert, Friedmann, & Regenbrecht, 2001). Immersion – Three levels: HMD with wide FOV; HMD with narrow FOV; and desktop. Interactivity – High: HMD with 6 DOF tracker. Median: HMD with 3 DOF tracker. Low: Desktop with Joystick.	Significant difference in presence was found only between the high and low immersion group. There was no significant difference in knowledge scores across the three groups.
†Chaturvedi et al. (2012)	Engineering Education.	Immersion.	Immersion is a realistic simulation of the experiment in a laboratory- like environment.	Comparison – Desktop VR vs. CAVE.	CAVE VR students outperformed Desktop VR students on the quiz.

(Continued)

Table 3.2 **(Continued)**

Study Listed by First Author	*Subject*	*Focus*	*Definitions*	*Setup and Measurement*	*Results*
Chen et al. (2019)	Physical Training (Taichi).	Presence.	None.	Comparison – CAVE, HMD, Desktop. Presence – Used items from Witmer and Singer (1998).	The HMD group scored higher in the sensory and realism category under presence, followed by CAVE and Desktop groups. Significantly better motion quality was found in CAVE despite the high presence perceived in HMD.
Chua et al. (2019)	Engineering.	Immersion. Interactivity.	Immersion – None. Interactivity – None.	Immersion – Comparison: iPad, magic window, Google Cardboard. Interactivity – Comparison: Passive consumption of video content vs. learner-paced interactive exploration.	Immersion – No significant differences was found on performance across devices. Interactivity – The difference in performance was not significant.
†Cooper et al. (2018)	Psychology. Engineering.	Presence. Immersion. Interactivity.	Presence – The subjective feeling of being present in the virtual environment, rather than the real space. Immersion – A subjective experience: The psychological state where one perceives himself as being included in and interacting with an environment. Interactivity – None.	Immersion/Presence – Presence Questionnaire (Witmer & Singer, 1998; Witmer et al., 2005). Interactivity – Level of interactivity is enhanced via provision of sensory cues (audio, tactile, and visual).	All three sensory cues contribute to the sense of presence. Immersion/Presence – A correlation analysis showed that increased presence is positively correlated with higher performance in VR contexts. Interactivity – The task was performed faster when audio and/or tactile cues were present.

†Eden and Passig (2007)	Concept of time.	Immersion.	None.	Comparison – Immersive 3D VR, pictorial representation, written representation, auditory representation.	The IVR group performed tasks with the smallest error rate compared to other groups.
†Eynard, Pallot, Christmann, and Richir (2015)	Collaborative tasks.	Presence.	Presence – The feeling of "being there" in the virtual environment. Social presence – The feeling of being present with another entity.	Comparison: Performing collaborative tasks with or without verbal communication. Igroup Presence Questionnaire (Schubert, Friedmann, & Regenbrecht, 1999). Co-presence – Networked Minds Questionnaire (Biocca, Harms, & Gregg, 2001).	Verbal communication had positive effects on some items in the presence and co-presence questionnaire. Participants with verbal communication enabled had better performances.
Ferguson, van den Broek, and van Oostendorp (2020)	Invention of vaccination.	Presence. Interactivity.	Presence – None. Interactivity – The extent to which users are allowed to explore the educational content and given choices on what to learn freely.	Presence – Igroup Presence Questionnaire (Schubert et al., 1999). Interactivity – Interactivity is represented by having navigation options.	Participants in the passive interaction perceived lower presence, had higher scores on factual knowledge, but showed no difference in spatial knowledge.
Formosa, Morrison, Hill, and Stone (2018)	Psychology. Education.	Presence.	Presence – The subjective experience of actually existing in the virtual environment (Slater and Steed, 2000; Witmer and Singer, 1998).	Presence – Survey items modified from Alexander, Brunyé, Sidman, and Weil (2005).	No correlation was found between presence and learning outcomes. All three learning outcomes in knowledge, attitudinal change, and empathetic understanding have significant improvement.

(Continued)

Table 3.2 **(Continued)**

Study Listed by First Author	*Subject*	*Focus*	*Definitions*	*Setup and Measurement*	*Results*
†Freina, Bottino, Tavella, and Chiorri (2017)	Spatial perspective taking.	Presence. Immersion.	Presence – The extent to which participants believe they are somewhere different from their actual physical location (Nichols, Haldane, & Wilson, 2000). Immersion – Spatial immersion refers to the technical capability of the system to deliver a surrounding and convincing environment.	Presence – Presence questionnaire (Slater, Usoh, & Steed, 1994). Immersion – Comparison: immersive group (HMD), semi-immersive (Desktop), non-immersive (Fixed picture).	The HMD group reported a higher degree of presence. It also performed significantly better than the Fixed-Picture group, but the same with the Desktop group.
George, Spitzer, and Hussmann (2018)	Memory and object-finding tasks.	Presence.	Spatial presence – A subjective measure of how "real" the virtual world is perceived in comparison to the real world. Social presence – The perception of interacting face-to-face with another real person.	Comparison: Using sound, webcam, or avatar as a guide. Presence – Igroup Presence Questionnaire (Schubert, 2003). Social Presence: SP questionnaire (Bailenson, Blascovich, Beall, & Loomis, 2001).	Statistically significant differences in social presences were found among the three conditions. No significant differences were found in spatial presence. No significant differences were reported in task performance.

†Giglioli, Vidal, and Raya (2019)	Cooking Tasks.	Presence.	The feeling of "being there."	Comparison: AR vs. VR. Presence –Slater et al. (1994). ITC-Sense of Presence Inventory (Lessiter, Freeman, Keogh, & Davidoff, 2001).	The VR group perceived a higher degree of presence and was better at keeping up with designated burning and cooling time.
†Gruchalla (2004)	Engineering.	Immersion.	None.	Comparison: Desktop VR vs. CAVE.	CAVE users produced significantly higher rates of correct solutions in a shorter amount of time.
Hedge, Weaver, and Schnall (2017)	Spatial Navigation.	Presence.	The subjective experience of being in the environment (Slater, 2003).	Comparison: Fulldome vs. Flat screen. Presence – PQ (Witmer and Singer, 1998).	Presence was significantly higher in the Fulldome setting. Males in the Fulldome condition performed better than males in the flat screen condition only in one of the four assessments.
†Huang (2020)	Exergame.	Presence.	A subjective experience of feeling immersed in a mediated environment.	Comparison: HMD vs. Large screen. Presence – Adopted from the MEC Spatial Presence Questionnaires (Vorderer et al., 2004).	HMD elicited a significantly higher presence. Presence was positively associated with participants' improvement in cognitive tasks.
Huang, Luo, Yang, Lu, and Chen (2020)	Biology Education.	Presence.	A sense of spatial immersion in a mediated environment (Weibel & Wissmath, 2011) and can be used to describe the intensity of emotional involvement.	The sense of presence questionnaire (Witmer et al., 2005).	The regression coefficient analysis showed that involvement/immersion and interface quality were negatively associated with performance in the knowledge test.

(Continued)

***Table 3.2* (Continued)**

Study Listed by First Author	*Subject*	*Focus*	*Definitions*	*Setup and Measurement*	*Results*
Huber et al. (2017)	Medical Training.	Presence.	None.	Comparison: Desktop VR vs. 360-degree IVR. Presence – Questionnaire (Nichols et al., 2000).	Presence – No comparison No significant difference was found in the overall performance. Participants' time for fine dissection was significantly longer, and the cholecystectomy task was with higher error rates during IVR.
Huber, Paschold, Hansen, Lang, and Kneist (2018)	Medical Training.	Presence.	None.	Comparison: Artificial graphic IVR vs. 360 immersive VR. Presence – Questionnaire (Nichols et al., 2000).	A significantly higher presence was reported in 360-degree IVR. No significant difference was found in the overall performance of the three surgical tasks.
†Johnston et al. (2018)	Education.	Interactivity.	None.	Comparison: Traditional lecture (control group) vs. traditional + VR (interactivity group).	Students who experienced VR showed a significant improvement in exam performance.

Kim, Gračanin, Yang, and Quek (2015)	Spatial Task.	Interactivity.	Interactivity is represented by various navigation methods.	Comparison: Finger walking (FWIP), Joystick, two feet (SF-WIP).	The FWIP navigation and the SF-WIP methods had better effects on route knowledge acquisition than the Joystick navigation technique did; however, there was no significant difference between the FWIP and SF-WIP technique. Participants in the FWIP and SF-WIP navigation groups acquired survey knowledge of the maze.
Kim, Rosenthal, Zielinski, and Brady (2014)	Psychology.	Presence.	The psychological perception of being in or existing in the virtual environment in which one is immersed (Heeter, 1992).	Comparison: CAVE, HMD, Desktop with low-stress or high-stress tasks. Presence Questionnaire (PQ; Witmer et al., 2005).	Presence was significantly higher in CAVE, followed by HMD and Desktop. No significant difference was reported in task accuracy across the three platforms. A significant interaction effect was found between VR systems and stress conditions.
Kwon (2019)	Science Education.	Presence. Interactivity.	Presence – The sense of being there (Heeter, 1992) and perceptual illusion of non-mediation (Lombard & Ditton 1997). Interactivity – The level of participation in editing the form and content of the mediated environment in real time (Steuer, 1992).	Comparison: HMD vs. HMD with motorized interactivity technology (AVR). Presence – Questionnaires by Schubert et al. (1999, 2001; Schubert, 2003). Interactivity – Tactile interactivity and locomotive interactivity were assessed by Witmer and Singer (1998).	Presence was significantly higher in AVR, but no difference was reported in locomotive interactivity. No difference in overall knowledge assessment. AVR participants performed better only in analyzing/evaluating/creating type of questions.

(Continued)

Table 3.2 **(Continued)**

Study Listed by First Author	*Subject*	*Focus*	*Definitions*	*Setup and Measurement*	*Results*
Lok, Naik, Whitton, and Brooks (2003)	Block arrangement task.	Presence.	How much participants believed they were "in" the virtual world.	Comparison: Real or virtual blocks with generic or visually faithful self-avatar. Steed-Usoh-Slater Presence Questionnaire (Slater et al., 1994).	No significant difference was found in presence across all the conditions. Interacting with real objects reduced task completion time.
Ma et al. (2006)	Sports.	Presence.	The sense of being physically present within a computer-generated or remote environment (Draper, Kaber, & Usher, 1998).	Comparison: Viewpoint, auditory cue type, visual background, shot distance. Presence – a) Two-item PQ developed by Draper and Blair (1996); b) an objective measurement using a secondary-monitoring task performance.	Viewpoint and auditory cue increased perceived presence; however, it had no effects on task performance.

Markowitz, Laha, Perone, Pea, and Bailenson (2018)	Climate Change.	Presence. Immersion.	Presence – How well an individual perceives the self in the virtual world and has the opportunity to act within the space (Wirth et al., 2007). Immersion – How well the technology approximates actions and movements in the virtual space.	Comparison: Study 1: Pre- and post- tests. Study 2: Avatar as Coral vs. Human Avatar. Study 3: Physical movement during IVR. Study 4: Swimming with arm movement or joystick. Presence – Presence Questionnaire (Yee & Bailenson, 2007). Immersion – None.	Study1: There was no difference in reported levels of presence between pre- and post- test. There was a significant increase in ocean acidification knowledge. Study2: Presence was positively associated with post-knowledge. Study 3: Physical movement predicted inquisitiveness but not attitude change. Study 4: Swimming methods had no impact on the knowledge test.
Meyer, Omdahl, and Makransky (2019)	Education.	Immersion.	An objective measure based on the vividness offered and the extent to which a medium shuts out the outside world (Cummings & Bailenson, 2016).	Comparison: IVR vs. video with or without pre-training.	There was no significant main effect of immersion on knowledge retention and transfer. The use of pre-training significantly increased knowledge and transfer in the immersive VR condition.

(Continued)

Table 3.2 **(Continued)**

Study Listed by First Author	*Subject*	*Focus*	*Definitions*	*Setup and Measurement*	*Results*
†Mills et al. (2019)	Medical Training.	Immersion.	Perception of being present in the nonphysical world.	Comparison: IVR vs. live simulation. Objective – Heart rate. Subjective – National Aeronautics and Space Administration Task Load Index (NASA-TLX), an instrument requiring students to rate their perceived burden of the simulation.	The live simulation generated a higher level of immersion compared to the VR platform. No differences were observed in clinical performance.
Moro, Štromberga, Raikos, and Stirling (2017)	Medical Training.	Immersion.	None.	Comparison: AR, IVR, tablet 3D.	No significant differences were reported on the learning outcomes.
Papachristos, Vrellis, and Mikropoulos (2017)	Science Education.	Presence.	The phenomenon where a person fails to perceive or acknowledge that a mediated experience is mediated. (Lombard & Ditton, 1997).	Comparison: High-end VR vs. mobile VR. Temple Presence Inventory (TPI; Lombard, Ditton, & Weinstein, 2009).	No significant difference was found in presence. No significant difference in the post-test scores between the two settings; only the increase between pre- and post- test for high-end VR was significant.

Parmar et al. (2016)	Education.	Presence.	None.	Comparison: HMD vs. Desktop. Witmer-Singer questionnaire (Witmer & Singer, 1998).	No significant difference was found in presence. HMD VR participants performed better in high-level cognitive tasks, while Desktop VR users did better with psychomotor tasks.
†Passig (2009)	Concept of Time.	Immersion. Interactivity.	Immersion – None. Interactivity – None.	Comparison: 3D IVR, 2D pictorial episodes, none.	Immersion and Interactivity – Participants with mental retardation who were exposed to the IVR program achieved a greater degree of sequential time perception than did those exposed to a 2D program, or those who were not exposed to any aid.
†Passig et al. (2010)	Concept of Time.	Immersion.	None.	Comparison: 3D immersive VR vs. 2D representation modes.	Participants in the 3D IVR demonstrated better performance.
Persky et al. (2009)	Health.	Presence.	Self-presence – A psychological state in which virtual selves are experienced as the actual self.	Comparison: Active vs. didactic learning environment. Presence – Items from Swinth and Blascovich (2001).	The active learning environment induced a significantly higher presence. No relationship was found between presence and learning outcomes in both environments.
Roussou and Slater (2017)	Math Education.	Immersion. Interactivity.	Immersion – None. Interactivity – None.	Immersion – Comparison: Immersion vs. non-immersion. Interactivity – Three levels: Interactive VR, Passive VR, Lego.	Immersion – No significant difference was found in the knowledge test. Interactivity – There was no significant difference in post-test scores across the three conditions.

(Continued)

***Table 3.2* (Continued)**

Study Listed by First Author	*Subject*	*Focus*	*Definitions*	*Setup and Measurement*	*Results*
Selzer, Gazcon, and Larrea (2019)	Traveling to a wetland.	Presence.	Being perceptually present in a virtual environment so deeply as "if the medium were not there." (Lombard & Ditton, 1997).	Comparison: high-end VR, low-end VR, desktop. Presence – Presence Questionnaire (PQ, Witmer et al., 2005). Bouchard's test (Bouchard et al., 2004).	A medium positive correlation was found between learning outcome and presence. The high-end VR and low-end VR groups had significantly better learning outcomes and a higher level of a perceived presence than the desktop condition did. No difference existed between high-end and low-end VR groups.
Stanney, Kingdon, Graeber, and Kennedy (2002)	Locomotion and Object Manipulation Tasks.	Presence. Interactivity.	Presence – A sense of being a part of the virtual world. Interactivity – The ability to traverse through and manipulate objects in a virtual environment.	Presence – Comparison: Exposure duration, scene complexity. The Presence Questionnaire (PQ; Lampton et al., 1994). Interactivity – Comparison: complete control vs. semi-control.	Presence – Duration of exposure did not significantly affect presence, while scene complexity did. Scene complexity did not significantly affect overall performance, while duration of exposure did. Interactivity – Users with complete control over movement achieved higher performance scores (26% higher) than users with semi-control.

Steed, Pan, Zisch, and Steptoe (2016)	Cognitive Task.	Presence.	None.	Comparison: Presence or absence of self-avatar, showing or hiding of hand movement.	For letter recall tasks, participants with self-avatar and hand movement showing significantly outperformed the rest. For spatial rotation tasks, the results were not significant.
Vargas-Orjuela, Uribe-Quevedo, Rojas, Kapralos, and Perez-Gutierrez (2017)	Medical Training.	Immersion.	None.	Comparison: Immersive VR vs. non-VR.	The authors found that the diagnosis of the immersive VR group was slightly better than the non-VR group, suggesting that immersion may have a positive effect on the murmur interpretation.
†Yang et al. (2002)	Motion Training.	Interactivity.	None.	Comparison: Ghost metaphor-based VR vs. real-world indirect training.	Subjects trained in the virtual environment performed better (that is, the rhythms of motion were better preserved). Nevertheless, there was no difference in knowledge retention on the second day.
†Yu, Saham, Sahami, Sessions, and Denn (2017)	Astronomy.	Immersion.	None.	Comparison: Fulldome, flat screen, no visualizations.	Fulldome students had the largest knowledge gain compared to the other two groups.
Zhang, Bowman, and Jones (2019)	Education.	Interactivity.	The ability to select virtual objects and apply intended effects, and the ability to access specific learning information in the environment.	Comparison: low, medium, and high.	No significant difference in students' objective learning gains across different levels of interactivity, although higher levels of interactivity seemed to be associated with a better learning experience.

Impact of Presence on Learning Outcomes

The research design in studies probing the effect of presence on learning outcomes typically had control and treatment groups using different devices for IVR experience. In the studies reviewed in our analysis, comparisons were made as follows: HMD vs. desktop, HMD vs. large screen, HMD vs. CAVE, fulldome vs. flat screen, and VR vs. augmented reality (AR). In other studies with different types of control and treatment settings, participants immersed in the IVR used the same device, but some factors like the complexity of the scene, visual cues, and exposure time were manipulated to examine the differences.

The results of the impact of presence on learning outcomes were mixed. Several studies reported that an increased presence promotes learning and training outcomes. In research examining whether IVR can be an effective tool in a four-week cognitive training program for adults over age 49, Huang (2020) arranged for participants to play a VR exergame with one group using HMDs (immersive) and the other using Kinect via a large monitor (non-immersive). His study confirmed that presence served a mediating role in IVR experience to promote selected executive functions, such as inhibition and task switching. He believed that the higher level of presence perceived by the participants made them feel as if they were moving in the IVR, which is a key to improving their inhibitory control and task switching. The improved cognitive abilities might be the result of the process of presence activating the brain areas associated with executive functions.

Selzer et al. (2019) also reported a moderate positive correlation between presence and learning outcomes based on an experiment to compare high-end VR (Oculus Rift CV1), low-end VR (mobile), and desktop VR. Their study involved participants virtually traveling to a wetland area of Villa del Mar (Turks and Caicos), and a pre- and post-test were completed to evaluate knowledge gain. The results of the presence questionnaire and knowledge tests indicated significant differences existing between desktop VR and the other two devices; however, no difference was found between high-end and low-end VR in terms of presence and learning outcomes.

Despite the fact that the HMDs often received higher user ratings in the reviewed studies, it has not always been reported as the most effective training tool. Chen et al. (2019) evaluated the effects of IVR in motion learning, using three different devices: HMD, CAVE, and desktop. They recorded participants' Tachi performance after following the movement the expert demonstrated in the VR. These performance clips were analyzed using a specific algorithm to assess motion quality. Although participants indicated that the HMD provided them with a higher level of sensory engagement and realism, the CAVE learners demonstrated a significantly higher motion quality.

In addition to comparisons made among various devices that might influence presence, some studies manipulated potential factors in the same IVR experience carrier to probe the relationship between presence and learning outcomes. Stanney et al. (2002) experimented to determine whether different setups for exposure duration, scene complexity, and movement control (interactivity) would affect presence and then affect learning outcomes. They also investigated how these three elements related to cybersickness. Their study involved more than 300 participants in an IVR for locomotion, object manipulation, recognition tasks, and so on based on the Virtual Environment Assessment Battery (Lampton et al., 1994). They concluded that exposure duration appeared to promote learning based on the overall task performance in their study, but it did not significantly affect presence. They further suggested that the first 15 minutes of exposure in a virtual environment are crucial for participants to perceive whether or not its design promotes a sense of presence. By contrast, scene complexity can enhance presence, but it did not significantly affect overall performance.

Ma and Kaber (2006) examined whether viewpoint, auditory cue type, and visual background can influence presence, and then they evaluated the relation among presence, mental workload, and performance. Based on an experiment using an IVR-based basketball free-throw task, they reported that viewpoint and auditory cue increased the level of perceived presence, but they had no effect on the task performance. They suggested that a greater sense of presence, leading to increased perception of mental demand and possible disengagement of participants during a difficult task, might account for the impaired performance.

Parmar et al. (2016) examined learning outcomes in terms of cognitive and psychomotor aspects in a study of HMD vs. desktop, using IVR for learning psychomotor skills related to electrical circuitry measurement. The overall level of perceived presence reported by the desktop and HMD groups was not significantly different, but they discovered that the HMD group scored higher in assessment items targeting higher-level cognitive domains, such as analysis and evaluation based on Bloom taxonomy. In the comparison of psychomotor performance based on Dave's psychomotor taxonomy (Krathwohl, 2002), the Desktop group performed better at the tasks on the imitation and precision levels.

Based on the review under this element, the increase of presence in IVR does not guarantee an improved learning performance. Factors related to cognitive load, such as exposure time, multisensory enhancements, task types, and difficulty level, can also be considered when designing an IVR learning experience.

Immersion

More than one-third of the reviewed studies probed the impact of immersion in an IVR learning environment, and some of them overlapped with the studies focused on presence, which can be explained by variation in the definition.

Definition and Measurement

Immersion has been defined in two ways. From a technological perspective, "immersion" refers to an objective measure of the system to deliver a convincing and vivid environment and the extent to which a medium shuts out the outside world (Cummings & Bailenson, 2016; Slater, 2003). Among the studies that investigated the impact of immersion on learning outcomes, 15 of them defined or measured immersion from this perspective (Buttussi & Chittaro, 2017; Chaturvedi et al., 2012; Chua et al., 2019; Eden & Passig, 2007; Freina et al., 2017; Gruchalla, 2004; Janssen, Tummel, Richert, & Isenhardt, 2016; Markowitz et al., 2018; Meyer et al., 2019; Moro et al., 2017; Passig, 2009; Passig & Eden, 2010; Roussou & Slater, 2017; Vargas-Orjuela et al., 2017; Yu et al., 2017). Immersion has also been defined from a user perspective, which emphasizes a user's subjective experience. From this perspective, immersion is defined as the degree to which users perceive themselves as being included in and interacting with an environment (Witmer et al., 2005; Witmer & Singer, 1998). Two of the reviewed studies investigated immersion from this perspective (Alrehaili & Al Osman, 2019; Cooper et al., 2018).

For the studies defining immersion from the technological perspective, the impact of immersion on learning outcomes was investigated primarily using experimental manipulation. Immersion levels were broadly manipulated with three conditions: a fully immersive VR using an HMD, CAVE, or fulldome; a semi-immersive desktop VR using a normal computer screen; and a non-immersive condition using a 2D representation. Five of the immersion studies collected subjective immersion data using self-report questionnaires (Alrehaili & Al Osman, 2019; Cooper et al., 2018; Janssen et al., 2016; Mills et al., 2019), such as the Immersive Tendency Questionnaire (Witmer & Singer, 1998). In one study, Mills et al. (2019) recorded heart-rate data as an objective indicator of immersion.

Impact of Immersion on Learning Outcomes

Similar to the findings under the presence element, the impact of immersion on learning outcomes varied. As suggested by the definition, studies focused on immersion more heavily emphasized comparing the technical attributes of the device to make the experience as real as possible in the learning process.

In a study of CAVE vs. desktop, Gruchalla (2004) compared participants' performance in tasks involving planning well. They reported that the CAVE users not only had significantly more correct answers but also came up with the correct answers in less time. Their observation based on task difficulty indicated that participants performed equally for simple spatial tasks in both environments and that performance gaps were reflected in more complicated tasks. Similar views on the value of immersion have been echoed by other researchers.

A series of studies using IVR to teach the concept of time confirmed that the immersion experience can make abstract concepts concrete, promoting learning outcomes. Eden and Passig (2007) conducted an experiment for young children (aged 4–10) learning the concept of time at four different levels of immersion involving IVR, pictorial representation, written representation, and audio representation. Based on the number of errors during the learning process, they reported that the IVR group significantly outperformed the learners in other groups. Two later experiments using a similar approach but on different groups of learners – one for a group with mild to moderate intellectual disabilities (Passig, 2009) and the other for children with hearing impairment (Passig & Eden, 2010) – have confirmed the effectiveness of using IVR to teach the concept of time. They ascribed the success to the immersive experience because it provides a sensation of real presence to engage learners.

Not all the studies reported a positive correlation between immersion and performance. A study on using IVR to teach spatial perspective-taking skills yielded mixed results. Freina et al. (2017) arranged an experiment in which participants were to play a game at three levels of immersion: immersive (HMD), semi-immersive (computer), and non-immersive (fixed pictures). The HMD group earned significantly higher scores in presence than the other two groups, but its performance was at the same level as that of the computer group. In a follow-up study they added a real-life setting, in which the participants played the game with the real props; however, no significant differences emerged in the performance across these four immersion settings. Mills et al. (2019) examined the effect of using IVR for triage training. A mass-casualty traffic incident was recreated, and the trainees were required to place a triage card to indicate ten patients' situations at the scene. In this unique disaster setting, they measured the trainees' heart rate and perceived task load (NASA-TLX) as indicators of immersion level. All 29 participants completed the training in both IVR and live simulation with a random sequence. The results showed that participants perceived significantly higher immersion in live simulations; however, their performances were not significantly different across these two settings. The authors noted that once the IVR was created, the cost of running it each time would be much lower compared to facilitating the live simulation.

Many of the studies reviewed under this element declared the level of immersion merely by the use of different delivery media, which made quantifying the difference in results difficult. To address this issue, some studies used other objective measures, such as heart rate or physiological indicators, to assess the influence of immersion. These types of measures might help with the distinction between immersion and presence in future IVR studies.

Interactivity

Fewer than one-third of the reviewed articles presented the impact of interactivity on learning outcomes. Unlike the previous two elements, in which learners are the recipients of IVR stimulation, interactivity focuses on what learners can do in IVR environments.

Definition and Measurement

"Interactivity" has most often been defined as "the extent to which users can participate in modifying the form and content of a mediated environment in real time" (Steuer, 1992, p. 84), which emphasizes users' autonomy, freedom, and initiative in the learning and interaction process. Focusing on the mode of communication, another definition of interactivity is the extent to which two parties in a medium can receive real-time feedback from one another (Liu & Shrum, 2002). Across all the studies under this element, data on interactivity were collected using experimental manipulation. For instance, in Roussou and Slater's (2017) study, three conditions with different levels of interactivity were designed to investigate its impact on conceptual learning. Although no widely used self-report questionnaire for assessing interactivity was used, we found that tactile interactivity and locomotive interactivity can be measured using questions from the Presence Questionnaire (Witmer & Singer, 1998) because these two constructs are similar to the control factor of presence (Kwon, 2019).

Impact of Interactivity on Learning Outcomes

The impact of interactivity on learning outcomes also varied. Its positive effects on learning and performance were reported in several studies (Bailenson et al., 2008; Johnston et al., 2018; Passig, 2009; Stanney et al., 2002; Yang & Kim, 2002). Notably, the same subject for IVR instruction can be designed with different foci. For example, one IVR for Taichi training noted earlier fell under the presence category (Chen et al., 2019), and in this section another Taichi instruction exploited the interactive element of IVR. Bailenson et al. (2008) emphasized the functionalities of capture, review, and third-person view on one's own movement in IVR, which provided learners with real-time feedback on their Taichi movement. The results indicated participants in the IVR condition outperformed participants in the video condition based on scores from two graders. A study by Yang and Kim (2002) on motion training that focused on offering instant visual feedback also reported a positive impact on the participants' performance. Similarly, two studies involved instruction on cells with one under the element of presence and the other under interactivity. Johnston et al. (2018) used interactive features in IVR that allowed participants to move between cell components to acquire information. They compared the exam results of students in a traditional lecture with the results of students in a hybrid lecture that combined traditional lecture and VR and found that IVR had a significant positive effect on students' understanding of cell biology. Three studies under the theme of interactivity reported nonsignificant results (Bailenson et al., 2008; Kwon, 2019; Yang & Kim, 2002). Kwon (2019) pointed out that when learning was measured at a low level of thinking complexity, such as remembering and understanding, no significant difference emerged in academic achievement between the authentic IVR condition (with high interactivity) and the IVR (with low interactivity) condition. In the remaining four studies, no statistically significant difference in learning outcome and performance was found between the interactivity intervention group and the control – comparison group (Chua et al., 2019; Ferguson et al., 2020; Roussou & Slater, 2017; Zhang et al., 2019).

With a randomized controlled experiment, Ferguson et al. (2020) found that participants in the passive interaction condition had higher scores on factual knowledge, compared to the participants in the active interaction condition. In addition to autonomy support and feedback exchange, one study (Kim et al., 2015) also probed ways to navigate the VR system. With the rise of user experience and user interface (UX – UI) studies in recent years, more studies exploring intuitive technologies that help transfer authentic interaction in IVR are expected.

DISCUSSIONS

Although not every study established the connection between learning outcomes and presence, immersion, or interactivity, the process documented in the reviewed studies provides a nuanced understanding of designing IVR for educational purposes.

Finding a Learning Theory for Design Framework

As noted by Radianti et al. (2020), learning theories frequently did not serve as design frameworks in IVR learning applications. Our review reached a similar conclusion. Although some studies refer to a learning theory to explain how presence, immersion, or interactivity can facilitate learning in IVR, only a few studies designed the IVR learning process based on a given theory. One such example is Alrehaili and Al Osman's (2019) study, in which Multimedia Learning Principles were referred to in the IVR design process. Educational theories that influence the design of IVR to promote learners' performance can be broadly classified into two categories, namely, the cognitive perspective and the constructivist perspective. Theories from the cognitive perspective, such as cognitive load theory (Sweller, Van Merrienboer, & Paas, 1998) and cognitive theory of multimedia learning (Mayer, 2014), focus on the impact of immersion, presence, and interactivity on essential, extraneous, and generative processing that occur during IVR learning (Makransky, Terkildsen, & Mayer, 2019). Given that learners acquire new knowledge with a limited working memory, instructional design that reduces extraneous processing tends to lead to desired learning outcomes and performance (Mayer & Mayer, 2005). From the view of constructivist learning, learners construct their new knowledge by actively interacting with the learning materials and environments and connecting the new information with their prior ideas and experiences (Huang, Rauch, & Liaw, 2010). Several teaching strategies and designs guided by constructivist learning principles, including experiential learning (e.g., Alrehaili & Al Osman, 2019), Voygotsky's ZPD (e.g., Ferguson et al., 2020), and situated learning (e.g., Kwon, 2019), have been incorporated into IVR learning environments to promote learning and performance.

IVR for Teaching Complicated Concepts or Higher-Order Thinking

Among the studies that reported a partial effect of IVR on learning outcomes were some that investigated why such disparity occurred.

They suggested that instruction of complicated concepts and higher-order thinking would likely benefit from using IVR (Bertrand et al., 2017; Ferguson et al., 2020; Gruchalla, 2004; Kwon, 2019; Parmar et al., 2016). For example, Ferguson et al. (2020) reported that participants in the active interaction and passive interaction groups performed equally well with questions on spatial knowledge but not on factual knowledge. They, therefore, suggested that factual knowledge might be more suitable to be taught with guidance as opposed to freely exploring in IVR. Because IVR is known to be associated with motion sickness, educators and designers must think about what aspects of learning should be kept in the IVR for learning efficiency. For instance, factual knowledge may be taught before students enter the IVR, where they can apply the knowledge in an authentic setting. This practice was also proposed by Meyer et al. (2019) in the form of pre training in an IVR lesson. Their study showed that IVR works better than a video only when learners acquire fundamental knowledge of the content prior to the IVR lesson.

Determining Level of Presence, Immersion, Interactivity Needed for Learning to Occur

At the outset of this review process, one of our underlying inquiries involved whether a threshold in the level of presence, immersion, or interactivity in IVR was needed for learning to occur. This chapter might not provide a definite quantitative answer, but our review shows this question can be considered across different contexts depending on the training goals. For example, Chen et al. (2019) reported that learners perceived a higher presence with HMD during a Taichi training despite demonstrating better motion quality with the CAVE environment. With this type of data at hand, instructors can make an informed decision on which setting is best suited to facilitate the desired learning outcomes. Another example comes from a study by Huber et al. (2018) in which two IVR settings were compared for surgical training. One setting was constructed with artificial graphics, and the other was built using 360-degree videos. Participants rated the 360-degree IVR with a significantly higher presence score, but their performance on three surgical tasks did not yield a significant difference; nevertheless, the authors observed that the cholecystectomy task had higher error rates in the 360-degree IVR setting, produced by participants with limited operating experience. They suspected this might have been caused by the distractions introduced in the 360-degree environment. Thus, if the training goal was to have participants perform the surgery in an environment with distractions, a highly immersive 360-degree VR would better fulfill this purpose.

CONCLUSION

As more reasonably priced consumer VR technologies enter the market, growing popularity is likely in the coming decades. Facebook CEO Mark Zuckerberg (2014) predicted a billion or more VR users in the future. VR has been used more heavily in gaming, but it presents a promising learning environment for its capacity to enhance presence, immersion, and interactivity. This chapter provides a comprehensive review of two decades of IVR studies to assess whether these three elements of IVR promote learning. We have examined how presence, immersion, and interactivity were defined in each study along with the scales employed to measure them. We have also reviewed the investigations of the relation between these elements and learning outcomes presented in these studies. Although we cannot definitively state that enhancing presence, immersion, and interaction promotes learning in IVR, this chapter nevertheless offers a rich context to review the positive and negative impact of these three elements on learning outcomes. We hope our findings will inform practitioners on how to incorporate these three elements to create effective educational IVR applications and direct future research toward understanding learners' cognitive and affective interaction in IVR learning environments. Based on this knowledge, we will be able to create an educational wonderland in the world of IVR for generations to come.

REFERENCES

Alexander, A. L., Brunyé, T., Sidman, J., & Weil, S. A. (2005). From gaming to training: A review of studies on fidelity, immersion, presence, and buy-in and their effects on transfer in pc-based simulations and games. *DARWARS Training Impact Group*, *5*, 1–14.

Alrehaili, E. A., & Al Osman, H. (2019). A virtual reality role-playing serious game for experiential learning. *Interactive Learning Environments*, 1–14. https://doi.org/10.1080/10494820.2019.1703008

Bailenson, J. N., Blascovich, J., Beall, A. C., & Loomis, J. M. (2001). Equilibrium theory revisited: Mutual gaze and personal space in virtual environments. *Presence: Teleoperators & Virtual Environments*, *10*(6), 583–598. https://doi.org/10.1162/105474601753272844

Bailenson, J. N., Patel, K., Nielsen, A., Bajscy, R., Jung, S.-H., & Kurillo, G. (2008). The effect of interactivity on learning physical actions in virtual reality. *Media Psychology*, *11*(3), 354–376. https://doi.org/10.1080/15213260802285214

Barré, J., Michelet, D., Truchot, J., Jolivet, E., Recanzone, T., Stiti, S., . . . & Pourcher, G. (2019). Virtual reality single-port sleeve gastrectomy training decreases physical and mental workload in novice surgeons: An exploratory study. *Obesity Surgery, 29*(4), 1309–1316. http://doi.org/10.1007/s11695-018-03680-9

Bertrand, J., Bhargava, A., Madathil, K. C., Gramopadhye, A., & Babu, S. V. (2017). The effects of presentation method and simulation fidelity on psychomotor education in a bimanual metrology training simulation. In *2017 IEEE symposium on 3D user interfaces* (pp. 59–68). Los Angeles, CA: IEEE. https://doi.org/10.1109/3DUI.2017.7893318

Biocca, F., Harms, C., & Gregg, J. (2001). The networked minds measure of social presence: Pilot test of the factor structure and concurrent validity. *The 4th annual international workshop on presence.* Philadelphia, PA.

Bouchard, S., Robillard, G., St-Jacques, J., Dumoulin, S., Patry, M. J., & Renaud, P. (2004, October). Reliability and validity of a single-item measure of presence in VR. In *The 3rd IEEE international workshop on haptic, audio and visual environments and their applications* (pp. 59–61). Ottawa, ON: IEEE. https://doi.org/10.1109/HAVE.2004.1391882

Buttussi, F., & Chittaro, L. (2018). Effects of different types of virtual reality display on presence and learning in a safety training scenario. *IEEE Transactions on Visualization and Computer Graphics, 24*(2), 1063–1076. https://doi.org/10.1109/TVCG.2017.2653117

Chaturvedi, S., Yoon, J., McKenzie, R., Katsioloudis, P. J., Garcia, H. M., & Ren, S. (2012). Implementation and assessment of a virtual reality experiment in the undergraduate themo-fluids laboratory. Paper presented at *the ASEE annual conference and exposition.* San Antonio, TX, June 10–13, 2012. Retrieved from https://digitalcommons.odu.edu/mae_fac_pubs/75

Chen, X., Chen, Z., Li, Y., He, T., Hou, J., Liu, S., & He, Y. (2019). ImmerTai: Immersive motion learning in VR environments. *Journal of Visual Communication and Image Representation, 58*, 416–427. https://doi.org/10.1016/j.jvcir.2018.11.039

Chua, Y., Sridhar, P. K., Zhang, H., Dissanayake, V., & Nanayakkara, S. (2019). Evaluating IVR in primary school classrooms. In *2019 IEEE international symposium on mixed and augmented reality adjunct (ISMAR-Adjunct)* (pp. 169–174). Beijing, China: IEEE. https://doi.org/10.1109/ISMAR-Adjunct.2019.00-53

Cooper, N., Milella, F., Pinto, C., Cant, I., White, M., & Meyer, G. (2018). The effects of substitute multisensory feedback on task performance and the sense of presence in a virtual reality environment. *PLoS ONE, 13*(2). https://doi.org/10.1371/journal.pone.0191846

Cox, C. B., House, A., Lopez, A., & Pool, G. J. (2017). The need for conceptual models of technology in training and development: How immersive does training need to be? *Industrial and Organizational Psychology, 10*(4), 696–701. https://doi.org/10.1017/iop.2017.78

Cummings, J. J., & Bailenson, J. N. (2016). How immersive is enough? A meta-analysis of the effect of immersive technology on user presence. *Media Psychology, 19*(2), 272–309. https://doi.org/10.1080/15213269.2015.1015740

Draper, J. V., & Blair, L. M. (1996). Workload, flow, and telepresence during teleoperation. In *Proceedings of IEEE international conference on robotics and automation* (Vol. 2, pp. 1030–1035). IEEE.

Draper, J. V., Kaber, D. B., & Usher, J. M. (1998). Telepresence. *Human Factors, 40*(3), 354–375.

Eden, S., & Passig, D. (2007). Three-dimensionality as an effective mode of representation for expressing sequential time perception. *Journal of Educational Computing Research, 36*(1), 51–63. https://doi.org/10.2190/J452-Q6H2-8695-475U

Eynard, R., Pallot, M., Christmann, O., & Richir, S. (2015). Impact of verbal communication on user experience in 3D immersive virtual environments. In *2015 IEEE international conference on engineering, technology, and innovation/international technology management conference (ICE/ITMC)* (pp. 1–8). IEEE. https://doi.org/10.1109/ICE.2015.7438679

Ferguson, C., van den Broek, E. L., & van Oostendorp, H. (2020). On the role of interaction mode and story structure in virtual reality serious games. *Computers & Education, 143*, 103671. https://doi.org/10.1016/j.compedu.2019.103671

Formosa, N. J., Morrison, B. W., Hill, G., & Stone, D. (2018). Testing the efficacy of a virtual reality-based simulation in enhancing users' knowledge, attitudes, and empathy relating to psychosis. *Australian Journal of Psychology, 70*(1), 57–65. https://doi.org/10.1111/ajpy.12167

Foucault, M. (1970). *The order of things: An archaeology of the human science* (Vintage Bo). London: Random House.

Fowler, C. (2015). Virtual reality and learning: Where is the pedagogy? *British Journal of Educational Technology, 46*(2), 412–422. https://doi.org/10.1111/bjet.12135

Freina, L., Bottino, R., Tavella, M., & Chiorri, C. (2017). Evaluation of spatial perspective taking skills using a digital game with different levels of immersion. *International Journal of Serious Games, 4*(3). https://doi.org/10.17083/ijsg.v4i3.178

Freina, L., & Ott, M. (2015). A literature review on immersive virtual reality in education: State of the art and perspectives. In *Proceedings of the international scientific conference elearning and software for education* (Vol. 1, No. 133, pp. 10–1007). Bucharest, Romania: eLSE.

Furht, B. (2008). *Encyclopedia of multimedia*. Boston, MA: Springer Science & Business Media. https://doi.org/10.1007/978-0-387-78414-4_85

George, C., Spitzer, M., & Hussmann, H. (2018). Training in IVR: Investigating the effect of instructor design on social presence and performance of the VR user. In *Proceedings of the 24th ACM symposium on virtual reality software and technology* (pp. 1–5). Tokyo, Japan: ACM. https://doi.org/10.1145/3281505.3281543

Giglioli, I. A. C., Vidal, C. B., & Raya, M. A. (2019). A virtual versus an augmented reality cooking task based tools: A behavioral and physiological study on the assessment of executive functions. *Frontiers in Psychology, 10*, 1–12. https://doi.org/10.3389/fpsyg.2019.02529

Gruchalla, K. (2004). Immersive well-path editing: Investigating the added value of immersion. In *IEEE annual international symposium virtual reality* (pp. 157–164). Chicago, IL: IEEE. https://doi.org/10.1109/VR.2004.1310069

Hedge, C., Weaver, R., & Schnall, S. (2017). Spatial learning and wayfinding in an immersive environment: The digital fulldome. *Cyberpsychology, Behavior, and Social Networking, 20*(5), 327–333. http://doi.org/10.1089/cyber.2016.0399

Heeter, C. (1992). Being there: The subjective experience of presence. *Presence: Teleoperators & Virtual Environments, 1*(2), 262–271. https://doi.org/10.1162/pres.1992.1.2.262

Huang, C. L., Luo, Y. F., Yang, S. C., Lu, C. M., & Chen, A. S. (2020). Influence of students' learning style, sense of presence, and cognitive load on learning outcomes in an immersive virtual reality learning environment. *Journal of Educational Computing Research, 58*(3), 596–615.

Huang, H.-M., Rauch, U., & Liaw, S.-S. (2010). Investigating learners' attitudes toward virtual reality learning environments: Based on a constructivist approach. *Computers & Education, 55*(3), 1171–1182. https://doi.org/10.1016/j.compedu.2010.05.014

Huang, K.-T. (2020). Exergaming executive functions: An immersive virtual reality-based cognitive training for adults aged 50 and older. *Cyberpsychology, Behavior, and Social Networking, 23*(3), 143–149. https://doi.org/10.1089/cyber.2019.0269

Huber, T., Paschold, M., Hansen, C., Lang, H., & Kneist, W. (2018). Artificial versus video-based immersive virtual surroundings: Analysis of performance and user's preference. *Surgical Innovation, 25*(3), 280–285. https://doi.org/10.1177/1553350618761756

Huber, T., Paschold, M., Hansen, C., Wunderling, T., Lang, H., & Kneist, W. (2017). New dimensions in surgical training: Immersive virtual reality laparoscopic simulation exhilarates surgical staff. *Surgical Endoscopy, 31*(11), 4472–4477. https://doi.org/10.1007/s00464-017-5500-6

Janssen, D., Tummel, C., Richert, A., & Isenhardt, I. (2016). Virtual environments in higher education – Immersion as a key construct for learning 4.0. *International Journal of Advanced Corporate Learning (iJAC), 9*(2), 20–26. https://doi.org/10.3991/ijac.v9i2.6000

Jensen, L., & Konradsen, F. (2018). A review of the use of virtual reality head-mounted displays in education and training. *Education and Information Technologies, 23*(4), 1515–1529. https://doi.org/10.1007/s10639-017-9676-0

Johnston, A. P., Rae, J., Ariotti, N., Bailey, B., Lilja, A., Webb, R., . . . & Parton, R. G. (2018). Journey to the centre of the cell: Virtual reality immersion into scientific data. *Traffic, 19*(2), 105–110. https://doi.org/10.1111/tra.12538

Kim, J.-S., Gračanin, D., Yang, T., & Quek, F. (2015). Action-transferred navigation technique design approach supporting human spatial learning. *ACM Transactions on Computer-Human Interaction (TOCHI), 22*(6), 1–42. https://doi.org/10.1145/2811258

Kim, K., Rosenthal, M. Z., Zielinski, D. J., & Brady, R. (2014). Effects of virtual environment platforms on emotional responses. *Computer Methods and Programs in Biomedicine, 113*(3), 882–893. https://doi.org/10.1016/j.cmpb.2013.12.024

Kiousis, S. (2002). Interactivity: A concept explication. *New Media & Society, 4*(3), 355–383.

Krathwohl, D. R. (2002). A revision of bloom's taxonomy: An overview. *Theory into Practice, 41*(4), 212–218. https://doi.org/10.1207/s15430421tip4104_2

Kwon, C. (2019). Verification of the possibility and effectiveness of experiential learning using HMD-based immersive VR technologies. *Virtual Reality, 23*(1), 101–118. https://doi.org/10.1007/s10055-018-0364-1

Lampton, D. R., Knerr, B. W., Goldberg, S. L., Bliss, J. P., Moshell, J. M., & Blau, B. (1994). The virtual environment performance assessment battery (VEPAB): Development and evaluation. *Presence: Teleoperators & Virtual Environments, 3*(2), 145–157. https://doi.org/10.1162/pres.1994.3.2.145

Lessiter, J., Freeman, J., Keogh, E., & Davidoff, J. (2001). A cross-media presence questionnaire: The ITC-sense of presence inventory. *Presence: Teleoperators & Virtual Environments, 10*(3), 282–297. http://doi:10.1162/105474601300343612

Lewis, P. H. (1994, September). Sound bytes; He added "virtual" to "reality". *The New York Times*. Retrieved from www.nytimes.com/1994/09/25/business/sound-bytes-he-added-virtual-to-reality.html

Liu, Y., & Shrum, L. J. (2002). What is interactivity and is it always such a good thing? Implications of definition, person, and situation for the influence of interactivity on advertising effectiveness. *Journal of Advertising, 31*(4), 53–64. https://doi.org/10.1080/00913367.2002.10673685

Lok, B., Naik, S., Whitton, M., & Brooks, F. P. (2003). Effects of handling real objects and self-avatar fidelity on cognitive task performance and sense of presence in virtual environments. *Presence: Teleoperators & Virtual Environments, 12*(6), 615–628. https://doi.org/10.1162/105474603322955914

Loke, S.-K. (2015). How do virtual world experiences bring about learning? A critical review of theories. *Australasian Journal of Educational Technology, 31*(1), 112–122. https://doi.org/10.14742/ajet.2532

Lombard, M., & Ditton, T. B. (1997). At the heart of it all: The concept of presence. *Journal of Computer-Mediated Communication, 3*(2), JCMC321. https://doi.org/10.1111/j.1083 6101.1997.tb00072.x

Lombard, M., Ditton, T. B., & Weinstein, L. (2009). Measuring presence: The temple presence inventory. In *Proceedings of the 12th annual international workshop on presence* (pp. 1–15). Los Angeles, CA: The International Society for Presence Research (ISPR).

Ma, R., & Kaber, D. B. (2006). Presence, workload and performance effects of synthetic environment design factors. *International Journal of Human-Computer Studies, 64*(6), 541–552. https://doi.org/10.1016/j.ijhcs.2005.12.003

Makransky, G., Terkildsen, T. S., & Mayer, R. E. (2019). Adding immersive virtual reality to a science lab simulation causes more presence but less learning. *Learning and Instruction, 60*, 225–236. https://doi.org/10.1016/j.learninstruc.2017.12.007.

Markowitz, D. M., Laha, R., Perone, B. P., Pea, R. D., & Bailenson, J. N. (2018). Immersive virtual reality field trips facilitate learning about climate change. *Frontiers in Psychology, 9*, 2364. https://doi.org/10.3389/fpsyg.2018.02364

Mayer, R. E. (2014). Incorporating motivation into multimedia learning. *Learning and Instruction, 29*, 171–173. https://doi.org/10.1016/j.learninstruc.2013.04.003

Mayer, R. E., & Mayer, R. E. (2005). *The Cambridge handbook of multimedia learning*. Cambridge: Cambridge University Press.

Meyer, O. A., Omdahl, M. K., & Makransky, G. (2019). Investigating the effect of pre-training when learning through immersive virtual reality and video: A media and methods experiment. *Computers & Education, 140*, 103603. https://doi.org/10.1016/j.compedu.2019.103603

Mikropoulos, T. A., & Natsis, A. (2011). Educational virtual environments: A ten-year review of empirical research (1999–2009). *Computers & Education, 56*(3), 769–780. https://doi.org/10.1016/j.compedu.2010.10.020

Mills, B., Dykstra, P., Hansen, S., Miles, A., Rankin, T., Hopper, L., . . . & Bartlett, D. (2019). Virtual reality triage training can provide comparable simulation efficacy for paramedicine students compared to live simulation-based scenarios. *Prehospital Emergency Care*, 525–536. https://doi.org/10.1080/10903127.2019.1676345

Moher, D., Liberati, A., Tetzlaff, J., Altman, D. G., & PRISMA Group. (2009). Preferred reporting items for systematic reviews and meta-analyses: The PRISMA statement. *PLoS Medicine, 6*(7), 1–6. https://doi.org/10.1371/journal.pmed.1000097

Moro, C., Štromberga, Z., Raikos, A., & Stirling, A. (2017). The effectiveness of virtual and augmented reality in health sciences and medical anatomy. *Anatomical Sciences Education, 10*(6), 549–559. https://doi.org/10.1002/ase.1696

Nichols, S., Haldane, C., & Wilson, J. R. (2000). Measurement of presence and its consequences in virtual environments. *International Journal of Human-Computer Studies, 52*(3), 471–491. https://doi.org/10.1006/ijhc.1999.0343

Papachristos, N. M., Vrellis, I., & Mikropoulos, T. A. (2017). A comparison between oculus rift and a low-cost smartphone VR headset: Immersive user experience and learning. In *2017 IEEE 17th international conference on advanced learning technologies (ICALT)* (pp. 477–481). Timisoara, Romania: IEEE. http://doi.org/10.1109/ICALT.2017.145

Parmar, D., Bertrand, J., Babu, S. V., Madathil, K., Zelaya, M., Wang, T., . . . & Frady, K. (2016). A comparative evaluation of viewing metaphors on psychophysical skills education in an interactive virtual environment. *Virtual Reality, 20*(3), 141–157. https://doi.org/10.1007/s10055-016-0287-7

Passig, D. (2009). Improving the sequential time perception of teenagers with mild to moderate mental retardation with 3D immersive virtual reality (IVR). *Journal of Educational Computing Research, 40*(3), 263–280. https://doi.org/10.2190/EC.40.3.a

Passig, D., & Eden, S. (2010). Enhancing time-connectives with 3D immersive virtual reality (IVR). *Journal of Educational Computing Research, 42*(3), 307–325. https://doi.org/10.2190/EC.42.3.d

Persky, S., Kaphingst, K. A., McCall, C., Lachance, C., Beall, A. C., & Blascovich, J. (2009). Presence relates to distinct outcomes in two virtual environments employing different learning modalities. *CyberPsychology & Behavior, 12*(3), 263–268. https://doi.org/10.1089/cpb.2008.0262

Phillips, V. (1998). Online universities teach knowledge beyond the books. *HR Magazine, 43*(8), 120–125.

Radianti, J., Majchrzak, T. A., Fromm, J., & Wohlgenannt, I. (2020). A systematic review of immersive virtual reality applications for higher education: Design elements, lessons learned, and research agenda. *Computers & Education, 147*, 103778. https://doi.org/10.1016/j.compedu.2019.103778

Rafaeli, S. (1988). Interactivity: From new media to communication. In R. P. Hawkins, J. M. Wiemann, & S. Pingree (Eds.), *Advancing communication science: Merging mass and interpersonal processes* (pp. 110–134). Beverly Hills, CA: Sage.

Robertson, G. G., Card, S. K., & Mackinlay, J. D. (1993). Three views of virtual reality: Nonimmersive virtual reality. *Computer, 26*(2), 81. https://doi.org/10.1109/2.192002

Roussou, M., & Slater, M. (2017). Comparison of the effect of interactive versus passive virtual reality learning activities in evoking and sustaining conceptual change. *IEEE Transactions on Emerging Topics in Computing, 8*(1), 233–244. https://doi.org/10.1109/TETC.2017.2737983

Schott, C., & Marshall, S. (2018). Virtual reality and situated experiential education: A conceptualization and exploratory trial. *Journal of Computer Assisted Learning, 34*(6), 843–852. https://doi.org/10.1111/jcal.12293

Schubert, T. W. (2003). The sense of presence in virtual environments: A three-component scale measuring spatial presence, involvement, and realness. *Z. für Medienpsychologie, 15*(2), 69–71.

Schubert, T. W., Friedmann, F., & Regenbrecht, H. (1999). Embodied presence in virtual environments. In R. Paton & I. Neilson (Eds.), *Visual representations and interpretations* (pp. 269–278). London: Springer. https://doi.org/10.1007/978-1-4471-0563-3_30

Schubert, T. W., Friedmann, F., & Regenbrecht, H. (2001). The experience of presence: Factor analytic insights. *Presence: Teleoperators & Virtual Environments, 10*(3), 266–281. https://doi.org/10.1162/105474601300343603

Selzer, M. N., Gazcon, N. F., & Larrea, M. L. (2019). Effects of virtual presence and learning outcome using low-end virtual reality systems. *Displays, 59*, 9–15. https://doi.org/10.1016/j.displa.2019.04.002

Slater, M. (2003). A note on presence terminology. *Presence Connect, 3*(3), 1–5.

Slater, M., & Steed, A. (2000). A virtual presence counter. *Presence: Teleoperators & Virtual Environments, 9*(5), 413–434. https://doi.org/10.1162/105474600566925

Slater, M., Usoh, M., & Steed, A. (1994). Depth of presence in virtual environments. *Presence: Teleoperators & Virtual Environments, 3*(2), 130–144. https://doi.org/10.1162/pres.1994.3.2.130

Stanney, K. M., Kingdon, K. S., Graeber, D., & Kennedy, R. S. (2002). Human performance in immersive virtual environments: Effects of exposure duration, user control, and scene complexity. *Human Performance, 15*(4), 339–366. https://doi.org/10.1207/S15327043HUP1504_03

Steed, A., Pan, Y., Zisch, F., & Steptoe, W. (2016). The impact of a self-avatar on cognitive load in immersive virtual reality. In *2016 IEEE annual international symposium virtual reality* (pp. 67–76). Greenville, SC: IEEE. https://doi.org/10.1109/VR.2016.7504689

Steuer, J. (1992). Defining virtual reality: Dimensions determining telepresence. *Journal of Communication, 42*(4), 73–93. https://doi.org/10.1111/j.1460-2466.1992.tb00812.x

Sutherland, I. E. (1964). Sketchpad a man-machine graphical communication system. *Simulation, 2*(5), R–3. https://doi.org/10.1177/003754976400200514

Sutherland, I. E. (1965). The ultimate display. In *Proceedings of IFIP congress* (pp. 506–508). Retrieved from http://citeseer.ist.psu.edu/viewdoc/summary?doi=10.1.1.136.3720

Sweller, J., Van Merrienboer, J. J., & Paas, F. G. (1998). Cognitive architecture and instructional design. *Educational Psychology Review, 10*(3), 251–296. https://doi.org/10.1023/A:1022193728205

Swinth, K. R., & Blascovich, J. (2001). Conformity to group norms in an immersive virtual environment. In *Hot topic paper presented at the annual meeting of the American Psychological Society*. Toronto, ON: APS.

Vargas-Orjuela, M., Uribe-Quevedo, A., Rojas, D., Kapralos, B., & Perez-Gutierrez, B. (2017). A mobile immersive virtual reality cardiac auscultation app. In *2017 IEEE 6th global conference on consumer electronics* (pp. 1–2). Nagoya, Japan: IEEE. https://doi.org/10.1109/GCCE.2017.8229276

Vorderer, P., Wirth, W., Gouveia, F. R., Biocca, F., Saari, T., Jäncke, F., . . . & Jäncke, P. (2004). MEC Spatial Presence Questionnaire (MECSPQ): Short documentation and instructions for application. *Report to the European community, project presence: MEC (IST-2001–37661)*. MEC. Retrieved from http://www.ijk.hmt-hannover.de/presence

Weibel, D., & Wissmath, B. (2011). Immersion in computer games: The role of spatial presence and flow. *International Journal of Computer Games Technology*, *2011*, 1–14. https://doi.org/10.1155/2011/282345

Wirth, W., Hartmann, T., Böcking, S., Vorderer, P., Klimmt, C., Schramm, H., . . . & Jäncke, P. (2007). A process model of the formation of spatial presence experiences. *Media Psychology*, *9*(3), 493–525. https://doi.org/10.1080/15213260701283079

Witmer, B. G., Jerome, C. J., & Singer, M. J. (2005). The factor structure of the presence questionnaire. *Presence: Teleoperators & Virtual Environments*, *14*(3), 298–312. https://doi.org/10.1162/105474605323384654

Witmer, B. G., & Singer, M. J. (1998). Measuring presence in virtual environments: A presence questionnaire. *Presence*, 7(3), 225–240. https://doi.org/10.1162/105474698565686

Wu, G. (1999). Perceived interactivity and attitude toward web sites. In *Proceedings of the conference-American academy of advertising* (pp. 254–262). American Academy of Advertising. Gainesville, FL: University of Florida.

Yang, U., & Kim, G. J. (2002). Implementation and evaluation of "just follow me": An immersive, VR-based, motion-training system. *Presence: Teleoperators & Virtual Environments*, *11*(3), 304–323. https://doi.org/10.1162/105474602317473240

Yee, N., & Bailenson, J. (2007). The Proteus effect: The effect of transformed self-representation on behavior. *Human Communication Research*, *33*(3), 271–290. https://doi.org/10.1111/j.1468-2958.2007.00299.x

Yu, K. C., Saham, K., Sahami, V., Sessions, L., & Denn, G. (2017). Group immersive education with digital fulldome planetariums. In *2017 IEEE annual international symposium virtual reality* (pp. 237–238).Los Angeles, CA: IEEE. https://doi.org/10.1109/VR.2017.7892264

Zhang, L., Bowman, D. A., & Jones, C. N. (2019). Exploring effects of interactivity on learning with interactive storytelling in immersive virtual reality. In *2019 11th international conference on virtual worlds and games for serious applications* (pp. 1–8). Vienna, Austria: IEEE. https://doi.org/10.1109/VS-Games.2019.8864531

Zuckerberg, M. (2014, March 24). Announcement to acquire Oculus VR. *Facebook*. Retrieved from www.facebook.com/zuck/posts/10101319050523971474

CHAPTER 4

Beyond Information Acquisition

A Critical Design Framework to Support Emancipatory Discourses and Thinking in a Transmedia Learning Experience

Scott J. Warren, Meranda M. Roy, and Heather A. Robinson

INTRODUCTION

In an economy rendered highly competitive by increases in digital automation, global pandemics, and resulting unemployment, students today must become prepared for an uncertain future to a greater degree than those in the past. Tomorrow's graduates must be ready to adapt to the rapidly changing demands of the economy and society, while employers expect students to enter their companies ready to collaborate with peers, solve complex problems with creative solutions, apply advanced skills, and think critically with little time for transition and limited company training. To borrow an old colloquialism: "Students entering today's workforce must be prepared to hit the ground running."

However, much of a university's curricula and instructional methods are rooted in past workforce demands. Courses are often designed so that students acquire decontextualized information and skills. Learners are tested on how much they can recall, not whether they can apply or transfer what they learned. There are few published alternative models of how to engage students in activities that promote forms of critical thinking and problem-solving the world now requires. In our experience, engineering such courses is challenging, because the design is complex, and learning outcomes are specific to the student.

The purpose of this chapter is to describe the design of a course that centers student learning in a transmedia learning game experience.

DOI: 10.4324/9781003089704-6

Students encounter real-world problems using the global United Nations (UN) Millennium Development Goals (MDG), which are now called the UN Sustainable Development Goals. These goals were written into online stories localized to the United States and applicable to other parts of the world. We explore the pedagogical model, instructional design process, specific learning activities, and reasons for our choices. Our goal is to communicate a framework for designing courses to prepare students for an uncertain future. Students are prepared to rely on their own ingenuity, adaptability, and empathy during diverse learning activities as they propose solutions to ever-evolving, complex environmental, social, and systemic problems. These challenges mimic the problems learners may encounter as they struggle to adapt to an ever-changing society and an unpredictable future world of work.

BACKGROUND

Theories of Power and Communication Applied to Educational Systems

For Foucault (1970), power and knowledge are often constructed through discourse or a conversation. For Habermas (1970, 1984, 1998), discourse exists between participants as a give and take of truth and as the social act of determining what is agreed to be true, whether someone can be seen to tell the truth, and whether there are systemic and technological distortions. Foucault and Habermas both critique truth claims, as well as existing knowledge as central to the process of developing shared understanding. Further such critique creates changes in what is deemed knowledge in a group or community, as part of a process of knowledge construction (Shih, Chen, Chang, & Kao, 2010). Understanding between speakers occurs as an act of engaged cognition regarding a topic, often framed as a problem to be solved in problem-based learning paradigms (Savery, 2006), in which participants discuss their different viewpoints on a subject, and even what they believe is true about the situation. Learning experiences designed this way require argumentation and proposition of theories and propositions of potential, testable solutions.

The Emancipatory Problem of Schooling in the United States

The transition from primary and secondary school systems (K–12) to the university system becomes especially problematic. Traditionally, university systems were intended to be somewhat emancipatory and allow some transfer of control to students over their behavior and choices about learning (e.g., location and time) (White, 1997). On the contrary, K–12 school students are commonly trained to view knowledge as fixed and correct in the form of information and facts. When asked to construct their own knowledge, or even to acknowledge their own powerful role in the educational process, they may become rebellious and angry when they discover their freedom (Freire, 1998). In other cases, learners may be passive and a recipient of knowledge from their teacher, which is common in accountability-focused, neoliberal educational systems of today (Berg, Huijbens, & Larsen, 2016; Saunders, 2010; Shore & Wright, 1999). However, learning is a product of thinking – a messy and complex process when coupled with content (Ritchhart, Church, & Morrison, 2011). Higher-order thinking requires problem-solving, making connections, taking action, and making decisions – not just strategically shared statements and facts to be recalled and repeated by students. Instead, knowledge is to be critiqued and applied when appropriate to support learning transfer.

Social Constructivist Pedagogical Processes

During this complex progression of meaning making and knowledge production, speaker and hearer(s) also concurrently generate propositions that may serve as an improved framework for organizing and applying knowledge in response to newly constructed agreements that emerged from their communication (Ritchhart et al., 2011). Despite its complexity, this process is described in different terms by Jonassen and Hernandez-Serrano (2002), Savery and Duffy (1995), and others in pedagogical models that fall under the social constructivist model, such as case-based reasoning and problem-based learning (PBL). Both examples are associated with improvements to student's critical thinking, creativity, and problem-solving skills (Belland, Glazewski, & Ertmer, 2009; Blackwell, 2013; Hmelo-Silver, 2004; Samsonov, Pedersen, & Hill, 2006). However, the challenge of designing such learning experiences (Hung, 2011) is offset by the difficulty of reaching such outcomes and limits of non-repeatable learning experiences. These challenges may render PBL a potentially costly and inefficient option when compared with direct instruction pedagogical models (Kirschner & Clark, 2006). It is through reflection and critique by both groups (i.e., speakers and hearers) that emancipatory educational communicative acts emerged and inspired *The 2015 Project*.

SUPPORTING EMANCIPATION: "THE 2015 PROJECT" GOALS

It was important for us to design an undergraduate course that did not focus on traditional testing and objectification of knowledge. How, then, do we develop curriculum that challenges students to consider how knowledge is used and established? Is it possible to overcome a system's influence that reduced student ability and willingness to engage in critical thinking, understand complex problems, or generate solutions? The design task, therefore, was to support the development of the higher-order thinking skills needed to emancipate students from their previous ways of thinking.

Metacognitive Reflection as a Means of Understanding Systemic Power and Liberation

The goal of emancipatory learning activities is to ask instructors and learners to use critical thinking to break away from traditional thoughts of existing knowledge as acceptable. Additionally, it communicates that students have personal power and agency to recommend and make changes that will either improve the system or free them from it. Guiding students and instructors to engage in metacognitive reflective acts, in thinking about their own thinking, centered on questioning one's own preconceived notions about the world, learning, teaching, and the roles of educational systems was a necessary first step.

Improving the Curriculum by Studying Past Designs

We hypothesized that learning activities could be designed to engage learners in a critical examination of their own individual and socially accepted forms of knowledge using complex, shared, global problems. Such ill-structured problems have no one correct answer and are rooted in case-based reasoning and problem-based learning approaches pioneered by Jonassen (1999, 2011), Hmelo-Silver (2004), Savery and Duffy (1995), and others. To develop these learning problems required leveraging the communicative social and cross-platform (i.e., transmedia) technology tools readily available rather than existing, fixed tools like learning management systems that tend to reify or "fix" the idea that there is only one form of correct knowledge, leading students to believe it is unchanging and cannot be challenged.

Before *The 2015 Project*, the undergraduate computer literacy course employed two other transmedia game-based approaches. The first, *The Door*, was an alternate reality game course that spanned the length of the class (Warren, Dondlinger, McLeod, & Bigenho, 2012). The design situated learning by providing students with a fictional narrative in which they would learn to use the tools by interacting with fictional clients. The second transmedia game, called *Broken Window* employed a similar game-based strategy for the first six weeks to immerse students in an alternate reality game (Warren, Beck, Najmi, & Darby, 2019). Learners were then asked to apply what they learned to a novel situation rooted in an online, transmedia game space (Warren & Lin, 2012; Warren & Najmi, 2013).

Transmedia game interactions were distributed across multiple internet media and platforms: blogs, Twitter, Facebook, websites, massive multi-player online games, virtual worlds, and learning management systems. Thus, the games are termed *transmedia* (Jenkins, 2003), because they take advantage of the separate visual, auditory, and communication affordances of different forms of media. What made them *transmedia learning games* was that these affordances were paired and designed to use the educational affordances of each to support skill and knowledge acquisition or construction. Our intention with *The 2015 Project* was to empower students using interactive learning experiences. The ill-structured problem-solving experiences were intended to provide students with both challenge and agency to work with peers to creatively address global challenges with no one correct answer.

ANALYSIS: PROBLEMS TO BE ADDRESSED

Students would "cheat" on *Broken Window* by using posted digital problem solutions and game outcomes for others to use. Unfortunately, this is a weakness of transmedia designs in general – they are usually single-use experiences. However, the benefit of short life cycles is that designers can refresh the learning experience and improve it more often than other forms of curriculum (Warren & Robinson, 2018).

The new project would need to be open-ended enough to allow for myriad solutions as called for in social constructivist methods. Based on previous research with *The Door* (Warren et al., 2012) and *Broken Window* (Warren et al., 2019), students must be taught self-regulation skills and computer literacy skills and then be able to apply them in familiar and novel contexts to demonstrate learning.

Based on research with *Broken Window* (Warren et al., 2019), instructors asked for more explicit learning activities in the curriculum to prepare learners for the transmedia experience. Specifically, this meant teaching students self-regulation skills, basic Microsoft Office skills, and how to challenge poorly formed knowledge as part of character role play. *The 2015 Project* used a blended design model to specify the transmedia learning experience and merge aspects of PBL, ADDIE, and game, as depicted in Figure 4.1.

The pedagogical components were operationalized within the narrative framing to immerse students in complex problems. Because we had limited time to produce the game (i.e., two months), the project leveraged a core mechanic from McGonigal (2011) and Eklund's *World*

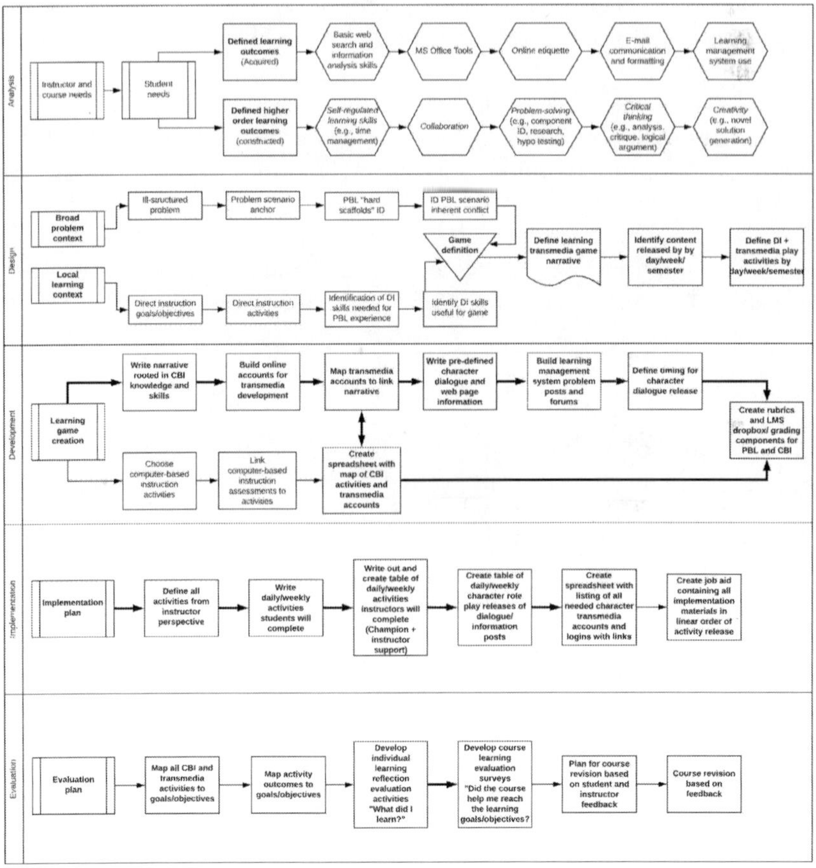

Figure 4.1 The 2015 Project Course Development Process Model

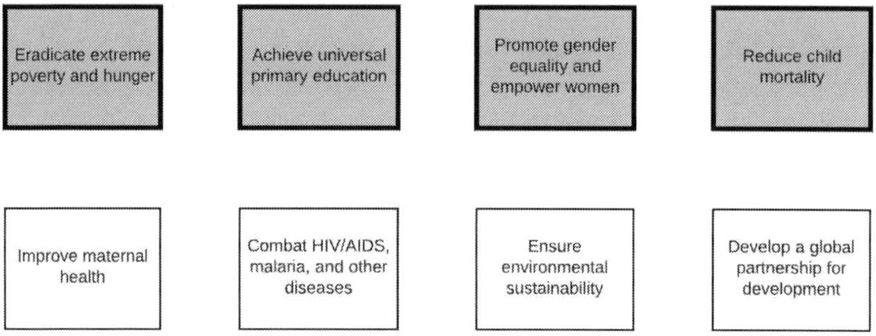

Figure 4.2 The UN MDGs With the Four Included in *The 2015 Project* Highlighted

Without Oil alternate reality game. The goal was for students to address (see Figure 4.2) the broad, highly complex problems facing the world, as defined by the United Nations Millennium Development Goals [UN MDG] (Warren & Wakefield, 2016).

Because the UN MDG problems are large and complex, they have no one correct answer and act as ill-structured problems to drive learning and play using problem-based learning (Savery & Duffy, 1995). Therefore, we designed game scenarios to allow students to generate diverse, defensible solutions using the computer literacy skills they acquired during computer-based instruction (CBI) to reduce instructor workload.

DEVELOPMENT: CBI, PROBLEM-BASED LEARNING, AND TRANSMEDIA PLAY

The learning experiences were rooted in Salen and Zimmerman's (2004) characteristics that qualify a play experience as a game. These components include *artificial conflict* to drive player actions, *interactive rules* governing play, and a *win scenario* to define the conclusion and rewards of play. Warren and Jones (2017) offered another necessary characteristic for a game to be educational; that is, it must *adequately model or simulate a version of reality*. The inclusion of simulation allows students to test the external views against their internal conceptions and supports transfer of learning to other contexts. Noting commonalities between problem-based learning requirements and educational games in the design of *The Door*, Warren, Dondlinger, McLeod, and Bigenho (2012, p. 400) noted that components listed (see Figure 4.3) are necessary for experiences to function as learning games.

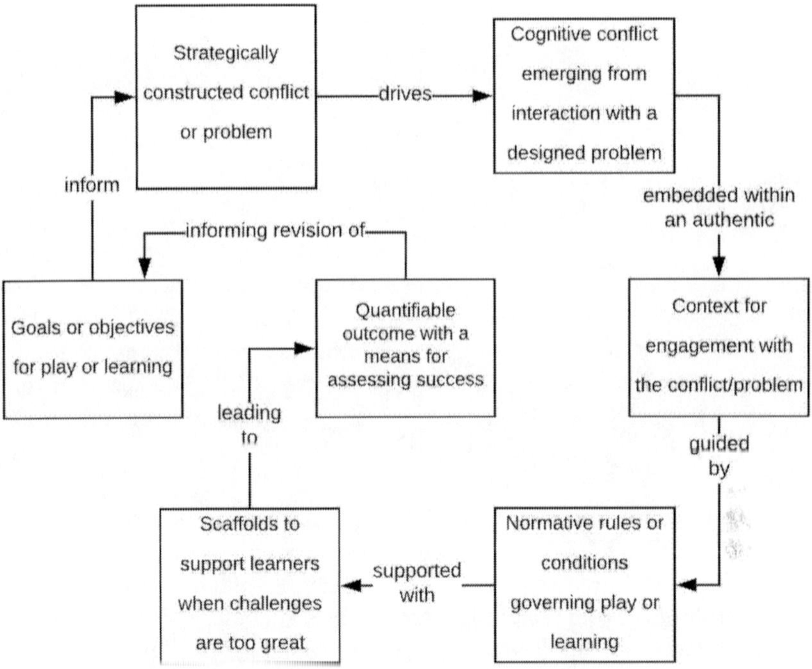

Figure 4.3 Cyclical Components Needed for a Learning Game

Learning in games requires ill-structured problems and cognitive conflict engendered by the open-ended nature of those challenges.

Course Structure

Weeks 1–8: Self-Regulated Learning and Computer-Based Instruction

The introductory college course began with an eight-week unit focused on teaching students how to perform rudimentary self-regulation skills. The purpose of the early activities was to help students break large tasks into smaller ones, communicate with peers, note-taking, time management, and other self-regulated skills that Zimmerman (1989, 1990, 2000) noted are important to student achievement. Previous observations of the course indicated students would enter with little to no knowledge of these skills. Therefore, they were explicitly taught skills followed by practice activities and quizzes to ensure students could recall and later apply skills to the transmedia PBL experience. Students were required to complete the self-regulation skill unit, read from a textbook, and complete CBI literacy simulations. This approach exposed learners to general computer literacy concepts, including hardware, software, and multimedia needed for gameplay.

Weeks 9–16: Transmedia Model

This course leveraged a distributed transmedia model where information and instruction were scaffolded, ill-structured learning activities were provided, and game play was distributed throughout the information given to students in weekly digital communications (Warren & Jones, 2017), including blogs, YouTube videos, Twitter, LMS, wikis, and virtual world spaces. Borrowing the term from Wittgenstein and Anscombe (1968), students *crisscrossed* various platforms, acting as detectives to uncover both tasks and narrative elements that helped drive game play and the learning experience. By distributing these resources across the internet and challenging students to locate them as part of building self-efficacy with online search and general research, students followed clues, sought solutions, and externally represented their own mental models using the tools they learned. Students encountered multiple problems intended to engender cognitive conflict that required communication with peers, critical thinking, and creative problem-solving to address global challenges.

Implementation: Instructor Roles in *The 2015 Project*

Instructors acted as MDG Champions who weekly provided current views on their MDG topic. This information was important because it linked global and local challenges to help students better understand the real-world impacts and complex causes of the crisis. Champions posted links and reflections about the topic in the discussion forum where students communicated with one another in teams called Working Groups. This approach helped model how to locate valuable resources students needed to argue their perspectives during the transmedia experience.

Instructors shared information such as the NIH starting a large-scale study of children's health in the US or how child welfare groups in Nebraska may shut down due to lack of funding. By situating the problem within the US, where the students live, the course sought to convey that the UN MDGs do not just impact people in poor and developing countries but also impact people near them. During week six, the first of four UN MDG problem descriptions were provided to students. The others were introduced in weeks eight, eleven, and thirteen, with the last serving as a culminating prompt to tie the learning experience together.

Problem A. Achieve universal primary education. This problem started with a description of a state budget crisis in Michigan in which the government must decide between paying interest on federal loans to avoid default and paying to keep its public schools open. The government is open to suggestions on how to solve the problem. At this point, the real crisis was weeks away, beginning when the balanced budget requirement impacts the new fiscal year budget beginning on October 1. The state legislature passed a law giving themselves a reprieve until December 1 but needed a solution by then.

Problem B. Eradicate extreme poverty and hunger. As this problem description began, climate change is harming California, Texas, Iowa, Florida, and several other states prone to flooding. This has driven up food prices rapidly during an economic downturn, and corporations as well as the state and federal government kept wages stagnant for government employees to maintain profits or to lower deficit spending. This drove white- and blue-collar workers into poverty.

Problem C. Promote gender equality and empower women. Several states cited reports showing that the gender wage gap/financial equity between men and women was inverted – a woman made 60.2 cents for every dollar earned by a man as part of a state law empowering women. Further, some municipalities considered laws barring men from appearing in public without a female relatives or escorts to prevent their harassment by powerful women.

Problem D. Reduce child mortality. At the time of course development, child health in the US was on the decline for more than a decade, while health care costs rose significantly. At the same time, preventable childhood diseases such as asthma and obesity were on the rise even as fewer Americans had access to health care. As the crisis hit three major metropolitan areas in the story, thousands of children arrived at hospitals with life-threatening asthma attacks in US cities. The following week, the real-world news reported US children having mild heart attacks, early onset diabetes, and being wheelchair bound due to obesity.

Forum Discussion, Critique, and Feedback

Champions and characters posted responses to students as a means of challenging the solutions and other resources they located. As part of their experiences, students were asked to use their Working Group discussion forum to post links to news and other useful research information. Learners discussed these solutions and gave feedback to one another through discussion forums as a means of vetting the veracity of located information while constructing knowledge together. As Champions, instructors critiqued student knowledge constructions through debate and provided feedback to correct poor mental models in keeping with social constructivist assertions.

The instructors responded to all students within a Working Group and role-played characters in response to student posts, which allowed extemporaneous building of the transmedia narrative in a way that was directly responsive to student posts and ideas, rather than generic and non-specific. Thus, the story emerged differently each time, because the transmedia experience unfolded in response to real world events and evolving student understanding. Discussion forums provided evidence of student learning through interaction with and struggle to understand and solve problems. Instructors could identify student growth over time based on diverse experiences without forcing students into a mold of standardized assessment.

Metacognition and Reflection Post

Each week students used the WordPress blog tool to create reflection posts about how and what they learned as well as what they did not understand and needed to learn more about. Students were also asked to think about how they used online and other computer tools to support their solution development and communication. Question prompts were used to encourage students to use newly acquired self-regulated learning skills. Other periodic reflections were mixed into weekly activities as a means of asking students to make connections between how they used the knowledge gained in the forums (e.g., news, research sources, character/Champion/peer discussions). These contemplations were used to support their acquisition of information or knowledge construction as well as ideas about how they could do better in the future. As with Savery and Duffy's (1995) problem-based learning and anchored instruction conceptions, these individual reflections provided instructors with evidence of student growth over time as they revised their mental models during interaction with ill-structured problems and critical thinking. In the accompanying study, we found students used these opportunities to learn more than the computer literacy tools. Our methods are described in the next section.

Research Methods

The 2015 Project employed qualitative methods to analyze student responses in the discussion forums and reflection blogs.

Setting

The study took place in three undergraduate pilot courses at a large public university in the southwest US. The setting was a 100% online course managed by one coordinator (tenured faculty) and three adjunct faculty members who were responsible for a single UN MDG topic as well as grading students in their own courses. All faculty had access to the CMS where the forums and other resources were housed and made available to students.

Participants

Twenty-four out of 94 students in the courses agreed to participate in the study. The students represented the overall demographic makeup of the university (i.e., 53% female; 48% white, 22% Hispanic, 14% African American, 26% all other ethnicities; 45% first-generation college student) and were approximately 18–20 years old.

Data Collection

For this study, data regarding student performance and experience were collected from discussion forums and student reflection blogs. The data were collected at the end of the semester once all postings were complete. The collected information was aggregated into Microsoft Word documents and then broken into spreadsheets for analysis.

Data Analysis

Student postings were analyzed using computer-mediated discourse analysis following the process developed by Herring (2004). Individual student blog utterances were placed in the spreadsheet in conjunction with student postings and responses to peers to make sense of their experience with the transmedia application of their acquired knowledge and skills. These posts were correlated with individual student reflections to examine what learners reported they learned and to confirm identified codes, categories, and themes generated by the analysts.

Findings

From analysis of student activities in the forums, coupled with their reflections, we found that there was significant value to providing the transmedia activities in terms of exposing students to new, complex global challenges to which they could apply their newly developed computer literacy skills. All students discussed in the following sections were assigned pseudonyms to protect their identities.

Theme 1: Value in Allowing Students to Explore and Define

The open-ended nature of what the instructors/Champions allowed in the discussion forums and blog postings resulted in significantly different levels of formality, and sometimes quality, in student postings despite clear directions regarding the requirements. However, simple exposure to the problem helped students better consider what they did not know about a topic and examine aspects their personally found motivating, as noted by Pamela:

> It is crazy to think how much I did not know about maternal health before I started this project. It seems like something that everyone women [sic] in not only America but also, all over the world, should be educated on.

The student further considered not only her own lack of knowledge about the complex problem but also how globally it remains, showing the value of connecting MDG challenges to both the international and local contexts to help better immerse learners in the problem narrative. Pamela named specific aspects of maternal health she learned from exposure to the transmedia course materials and sharing with peers in the forum:

> I learned so much about how most developing countries don't have the supplies and assistance they need to have a safe delivery. I learned that many women in those countries, and even women here in America, aren't educated on how to have a healthy pregnancy in order to avoid complications.

Another student, Ursula, responded directly to Pamela by posting a video in the forum about maternal mortality rates, also linking under-developed countries' problems to the US: http://abclocal.go.com/kgo/video?id=7254220:

> This is a video from the news that was aired on ABC. I was alarmed when I watched it. It describes that women giving birth in California are just as at-risk for mortality as those giving birth in underdeveloped countries. The maternal mortality rate compares to that of the 70's. . . . A scary thought!

In response to Ursula, Kristen posted her related reflection to another piece of media she had located on the topic:

> I recently found a chart containing alarming rates of maternal death rates in California. I was just as surprised to see that mothers in our country are not able to get the care they need to deliver a child with little complication.

Interactions among students included resources they located through their own research and shared knowledge regarding the topic of maternal mortality by linking what many students believed to be a problem impacted only on people in countries lacking resources, rather than one that continues to harm the US due to inequality and other complex issues. One challenge we noted was that these posts often did not include workable solutions; however, some students, like Ophelia, proposed a solution to the ill-structured problem that also included success measures:

> When I first read this, I was kind of unsure if it was true. But after I watched the video I could not believe the statics [sic] of mothers dieing [sic]! It is alarming to know that people living in the United States are at a risk just as much as mothers in third world countries for maternal mortality. I think a solution that can help this would be for mothers to be required to take a class in the risk of maternal mortality. It would be interesting to see statics [sic] of mortality rates after mothers go to the class then [sic] before when the mothers did not attend.

While students were not asked to consider measuring impacts, only to generate solutions, many also found it was important to develop some way to determine if their solutions were effective. By keeping some of the directions more open-ended, students were liberated to define their own approach to learning in a manner they may not have used if we had provided too much direction.

Theme 2: Students Learned the Intended Computer Literacy Skills

The central purpose of the course was to teach basic computer literacy skills (e.g., Microsoft Office, netiquette), so an early design concern was whether asking students to complete learning transfer tasks in a new context (i.e., UN MDGs) might interfere with their acquisition of the primary course content. However, students reported that they learned more because they had to apply those skills in a naturalistic manner, helping them grow further, as noted by Isabelle:

> I knew a lot about Microsoft Office before because I used it at work and at my house. The things I learned in this class were faster ways and little tricks here and there that helped me be more efficient when working on things. . . . This project taught me a lot about maternal health that I probably would have never known otherwise. The issues within maternal health make this subject so hard to wrap your brain around. Once you think you know something, something else pops out of nowhere and adds to the confusion.

The complexity of the larger, more abstract solution creation with maternal health in this instance took student focus away from just learning a tool and helped give a reason to use it. As Luke noted, he still acquired the needed knowledge and skills, but also took away something more:

> This [class] has given me a lot to learn when it comes to Maternal Health and just how to use the basic features of Word, Excel, and PowerPoint. I already knew a lot about Word and PowerPoint, but this class definitely helped refine my tools and learn a lot more with Excel. As far as Maternal Health, I learned a lot that I never had known. Putting it all together into a letter and slide show has made it easier and more fun too.

Similarly, Abigail stated that the value of the transmedia learning products was supportive of learning and increased her engagement:

> This project has taken a lot of time and work, but it has been worth it. I have gained such a deeper understanding of worldwide issues. When I first started this project I mainly worked to get myself familiar with the material provided; then I became extremely interested in the other information that was available, so I began researching it. When we began composing our letters I became even more determined to find valuable information on the topic. It

> has taken weeks to come to a final result for the powerpoint [sic] and letter, but now that it is done I'm proud of the knowledge I've gained.

Overall, students reported that their experience with the transmedia materials, computer literacy CBI, interactions with peers, and work to explore the complex problems helped them grow and provided them with the opportunity to work in the direction that most interested them.

CONCLUSION

The 2015 Project experience was rooted in transmedia games that challenged individuals to critique the state of the world and generate solutions to messy problems with no one right answer. However, our past research with transmedia experiences found that the messiness led to inefficiency of design and delivery, because students often did not have the core knowledge and skills needed to participate in the complex, abstract reasoning that problem-based learning experiences require. This led to the creation of a different digital model that leveraged low cost, distributed digital technologies, and activities used to support student emancipation from their past educational experiences. These taught self-regulated learning and computer-literacy skills needed to participate in higher-order creative problem-solving.

Our future work will leverage the lessons learned in the design of this course. We learned to use technology creatively to both improve the simulation components of the transmedia experience as well as increase the efficiency of delivery and further reduce the workload of instructors. While design was imperfect, the digital learning components that encouraged research, reflection, sharing, and critique were valuable for encouraging student independent learning and experience in a manner that our previous designs were not. *The 2015 Project* provided students diverse opportunities to critique local and global systems students; our hope is that improving student ability to learn from and adapt to ill-structured challenges will better prepare students for a future we cannot imagine.

REFERENCES

Belland, B., Glazewski, K., & Ertmer, P. (2009). Inclusion and problem-based learning: Roles of students in a mixed-ability group. *RMLE Online*, *32*(1), 1–19. https://doi.org/10.1080/19404476.2009.11462062

Berg, L. D., Huijbens, E. H., & Larsen, H. G. (2016). Producing anxiety in the neoliberal university. *The Canadian Geographer/Le Géographe Canadien, 60*(2), 168–180. https://doi.org/10.1111/cag.12261

Blackwell, D. (2013). *Effects of problem-based learning on a fifth grade language arts classroom* [Doctoral Dissertation], University of North Texas. UNT Digital Library. Retrieved from https://digital.library.unt.edu/ark:/67531/metadc271781/?q=blackwell

Foucault, M. (1970). *The order of things: An archaeology of the human science* (Vintage Bo). London: Random House.

Freire, P. (1998). *Pedagogy of freedom*. New York: Rowman & Littlefield. https://doi.org/10.1017/CBO9781107415324.004

Habermas, J. (1970). On systematically distorted communication. *Inquiry, 13*(1–4), 205–218. https://doi.org/10.1080/00201747008601590

Habermas, J. (1984). *The theory of communicative action: Volume 1. Reason and the rationalization of society* (English tr ed. Vol. 1). Boston, MA: Beacon Press. https://doi.org/10.2307/1955926

Habermas, J. (1998). *On the pragmatics of communication* (M. Cooke, Ed.). Cambridge, MA: The MIT Press. http://doi.org/10.2307/2655274

Herring, S. C. (2004). Computer-mediated discourse analysis: An approach to researching online behavior. In S. A. Barab, R. Kling, & J. H. Gray (Eds.), *Designing virtual communities in the service of learning* (pp. 338–376). Cambridge: Cambridge University Press. https://doi.org/10.1017/CBO9780511805080.016

Hmelo-Silver, C. E. (2004). Problem-based learning: What and how do students learn? *Educational Psychology Review, 16*(3), 235. https://doi.org/10.1023/B:EDPR.0000034022.16470.f3

Hung, W. (2011). Theory to reality: a few issues in implementing problem-based learning. *Educational Technology Research and Development, 59*(4), 529–552. https://doi.org/10.1007/s11423-011-9198-1

Jenkins, H. (2003). Transmedia storytelling. *MIT Technology Review*. Retrieved from www.technologyreview.com/s/401760/transmedia-storytelling/

Jonassen, D. H. (1999). Designing constructivist learning environments. In C. M. Reigeluth (Ed.), *Instructional design theories and models: A new paradigm of instructional theory* (Vol. 2, pp. 215–239). Mahwah, NJ: Lawrence Erlbaum Associates. https://doi.org/10.1007/BF02299477

Jonassen, D. H. (2011). *Learning to solve problems: A handbook for designing problem-solving learning environments*. New York: Routledge. https://doi.org/10.4324/9780203847527

Jonassen, D. H., & Hernandez-Serrano, J. (2002). Case-based reasoning and instructional design: Using stories to support problem solving. *Educational Technology Research & Development, 50*(2), 65–77. https://doi.org/10.1007/BF02504994

Kirschner, P. A., & Clark, R. E. (2006). An analysis of the failure of constructivist, discovery, problem-based, experiential, and inquiry-based teaching. *Learning, 41*(2), 75–86. https://doi.org/10.1207/s15326985ep4102_1

McGonigal, J. (2011). *Reality is broken: Why games make us better and how they can change the world* (1st ed.). London: Penguin Books. https://doi.org/10.5860/choice.49-6095

Ritchhart, R., Church, M., & Morrison, K. (2011). *Making thinking visible: How to promote engagement, understanding, and independence for all learners*. San Francisco, CA: Jossey-Bass. https://doi.org/10.1111/j.1467-9604.2012.01520.x

Salen, K., & Zimmerman, E. (2004). *Rules of play: Game design fundamentals*. Cambridge, MA: MIT Press. https://doi.org/10.1162/dram.2007.51.1.183

Samsonov, P., Pedersen, S., & Hill, C. (2006). Using problem-based learning software with at-risk students: A case study. *Computers in Schools*, *23*(1/2), 111–124.

Saunders, D. B. (2010). Neoliberal ideology and public higher education in the United States. *Journal for Critical Education Policy Studies*, *8*(1), 42–74.

Savery, J. R. (2006). Overview of PBL: Definitions and distinctions. *Interdisciplinary Journal of Problem-Based Learning*, *1*(1), 9–20. https://doi.org/10.7771/1541-5015.1002

Savery, J. R., & Duffy, T. M. (1995). Problem based learning: An instructional model and its constructivist framework. *Educational Technology*, *35*, 31–38.

Shih, K. P., Chen, H. C., Chang, C. Y., & Kao, T. C. (2010). The development and implementation of scaffolding-based self-regulated learning system for e/m-learning. *Educational Technology & Society*, *13*(1), 80–93. ISSN 1436-4522.

Shore, C., & Wright, S. (1999). Audit culture and anthropology: Neo-Liberalism in British higher education. *The Journal of the Royal Anthropological Institute*, *5*(4), 557–575. https://doi.org/10.2307/2661148

Warren, S. J., Beck, D. E., Najmi, A., & Darby, D. (2019). Transmedia play to teach computer literacy, global thinking, and rudimentary instructional design: Instructors reflect on teaching with Broken Window. *Journal of Interactive Learning Research*, *30*(4), 505–537. Retrieved from www.learntechlib.org/primary/p/180397/

Warren, S. J., Dondlinger, M. J., McLeod, J., & Bigenho, C. (2012). Opening the door: An evaluation of the efficacy of a problem-based learning game. *Computers & Education*, *58*(1), 397–412. https://doi.org/10.1016/j.compedu.2011.08.012

Warren, S. J., & Jones, G. (2017). *Learning games: The science and art of development* (D. Ifenthaler, S. Warren, & D. Esreyel, Eds.). Cham, Switzerland: Springer. https://doi.org/10.1007/978-3-319-46829-7_1

Warren, S. J., & Lin, L. (2012). Ethical considerations in the design and use of educational games. In H. H. Yang & S. C.-Y. Yuen (Eds.), *Handbook of research on practices and outcomes in virtual worlds and environments* (1st ed., Vol. 1, pp. 1–18). Hershey, PA: IGI Global. https://doi.org/10.4018/978-1-60960-762-3.ch00

Warren, S. J., & Najmi, A. (2013). Learning and teaching as communicative actions: Broken window as a model of transmedia game learning. In Y. Baek & N. Whitton (Eds.), *Cases on digital game-based learning: Methods, models, and strategies* (pp. 199–226). Hershey, PA: Information Science Reference. https://doi.org/10.4018/978-1-4666-2848-9.ch011

Warren, S. J., & Robinson, H. (2018). Improving an organization's knowledge and innovation capabilities with a cognitive science view of learning. In *Product innovation and technology management track*. Houston, TX: Production and Operations Management Society.

Warren, S. J., & Wakefield, J. S. (2016). Affect in online discourse: The case of the UN millennial goals topics. In S. Tettegah & M. McCreery (Eds.), *Emotions, technology, and learning* (1st ed., pp. 43–67). Amsterdam: Elsevier. https://doi.org/https://doi.org/10.1016/C2013-0-18514-5

White, J. (1997). Philosophy and the aims of higher education. *Studies in Higher Education*, *22*(1), 7–17. https://doi.org/10.1080/03075079712331381101

Wittgenstein, L. (1968). *Philosophical investigations* (2nd ed.). Hoboken, NJ: Blackwell. https://doi.org/10.4236/ojpp.2019.91005

Zimmerman, B. J. (1989). Self-regulated learning and academic achievement: An overview. *Educational Psychologist, 25*, 3–17. https://doi.org/10.1207/s15326985ep2501_2

Zimmerman, B. J. (1990). Self-regulated learning and academic achievement: An overview. *Educational Psychologist, 25*, 3–17.

Zimmerman, B. J. (2000). Attaining self-regulation: A social cognitive perspective. In M. Boekaerts, P. Pintrich, & M. Seidner (Eds.), *Self-regulation: Theory, research and applications* (pp. 1–39). Cambridge, MA: Academic Press. https://doi.org/10.1016/B978-012109890-2/50031-7

UNIT II

Diversifying Instruction

CHAPTER 5

Oral Interaction in Technology Education

Wendy Fox-Turnbull

INTRODUCTION

Technology education is fundamentally about the development of the technological world to enhance people's experiences of, in, and with the world. Today's world is technological in nature. We engage with and use technology from birth or maybe even before. Students therefore must be educated about technology, how it is developed, how it influences and impacts lives, and how to develop it ethically and sustainably. For students to flourish in a technological world, it is important that they become technologically literate; that is, develop technacy (Seemann & Talbot, 1995).

Technological literacy is defined in a number of different ways. In this chapter the term technacy is used to differentiate it from definitions of technological literacy that are narrower and restricted to the use of technologies (Seemann & Talbot, 1995). We refer to technacy as a means to acquire a level of literacy that is needed to understand, operate, and develop ethical and sustainable technologies and to understand the influences and impacts of technology necessary to succeed within today's technological world.

People need not only to read and write (language literacy) and engage with and use numbers (numeracy or number literacy) but they also need to be able to engage with, critique, and develop technology (technacy). Knowledge in technology is often difficult to define, but includes not only "knowing that" but also "knowing how" and "knowing why." Early philosophers of technology often identified knowledge deployed in the development of artifacts as being borrowed from science, but we now know that technology is a body of knowledge in its own right and that

DOI: 10.4324/9781003089704-8

people who use technology have knowledge and understanding that differ from that of technology developers. These knowledge categories are particularly relevant to technological knowledge: "those who do" and "those who use" technology (de Vries, 2017). This chapter explores the role oral interaction plays in developing technacy as an ultimate goal of technology education.

TECHNOLOGY EDUCATION AND EDUCATIONAL TECHNOLOGIES

Technology Education is not to be confused with educational technology, which involves teachers and children using technology as teaching learning tools. Technology education is a curriculum learning area or school subject sometimes taught alone and sometimes combined with other learning areas such as science. Education technologies focuses on the use of tools to facilitate and enhance teaching and learning (Fox-Turnbull, Reinsfield, & Forret, 2021). Table 5.1 summarizes the key ideas differentiating technology education and educational technology.

Technology education explicitly deals with the technological processes of investigating, critiquing, designing, making, and appraising technological solutions to address identified technological problems or to recognize and realize opportunities within any given social and cultural context. Programs of learning in technology education use authentic learning contexts and are particularly well suited for inquiry-based learning. Technology education frequently facilitates integration of a range of other learning areas or subjects. It is interdisciplinary and requires students to work as technologists and at times with technologists. A central aspect of technacy is the understanding that intellectual and practical resources are used to intervene in the world through the development of products and systems (Ministry of Education, 2007).

Creativity and innovation are critical aspects of successful technology practice (Spendlove, 2015). Innovative technological practice is collaborative in nature and requires communication and conversation with others throughout. It is during these often meaningful conversations that students may draw on their cultural funds of knowledge. They may have cultural experience, skills, and knowledge that other group members do not have. In such cases, they give value to often undervalued cultural knowledge and skills or funds of knowledge (Fox-Turnbull, 2013). Through technological practice, students converse with peers and professionals, deploy funds of knowledge, make connections, and develop new insights during the process of designing and developing technological outcomes.

Table 5.1 **Differentiating Technology Education and Educational Technology**

Technology Education	*Educational Technology*
In technology education, students learn:	*By engaging educational technologies, teachers and students understand:*
the impacts technology has on their own and others' lives	that educational technologies are tools to facilitate and enhance learning
the influences of technology on humans and the environment	and learn to use technology to enhance teaching and learning
the influences humans have on technological development	and learn to use technology to share teaching and learning
to critique existing technologies in order to inform future practice	that educational technologies facilitate different ways of doing and thinking
to plan and undertake technological practice	that educational technology both includes distance learning and enhances face-to-face learning
to design ethical and authentic technological outcomes in order to address needs or opportunities	that educational technology does not include designing and developing digital technologies, only using them for learning
to skillfully develop the above outcomes	how to use technology to enhance teaching and learning
to evaluate designed outcomes using stakeholder feedback and developed attributes and specifications	that technologies influence ways of learning
to develop strong technacy (technological literacy)	that different pedagogical approaches can be deployed

Source: Adapted from Fox-Turnbull et al. (2021).

DEFINING ORAL INTERACTION-TALK

Constructivist theories identify talk as a result of thinking and learning. However, in social constructivism and sociocultural theories, the reverse is true. Learning occurs as a result of talk (Coffer, 2017; Fox-Turnbull, 2016). This is the perspective taken in this chapter, as it is particularly relevant to technology education (Fox-Turnbull, 2013). From a socio-cultural perspective, interaction between people is a central aspect of cognitive, social, and cultural development (Black, 2008). As stated earlier, technological practice is frequently collaborative. Language and social interaction are vital components of working collaboratively; thus, quality oral interaction is a critical component in the success of technology practice, especially in the classroom (Coffer, 2017). When undertaking technology practice, students undertake collaborative problem-solving and frequently work within social constructivist and sociocultural paradigms (Fox-Turnbull, 2016).

Vygotsky (1978) emphasized the need for two opposing tendencies in quality social interaction. The first, Intersubjective Dialogue, occurs between a novice and an expert and works toward developing shared definition, aiming to move the novice to task independence. As people interact, they construct their world. This is illustrated in technology education when a student is guided by their teacher. As a facilitator of learning, a teacher must recognize when students are struggling with an issue or perhaps heading off on the wrong pathway. Teachers can probe and question students, facilitate reflection on, and alter their technology practice pathway. Joint problem-solving uses debate as a major force in cognitive development.

Alterity is concerned with the distinction between self and others when discrepancy or conflict of opinion occurs between personal and others' points-of-view. Alterity sparks cognitive development if the listener perceives and understands meaning, simultaneously responding actively, either agreeing or disagreeing partially or completely. This event is clearly illustrated in technology when two students are working on the design of a common outcome with different initial concept designs. By discussing, reflecting on, and defending their design ideas, they eventually arrive at an agreed solution that takes aspects of each of the initial designs. Their alterity led to the design of a better outcome than either of them could have achieved individually.

Language is not a system of set meanings for everyone. Single statements can mean different things to different people, thus presenting opportunity for misunderstanding and conflict (Mercer, 1995). For example, the statement/question "Did you do that?" can mean a range of things. It might mean the person is being accused of doing something wrong, or that they are being asked whether they are responsible for doing something unexpected or challenging. Oral language is interpreted by the listener, taking context, emphasis, tone, and nonverbal cues into consideration in order to make meaning. Discussion that takes place during the course of education activities is called dialogue. Within everyday dialogue the speaker regularly considers the listener's response, giving insight into variability of meaning. When this response aligns with the speaker's understanding, the conversation is enriched. On the other hand, when the listener's understanding differs, the speaker can sense resistance. Beliefs, values, and attitudes inform the way people act, read, what they say, and how they interact. However, these are not static and change as people read, experience, observe, and adapt to new situations (Mercer & Hodgkinson, 2008; Shields & Edwards, 2005).

DIALOGUE AND EXPLORATORY TALK

Dialogue and Exploratory talk are much more than just talk. They are complex and dynamic, often involving vastly different cultures, perspectives, values, ideas, and points of view. They generally involve the use of words with deep engagement from participants. Dialogue can bring moments of intense connection with another person with feelings of remarkable openness, deeply affirming and highly exhilarating moments (Mercer, 2006). Exploratory talk involves retrieval and questioning of what is known (Webb, Whitlow, & Venter, 2016).

> Exploratory talk might be effective because implementing it also embodies retrieval practice. That is, in order to make an argument, one has to remember the facts and concepts that one has studied to construct the argument. Exploratory talk might also implicitly provide distributed practice in that the process of developing and presenting argument is likely to involve coming back to the same material at different times. Similarly, developing an argument often requires a combination of reviewing past history, analyzing data from current findings and constructing a coherent narrative, a process that interleaves different tasks to complete a project.
>
> (Webb et al., 2016, pp. 575–576)

Exploratory dialogue is critical in learning and considerably more important than has been demonstrated in schools in the past. Educational success and failure may be explained by the quality of educational dialogue rather than by the capability of individual students or the skill of their teachers (Mercer, 2006; Robertson & Graven, 2019).

When people work together in problem-solving situations they do much more than just talk together. They "inter-think" by combining shared understandings and combining their intellects in creative ways, often reaching outcomes that are well above the capability of each individual. Problem-solving situations involve a dynamic engagement of ideas with rich conversation as the principal means used to establish a shared understanding, testing solutions, and reaching agreement or compromise. Exploratory dialogue is about thinking together and an important part of education that has long been ignored or actively discouraged in schools (Shields & Edwards, 2005).

Teachers need to engage in quality talk with students (and parents) to assist with cognitive and experiential understanding of the world in which they live. They also need to facilitate this talk between students (Fox-Turnbull, 2019). Teachers make powerful contributions to the way children think and talk and convey powerful messages about thinking by the way they structure classroom activity and talk. Students need to be engaged in thoughtful and reasoned talk, which teachers need to model and scaffold using appropriate language strategies to extend thinking. Students need regular opportunities to practice using talk to reflect, enquire, and explain their thinking to others. They need to be able to seek and compare points of view, debate and reconcile questions, taking learning beyond teachers' factual questions. Spoken language is one of the tools students use to make sense of the world and should be a teacher's main pedagogical tool.

INTERCOGNITIVE CONVERSATIONS

As stated earlier, exploratory dialogue occurs as students inter-think. Intercognitive conversations are conversations within which all participants learn through participation in exploratory dialogue and then have the ability and willingness to reflect on their own and others' views and knowledge. Working within a common context and engagement in the talk described, students are able to teach other and advance their own knowledge and understanding in their given context. Debate, argument, and disagreement assist students' understanding and helps to reposition existing information and position new information. However this cognitive growth only occurs if and when participants are open to change and new ideas (Fox-Turnbull, 2013). Intercognitive conversations can only occur in a classroom where the class climate allows risk-taking and exploration. Students need to understand that the purpose of teachers' questions is not to find the "right" answer but to explore thinking (Robertson & Graven, 2019).

There are two types of intercognitive conversations. The first, Convergent Growth Conversation (CGC), describes conversations within which cognitive growth occurs in the same field of learning or within the same context. This is exemplified when two students have a conversation, and each contributes what they know. Through the conversation, both participants combine and reshape their existing knowledge and skills, subsequently expanding their own understanding and each experiencing a shift in cognitive thinking (Fox-Turnbull, 2013). This phenomenon was illustrated in a study by Fox-Turnbull (2013). A group of three students was tasked to design a 1930's style microphone as a prop for their class production. During the initial sketch phase of their practice, one student, Molly (not her real name) drew a common hand-held cylindrical microphone, another student (Alan) drew an older-style rectangular shaped one, set on a long stand. The resulting conversation with their teacher facilitated growth for all. Molly realized that her sketch was of a microphone from a more recent era than needed and that the style assisted the audiences in determining the historical period. Alan shared that he had seen older-style microphones in movies but learned that microphones could either be hand-held or on a stand. The students were able to reach conclusions about an agreed final design that was true to the required era and flexible in its use. This conversation exemplified CGC. The teacher assisting the conversation gained insight into how students learned about technology and that to succeed, students need to be open to critique and new ideas.

The second type of intercognitive conversations is the Divergent Growth Conversation (DGC), which occurs when participants learn in different fields and for different purposes. For example, such a conversation might occur in teachers' conversations with students, as illustrated in the previous paragraph. Teacher questions assist the student to make new connections about their current context of learning. At the same time, teachers gain new knowledge about students' learning strategies and successful pedagogical approaches (Fox-Turnbull, 2013). With the assistance of reflective thinking, teachers undertake personal professional development on pedagogical context knowledge and possibly content knowledge as they talk with their students.

TALK TO LEARN TECHNOLOGY – INTERCOGNITIVE TALK

It is critical to understand the significance of conversations in learning. Through conversations, teachers and parents can encourage children to reshape their thoughts (Mercer, 1995). There are very clear implications here for technology given the collaborative nature of problem-solving required to develop technological outcomes. Intercognitive talk is particularly relevant because students often work collaboratively on a single technological outcome. To succeed, group members must talk about their ideas, listen to and accept others' ideas, clearly articulate their own thinking and reasoning, and make a shift in their own thinking when compromise or change is needed. Common ground must be identified in order for a group of students to be able to design and develop a single outcome to meet the identified need (Fox-Turnbull, 2017). This was illustrated by Molly and Alan who were tasked with develop one 1930's microphone. Both had vastly different initial design ideas that needed to be modified in order to succeed. Technology cannot be learned by rote (Black, 2008; Coffer, 2017). The only way forward for these two was open dialogue and intercognitive conversation to ensure new understandings about a way forward emerged. There are five critical components to having rich intercognitive conversations in the classroom: inclusive classroom climate, rich questions, encouragement of open discussion, strategies to support participation, and a willingness to have ideas challenged and to learn.

An inclusive classroom climate is one in which students feel they belong and are able to take risks. Teachers need to hold a growth mindset to learning, believing every child has the potential to learn, and actively fostering this belief in their students. Students need to understand that their intelligence is expandable. They need to embrace challenge, develop resilience and persistence after a setback, and understand that effort will be rewarded and learning takes place when constructive feedback and criticism are present (Clarke, 2014). In technology, students need to be comfortable exploring wacky design ideas and making design mistakes. They are less likely to do this if they feel that they are different or laughed at. Funds of knowledge of other cultures are more likely to be deployed during technology practice if students understand that they are included in their classroom and that their cultural knowledge is valued.

Schut, Klapwijk, Gielen, and de Vries (2019) also suggest that higher-level rich questions are a good tool for providing divergent feedback on design and creativity. At this stage, it is important to acknowledge that rich questioning does not only occur orally; however, there are several advantages of oral questioning. These include immediacy, co-presence, visibility, and co-temporality (Fox-Turnbull, 2013).

An inclusive classroom climate will go some way to encouraging open discussion in the classroom, but there are additional strategies to support participation. The use of talking partners and the "no hands up" rule are a start. Talking partners are selected randomly and changed often. They are peers with whom students discuss their thinking, ideas, and learning. Students need to be taught how to be a successful talking partner. Rules guide behavior. These include acceptance of what is being said, understanding that accepting ideas is not the same as agreeing with them, giving eye contact, looking interested, avoiding distractions, thinking about what the talking partner is saying, staying focused, letting go of some ideas so as not to disturb the talker's train of thought, saying more than one or two words and being prepared to compromise or constructively persuade (Clarke, 2005). This strategy is often coupled with "no hands up." When deployed, this strategy implies that everyone in the class has something to say and that any pair of talking partners may be called on to share their collective thinking. These two strategies promote deeper-level thinking and talking that creates opportunities for students to evaluate, analyze, and synthesize rather than merely recall and comprehend ideas (Bloom, 1956). Understanding the importance of and facilitating student-teacher and student-student dialogue is also particularly relevant to technology education because of the practical nature of many lessons. Teachers are often easily distracted by organization of activities and management of the children's behavior. Discipline is needed to ensure these things do not distract them from engaging the children in conversation about their learning and practice. Technology education allows children to use creativity and innovative thinking; it lets them move in directions very different from current thinking or thinking of their peers, offering teachers unique opportunities and insight into their students' thinking.

The difference this can make for some students was illustrated in a study undertaken by the author. The class task was to design a futuristic car. Issy, a very quiet, shy six-year-old girl, rarely contributed orally in class. After talking her ideas through with her talking partner about her design ideas, she began to share with her class for the first time. Her teacher saw, for the first time, her creative and innovative thinking. Issy's design was a car with wings rather than wheels. She had identified that cars in the future might have wings instead of wheels. During the same conversations, Issy was able to reflect on some of the issues associated with flying cars such as flying over people's houses and stopping for other "cars." Dialogue between her teacher and Issy enabled insight into her forward thinking and understanding that previously had not been identified by the classroom teacher. Her ideas were considerably more sophisticated than those of her peers. This is an example of a DGC intercognitive conversation. The conversation enabled Issy to identify and articulate potential issues of her designed technology outcome. The classroom teacher learned about Issy's sophisticated designerly thinking.

Another conversation with a child, told in first person for effect, is worth sharing here, as it again illustrates the power of teacher-student conversation. The conversation occurred between Rex (not his real name) an eight-year-old boy from a low-decile school in Christchurch, New Zealand, and the author in her role as a technology education lecturer at the local pre-service teacher education provider. Rex was in a Year 4 class. In appreciation of some work undertaken with the class, I offered to resource and teach a technology unit with the class. The classroom teacher requested a Christmas theme. At my suggestion, the classroom teacher bought a Christmas tree for the class and we posed the problem that the tree had no decorations and with no money to buy them we suggested the children design and develop chocolate Christmas tree decorations to adorn the tree. Over a period of a week the students undertook a number of activities to enhance their understanding of Christmas decorations, symbols of Christmas, of physical and functional features of molds and the vacuum forming process used to construct the plastic molds for chocolates. Subsequently the students sketched three possible ideas for their decoration, selected one, and created a pattern of their intended design in ceramic dough, cooked for hardening. During the sketching process, I circulated around the room looking at the students' options and preferred designs. I noticed that one boy, Rex, had three sketches on his paper; two traditional Christmas designs and one that looked like a sausage with a face rather like a papoose. I asked him which one he was going to develop into the actual decoration. He pointed to the papoose. "A strange choice," I thought and wandered on to the next child. Later that week when the students had completed their patterns I noticed Rex carefully cradling his "papoose" in his little hands. I stopped and asked him to tell me about his design. He explained to me that his design was for his mother. He went on to say that two years previously he had had a baby brother, born prematurely, who lived only two days. Every year the family hung a decoration on their Christmas tree to remember him. Rex had designed a representation of his little brother that he was going to give to his mother to hang on their tree at home. The story still moves me every time I read it or retell it. On reflection, I realized how easily I could have missed this conversation with Rex. From my perspective, his design could have just been a sausage with a face. On hearing his story, I had a much better appreciation of the thinking and reasoning that had gone into Rex's technological solution. I began to wonder how much teachers miss when they don't have these conversations with their students and what insights these conversations give us into learning in technology.

Understanding the power of exploratory dialogue and intercognitive conversation led to the development of a conversation framework designed to enable student-teacher conversations. It must be acknowledged here the student-student conversations are equally if not more important than teacher-student conversations. However, in order to teach students to talk to each other constructively to facilitate higher thinking, their teachers must first model and then scaffold appropriate conversations. The Technology Observation and Conversation Framework assists this process.

TECHNOLOGY OBSERVATIONS AND CONVERSATION FRAMEWORK

Developed to assist teachers' facilitation of quality exploratory dialogue and intercognitive conversation while they work in technology, the TOCF offers a large number of questions teachers can select from to initiate conversations with students. It gives suggestions as to the types of comments that might be useful and makes suggestions for behaviors to observe. The TOCF has a dual role, also assisting in the development of teachers' understanding of technology and facilitating students-teacher higher-level thinking in technology. Using the framework, teachers facilitate exploratory dialogue with students, some of which will become intercognitive in nature.

The framework identifies five desirable behaviors for success in learning technology: resilience, transference, flexibility and sophistication, reflection, and socialization. These desirable technology behaviors (DTB) were identified from Claxton, Chambers, Powell, and Lucas's (2013) work on building learning power. Given the collaborative, academic and practical natures of technology education, the author identified and modified them as needed. The first behavior, "resilience," includes capabilities of perseverance, especially after initial failure; managing distractions from peers, other activities, and people around them; and absorption in any given task. Absorption, likened to Csikszentmihalyi's (1990) state of "flow," is described as a state of deep mental involvement in an activity that is intrinsically enjoyable, as when artists and athletes are focused on their performance or play. This is clearly relevant to technology. Students must be able to fail repeatedly when designing and testing technology outcomes. Modeling should be about discovering what works; mistakes should be celebrated, with each identifying something that does not work "yet" or suggesting that a solution may lie elsewhere.

The transference of knowledge occurs when students develop understanding in one context and apply it successfully to another context. It may not occur naturally for students; however, teachers can facilitate transference with a keen awareness of their students, good understanding of content knowledge, and the ability to make authentic connections.

Transference includes making links to technologies experienced or seen and to experiences undertaken previously. Transference also draws on students' Funds of Knowledge (Fox-Turnbull, 2012). It also includes students reflecting on and questioning the relevance of previous experiences, knowledge, and skills and what can be used again in the current context. The relevance to technology is once again clear. As students design and develop their technological outcomes, opportunities to use knowledge and skills from other subjects arise. Mathematics, writing, reading, social studies, and science are significant contributors to technology, but teachers frequently need to bridge the gap between the learning areas (Jones, 2009).

The ability to think flexibly and sophisticatedly includes questioning others to learn more and getting below the surface of ideas and artifacts. Flexibility and sophistication indicate a depth to understanding as well as an openness to potentially strange ideas. Critical components include the use of reasoning to evaluate, the ability to distill information in order to understand, planning ideas and actions, and capitalizing or making the best use of resources. There is an intuitive connection between creativity and cognition. Increased sophistication is linked to thinking creatively and flexibly. Spendlove (2015) identifies strong societal benefits of being creative within technology education. We can illustrate this through the New Zealand (NZ) context. Important documents that assist teachers' understanding of how technology knowledge and understanding develop in flexibility and sophistication as students' progress include the achievement objects in *The New Zealand Curriculum* (NZC) (Ministry of Education, 2007) and the *Indicators of Progression* (Ministry of Education, 2009). Table 5.2 illustrates increased flexibility and sophistication of thinking across two of the achievement objectives: brief development and characteristics of technology, guided by the indicators. The third column in the table explicitly identifies ideas that are developed between curriculum levels 1 and 4, representing learning expected at Year 1 (5- to 6-year-olds) and Year 4 (11 to 13-year-olds), respectively (Fox-Turnbull et al., 2021).

Reflection is a critical component of technology practice. It describes the strategic and self-managing aspect of learning. It includes distilling information for potential or future use, the planning and anticipation of issues, and metacognitive thinking. Evaluation of prior learning is a part of distilling information to identify relevant learning for a new context. Self-generated questioning and self- monitoring of progress by being cognizant of what, how, and why learning is taking place are critical. To

Table 5.2 **Sophistication and Flexibility of Thinking Across Two NZC Achievement Objectives**

Achievement Objective	*Indicators of Progression*	*Increased Sophistication and Flexibility*
Brief Development		
Level 1: The students will describe the outcome they are developing and identify the attributes it should have, taking account of the need or opportunity and the resources available.	*Students can:* • Communicate the outcome to be produced. • Identify attributes for an outcome.	The students develop flexibility and sophistication by progressing ***from*** the ability to: • Articulate what they are developing ***to*** identifying a need or opportunity within a given context. • Identify some attributes for their intended outcome ***to*** writing of a conceptual statement that describes and justifies their outcome. • Identify list of attributes ***to*** establish and justify key attributes developed from stakeholder's needs and feedback.
Level 4: Justify the nature of an intended outcome in relation to the need or opportunity. Describe the key attributes identified in stakeholder feedback, which will inform the development of an outcome and its evaluation.	• Identify a need or opportunity from the given context and issue. • Establish a conceptual statement that communicates the nature of the outcome and why such an outcome should be developed. • Establish the key attributes for an outcome informed by stakeholder considerations. • Communicate key attributes that allow an outcome to be evaluated as fit for purpose.	
Characteristics of Technology		
Level 1: The students will understand that technology is purposeful intervention through design.	*Students can:* • Identify that technology helps to create the made world. • Identify that technology involves people designing and making technological outcomes for an identified purpose. • Identify that technological practice involves knowing what you are making and why, planning what to do and what resources are needed, and making and evaluating an outcome.	The students develop flexibility and sophistication by progressing ***from*** the ability to: • Identify that technology creates the "made world" ***to*** understanding that technology changes people's abilities, perceptions, and experiences of the world. • Understand that technology is around us ***to*** understanding technology has short- and long-term impacts on the world.

Table 5.2 (Continued)

Achievement Objective	*Indicators of Progression*	*Increased Sophistication and Flexibility*
Level 4: Understand how technological development expands human possibilities and how technology draws on knowledge from a wide range of disciplines.	• Identify examples where technology has changed people's sensory perception and/or physical abilities and discuss the potential short and long term impacts of these. • Identify examples of creative and critical thinking in technological practice. • Identify and categorize knowledge and skills from technology and other disciplines that have informed decisions in technological development and manufacture.	• Understand that people make technology for a reason or purpose ***to*** understanding people think critically and creatively when developing technology to meet a need or opportunity. • Understand the process of making technology involves knowing what is being made, the resources needed, and why ***to*** understanding technology practice involves recognizing and deploying skills and knowledge from technology and other disciplines. • Understand technology practice involves design and outcome evaluation ***to*** understanding that evaluation of technology design and outcomes includes technological development and manufacture.

Source: Adapted from Fox-Turnbull et al. (2021).

successfully design and develop technological outcomes, reflection must be active, continuous, and informative.

Socialization identifies with the inherently social nature of being human. Technology is a human activity with significant physical, social, and environmental impacts. Whether engaging in the use of or the developing of technology, students interact socially. When collaborating with others to develop single or parallel technologies, they experience interdependence, thus balancing self-reliance and socialization. Even when interacting with technology in a solitary manner, children are still engaging with people. Their evaluation of the technology and decisions about whether to come back for further engagement will impact other

Table 5.3 **Capabilities Within Desirable Technology Behaviors**

Behaviors: Demonstration of:	*Resilience*	*Transference*	*Flexibility and Sophistication*	*Reflection*	*Socialization*
Capabilities	Perseverance Managing Distractions Absorption	Making Links Imaging Noticing Questioning	Planning Distilling Reasoning Imagining Capitalizing Evaluating	Questioning Distilling Revising Meta Learning Evaluating	Empathy and Listening Collaboration Interdependence Imitating

people in the long term, if not sooner. For example, teachers will not purchase a technological device, toy, or piece of equipment that their students choose not to engage with. Technology practice also requires students to engage with clients and stakeholders.

The desirable technology behaviors outlined in the preceding paragraphs each incorporates a number of capabilities (see Table 5.3). These DTBs assist teachers in their recognition of the behaviors and teaching of technology through enhancement of the DTB.

The TOCF uses the aforementioned behaviors and capabilities coupled with the components of technology identified through analysis of three national technology curricula (England, Sweden, and New Zealand) to create sets of questions enabling the facilitation of teachers' exploratory dialogue with students to assist learning in technology. It is aimed at both improving learning for students and developing teachers' understanding of technology content and pedagogical content knowledge. The framework was originally produced to work with students 4–6 years of age. This version has been published in the *International Journal of Technology Education* (Fox-Turnbull, 2019).

Parts of the TOCF version for students 11–13 years of age are included in Table 5.4. When using the framework to assist conversations with students, teachers should concentrate on one technology component or objective. Table 5.4 focuses on aspects of the nature of technology. By drawing on questions from this framework, teachers are able to facilitate conversation and thinking about the deeper features of technology. Note that where "X" is used, a specific technological product or system should be substituted.

Table 5.4 **TOCF Nature of Technology**

	Desirable Behaviors to Support Technology Learning				
Strand and Achievement Objective	*Resilience*	*Transference*	*Reflection*	*Flexibility and Sophistication*	*Socialization*
	Look for: Evidence of understanding the developing technology may require repeated failure and modification. Perseverance with and through issues. Total absorption while others are working around them.	Look for: Students drawing on knowledge from other learning areas and technology learning to enhance their understanding of technology and to inform their technology practice.	Look for: Critical analysis of technologies from the past, present, and future. Questioning and critique of existing technologies. Questioning and critique of their own design decisions.	Look for: Advancement of key ideas and the ability to take thinking in different directions when considering past, present, and future technologies.	Look for: Understanding that technology is for people. Technology impacts and influences people. People influence technological design and development. Technology practice is a collaborative process. Technologists rely on others even when working on an individual project.
What is Technology	How has repeated failure from the designer improved the functionality of this technology?	Tell me which knowledge and skills from other learning areas (e.g., mathematics, social sciences) assist the technologist as they design and make technology?	There are two ways of making a critical technology. One requires an extra month to manufacture it and the other requires extra material to manufacture. Either way the manufacturing cost is the same. Which way would you choose and why?	How has this example of a technology that has changed human physical limitations – either positively or negatively?	Some technologies work but were not accepted by people? (Google Glasses, Segway are good examples) Why do you think people did not accept some technology?

	Identify three potential negative impacts of technology. What causes these impacts?	Tell me which knowledge and skills from other areas of technology (e.g., digital, food technologies) assist technologists as they design and make technology?	If everyone could have X technology how would your life change?	Give an example of features in technology that you think are creative and well thought out. Why do you think so?	How does the role of society affect the way in which technology is used and produced?
	What could be done to prevent this impact or make the impact less severe?		How would your life change without technology?		
What Characterizes Technology Outcomes?	Take any obsolete technology from the past (example typewriter, pagers). Why are they obsolete today? What has replaced this technology? Why?	In this product design, what knowledge has been used from other subjects or areas like science or mathematics?	What about this design that confuses you? What kind of knowledge do you think you might lack in order to understand this thoroughly?	What is the key or primary function of this *technology*? How do you know this?	How do you think people in a colder, hotter, richer, poorer, more religious country would rate this product? Why? Do you think they would find it meets their needs in the same way?

(Continued)

Table 5.4 **(Continued)**

	Desirable Behaviors to Support Technology Learning				
Strand and Achievement Objective	*Resilience*	*Transference*	*Reflection*	*Flexibility and Sophistication*	*Socialization*
	If you were a technologist, what steps would you take to make sure that your designed technology does not become obsolete?	In this product, X (name a specific technology), how has the technologist used understanding of function and aesthetics to make their design better?	If it was your job to design this technology X (name a specific technology), what information do you think you would need to get a good outcome for your stakeholder?	Look at X. Identify a technology that has alternative functions to that of its original design. What influenced/ instigated this alternative use?	What kind of attributes do you think your parents/ grandparents/ Captain Cook *(or other famous person from history)* wanted for travel/communication/ food? How are your criteria for that different?
				Give an example of a technology from the past that we no longer use. Why do you think this technology was developed in that time and why isn't it around now?	Think of your life without X (name a specific technology), how would your life change?

FUNDS OF KNOWLEDGE

Technology education gives students unique opportunities to draw on their cultural knowledge to enhance their own and possibly others' learning. It facilitates useful interaction between knowledge found inside and outside the classroom and provides opportunity for rich conversations between students and teachers and between students. For students who have English as a second language, oral dialogue about their cultural funds of knowledge has the potential to assist making connections with their classmates. For teachers it provides opportunities for insight into the worlds of their students. González, Moll, and Amanti (2005) found that the more teachers know about the home and cultural activities and experiences of their students, the better informed they are to maximize learning opportunities, thus making the most of knowledge and skills already accessible to some students. Students deploy funds of knowledge in technology education from two sources: participatory enculturation and passive observation (Fox-Turnbull, 2012).

Sources of Funds of Knowledge

Awareness of these two sources can again assist teachers' facilitation of conversations with their students, enabling students to value and transfer their cultural knowledge to their technology practice, gaining recognition and helping their peers as well as enhancing their technology practice.

Participatory Enculturation

Gaining knowledge through participatory enculturation provides students with opportunities to learn and share information their peers may be unfamiliar with and to involve practices unique to their family and culture. Skills and knowledge learned from active engagement in activity resulting in transferable knowledge are funds of knowledge through participatory enculturation. This engagement includes active participation, where the student is involved in the activity, or peripheral participation where they are on the periphery of the activity but able to engage through questions, conversation, and "helping out." This might be a part of gaining knowledge and skills from expert to novice, such as mother to son or grandparent to grandchild. Knowledge gained from these experiences can provide students status within their peer group. This is more likely to occur in an inclusive class climate discussed earlier in the chapter. There are a number of avenues from which students gain funds

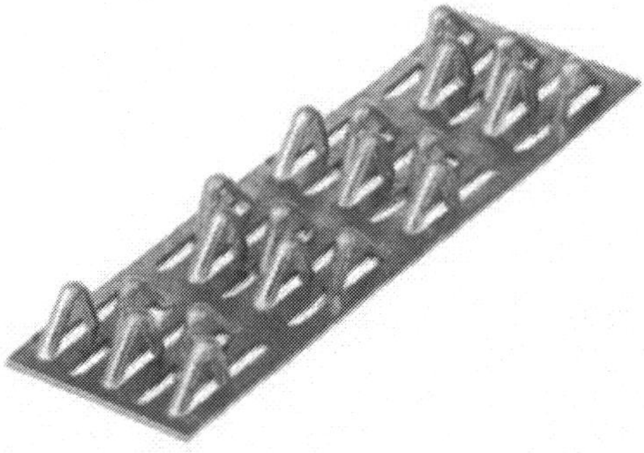

Figure 5.1 A Tylok Plate for Wood

of knowledge through participatory enculturation: family cultural, social, and cooperative practices; family activity; after school activities; parents' occupation; and interests and artifacts used at home. This was illustrated when Maddison (10) assisted her peers in designing and building their play prop, a representation of a large 1930's-style radio. The frame was to be built from trellis wood. She had recently helped her dad build a tree house and knew that Tylok Plates (see Figure 5.1) assisted the joining of flat wood. She assisted her group by sharing this information and requesting the purchase of some Tylok Plates from her teacher, thus leading to a successful outcome that otherwise would have been difficult to achieve for this group of students.

Edgar also illustrated this use of Funds of Knowledge (FOK) when he helped Debbie to create a papier-mâché fish, again as a prop for their school production. Before the layers of paper and glue were added, the children stuffed the stomach of their fish with paper to give it a three-dimensional effect. As he was pushing paper into the stomach, Edgar said to Debbie that it reminded him of gutting a fish, only backwards. Edgar and his grandfather often went fishing. He recognized that fish normally did have "stuff" in their stomach and therefore their task was authentic.

Passive Observation

Learning technology through Passive Observation FOK occurs when students are non-participatory passive observers, such as by watching movies, television, or reading books. This knowledge is then applied in their technology practice. Passive Observation includes the location of technology in historical and cultural contexts. The next story illustrates using FOK through passive means to make sense of a historical location.

A class of 10-year-old students were required to design and make historically situated props for their school production. They had learned that props assisted in the historical location of a play or setting. In an activity aimed at understanding the role of props in a play, the students were given a range of photographs of play props. Minnie recognized a cart and knew they were from the past. She had seen them in a video *Little House on the Prairie* – set in pioneer times in the Midwest of the United States of America. Minnie used prior observation to assist her personal construct of an object from a different era. In addition, a class of six-year-olds listened the props manager from the local Court Theatre explain the purpose and function of props. He illustrated his talk with a range of props his company used in the past. He discussed how each was used in situ. Issy was reminded of a show she has seen in the previous school holidays. As an audience member, she observed one particular prop used in a variety of ways. She was able to use knowledge gained from attending the theatre to assist her understanding of the definition of a technological outcome. Issy's input to the conversation indicated that she understood that props might have multiple purposes.

CONCLUSION

Teachers need to engage in quality intercognitive conversation with their students to help them make sense both cognitively and experientially of the world in which they live, learn, and work. Technology education involves a rich combination of academic and practical activity and requires students to take risks and work collaboratively. Teachers need to know and understand their students and their communities and cultural practices to maximize learning opportunities in the classroom. Several considerations and strategies to assist this have been presented in this chapter. Teachers must have a rich understanding of technology education. Understanding the nature of and facilitating intercognitive conversations will assist teachers in this endeavor. This chapter includes a number of strategies to facilitate teacher professional development and enhance the quality of classroom interaction. TOCF assists teachers with student questioning. It may also provide teachers with scaffolding needed to enhance their understanding of technology. Awareness of and understanding of the role and values of students' FOK, assist teachers in making connections with students and ensure the taking of specific steps to provide an inclusive, safe classroom where students are comfortable to take risks and fail. Using strategies such as talking partners and "no hands up" within this safe environment gives students the freedom to explore their thinking orally and learn in a nonjudgmental manner, thus enabling them to articulate and shift thinking if necessary, thus sparking cognitive growth.

REFERENCES

Black, P. (2008). Formative assessment in the learning and teaching of design and technology. *Design and Technology Education: An International Journal, 13*(3), 19–26.

Bloom, B. (Ed.). (1956). *Taxonomy of educational objectives: The classification of educational goals* (1st ed., Vol. 1). New York: Longmans, Green and Co Inc.

Clarke, S. (2005). *Formative assessment in action: Weaving the elements together*. Oxon: Hodder Murray.

Clarke, S. (2014). *Outstanding formative assessment: Culture and practice*. London: Hodder Education.

Claxton, G., Chambers, M., Powell, G., & Lucas, B. (2013). *The learning powered school: Pioneering 21st century education*. Bristol: TLO Limited.

Coffer, C. (2017). Exploratory and dialogic talk and creative learning. In C. Benson & S. Lawson (Eds.), *Teaching design and technology creatively*. Oxon: Routledge.

Csikszentmihalyi, M. (1990). *Flow: The psychology of optimal experience*. New York: Harper-Perennial.

de Vries, M. (2017). Philosophy of technology: Themes and topics. In M. de Vries (Ed.), *Handbook of technology education* (pp. 7–16). Cham, Switzerland: Springer.

Fox-Turnbull, W. (2012, June 26–30). *Funds of knowledge in technology education*. Paper presented at the PATT 26, Stockholm, Sweden.

Fox-Turnbull, W. (2013). *The nature of conversation of primary students in technology education: Implications for teaching and learning* [PhD], University of Waikato.

Fox-Turnbull, W. (2016). The nature of primary students' conversation in technology education. *International Journal of Technology and Design Education, 26*(1), 21–41.

Fox-Turnbull, W. (2017). Let's get kids talking in technology: Implications for teachers. In P. J. Williams & D. Barlex (Eds.), *Comtemporary research in technology*. Singapore: Springer.

Fox-Turnbull, W. (2019). Assisting teachers' understanding of student learning in technology. *International Journal of Technology and Design Education, 29*(29), 1133–1152. https://doi.org/doi.org.10.007/s10798-018-9484-x

Fox-Turnbull, W., Reinsfield, E., & Forret, M. (2021). *Technology education in New Zealand: A guide for teachers*. New York: Routledge.

González, N., Moll, L. C., & Amanti, C. (Eds.). (2005). *Funds of knowledge* (1st ed., Vol. 2009 Reprint). New York: Routledge.

Jones, A. (2009). Towards an articulation of students making progress in learning technological concepts and processes. In A. Jones & M. de Vries (Eds.), *International handbook of research and development in technology education*. Rotterdam: Sense Publishers.

Mercer, N. (1995). *The guided construction of knowledge-talk amongst teachers and learners*. Avon, UK: Multilingual Matters Ltd.

Mercer, N. (2006). *Words & minds: How we use language to think together*. Abingdon, Oxon: Routledge.

Mercer, N., & Hodgkinson, S. (Eds.). (2008). *Exploring talk in school.* London: Sage Publications Ltd.

Ministry of Education. (1995). *Technology in the New Zealand curriculum.* Wellington: Learning Media.

Ministry of Education. (2007). *The New Zealand curriculum.* Wellington: Learning Media.

Ministry of Education. (2009). *Indicators of achievement.* IPENZ. Retrieved March 9 from www.techlink.org.nz/curriculum-support/

Robertson, S.-A., & Graven, M. (2019). Exploratory mathematics talk in a second language: A sociolinguistic perspective. *Educational Studies in Mathematics, 101,* 215–232. https://doi.org/https://doi.org/10.1007/s10649-018-9840-5

Schut, A., Klapwijk, R. M., Gielen, M., & de Vries, M. (2019). Children's responses to divergent and convergent design feedback. *Design and Technology Education: An International Journal, 24*(2), 67–89. https://ojs.lboro.ac.uk/DATE/article/view/2611

Seemann, K., & Talbot, R. (1995). Technacy: Towards a holistic understanding of technology teaching and learning among Aboriginal Australians. *Prospects, 25*(4), 14.

Shields, C., & Edwards, M. (2005). *Dialogue is not just talk: A new ground for educational leadership.* New York: Peter Lang Publishing Inc.

Spendlove, D. (2015). Developing deeper understanding of design. In P. J. Williams (Ed.), *The future of technology education: contemporary issues in technology education.* Singapore: Springer.

Vygotsky, L. S. (1978). *Mind in society: The development of higher psychological processes.* M. Cole, V. John-Steiner, & E. Souberman (Eds.). Cambridge, MA: Harvard University Press.

Webb, P., Whitlow, J. W., Jr., & Venter, D. (2016). From exploratory talk to abstract reasoning: A case for far transfer? *Educational Psychology Review, 29*(3), 565–581.

CHAPTER 6

Using Sound to Enhance Interactions in an Online Learning Environment

Yun Li and Sherman Finch

INTRODUCTION

Moreno and Mayer (2007) published an article entitled "Interactive Multimodal Learning Environments," in which they defined such an environment as "one in which what happens depends on the actions of the learner" (p. 310). This definition highlights the importance of interactivity in learning and explains learning in the view of knowledge construction. Unlike noninteractive learning environments where all the instructional messages are presented regardless of what learners do during learning, learners are actively engaged in the knowledge construction process by interacting with the instructional materials in interactive learning environments (Moreno & Mayer, 2007). Typical examples of highly interactive instructional programs are educational video games and instructional simulations. While such highly interactive environments open new opportunities to improve learning, sophisticated interactivity can increase extraneous cognitive processing and disrupt generative cognitive processing (Moreno & Mayer, 2007).

Another distinctive attribute of the interactive multimodal learning environment is conveying information using mixed-modality presentations. The integrated use of visual and auditory information is believed to avoid cognitive overload by processing information in separate visual and auditory channels (Bétrancourt, 2005; Mayer, 2005; Mayer, Heiser, & Lonn, 2001; Mayer & Moreno, 2003). In the past several decades, instructional designers have sought to apply this modality principle in various learning environments, and the predominant use of auditory

DOI: 10.4324/9781003089704-9

information is in the form of speech audio (i.e., spoken words). However, auditory representations are not limited to speech but include unaltered or slightly altered nonspeech sound such as environmental sound, computer-generated tones, and instrumental music (Csapó & Wersényi, 2013; Wersényi, 2010).

Nonspeech sound serves as one of the critical information sources to guide our actions when we interact with the complex external environment and build our understanding of the surroundings. For example, when we drive, our visual system focuses on obtaining information from the field in front of the vehicle, and our hearing system receives signals outside of our peripheral vision. When we hear car horns, we can detect the position of the car even if the car is out of sight. When we interact with the external world, nonspeech sound gives complementary information from all around us, and with that information we determine and perform the required actions. We depend on both visual and auditory information sources to guide our behavior and to modify our actions to better accomplish tasks in everyday life.

Despite the fact that nonspeech sound is an essential type of auditory information source, it seems to be overlooked when designing a multimodal learning environment (Bajaj et al., 2015; Bishop, Amankwatia, & Cates, 2008; Bishop & Sonnenschein, 2012). A possible reason why nonspeech sound is ignored is that the understanding of the modality principle is extensively based on the research findings in noninteractive and limited interactive multimodal learning environments (Mayer 2002; Mayer & Moreno 2003; Sweller, 1999). A noninteractive and limited interactive multimodal learning environment presents instructional content, including verbal and visual presentations, and learners can listen or read information without interacting with the instructional programs (Moreno & Mayer, 2007). However, as new learning technologies are getting increasingly interactive, it is time to notice the importance of nonspeech sound and discover how sound could be integrated into interactive learning environments to facilitate the learning process.

In this chapter we first review existing research to build a deeper understanding of the circumstances in which nonspeech sound is being used in the field of education. We then discuss how nonspeech sound can be integrated into the interaction process from the perspective of human-computer interaction. We conclude the chapter with a presentation of our rapid prototyping example. We hope our attempt will draw some degree of attention to sonic interaction that has the potential to better engage learners in the learning process behaviorally and cognitively.

REVIEW OF LITERATURE ON THE USE OF NONSPEECH SOUND IN EDUCATION

The number of studies that focus on the use of nonspeech sound for learning is fairly limited. In the available literature, nonspeech sound is used to trigger attention, regulate emotions, and convey information.

Auditory Stimuli to Trigger Attention

In the existing literature, nonspeech sound is mainly used as auditory stimuli to direct learners' attention to the important information presented in multimedia learning materials (Bajaj, 2015; Boltz, Schulkind, & Kantra, 1991; Calvert & Scott, 1987, 1989; Hativa, 1987; Hupp & Allen, 2005; Mann, 1979). Nonspeech sound can be environmental sound, computer-generated tones, and instrumental music. When using environmental sound to trigger learners' attention, nonspeech sound is closely associated with the key concepts (Bajaj, 2015; Mann, 1979). For example, the sound of water flowing through a tap is presented together with a narration that described how to add water to a chemical compound in an instructional video (Bajaj, 2015), and clinking dishes and muffled conversations along with visual images are used to cue student attention to certain areas in presented images of a restaurant in an e-learning course (Bishop, 2000). When choosing computer-generated tones to attract learners' attention, these random brief tones are not directly related to the event with which they are associated. In this case, nonspeech sound is normally implemented in proximity to key content areas to be effective (Bajaj, 2015; Calvert & Scott, 1987, 1989; Hativa, 1987; Hupp & Allen, 2005). For example, the sound of a slide whistle is used in videos to direct student's attention to critical scenes (Calvert & Scott, 1987, 1989). A burp sound is associated with the key concept of acidity in a video instruction of Chemistry (Bajaj, 2015). When using instrumental music to cue critical scenes, auditory story clips, or video stories, information retrieval is significantly enhanced if the mood of instrumental music is congruent with the associated scene (Boltz et al., 1991).

When serving as auditory stimuli, nonspeech sound is believed to benefit learning in the following three ways. First, nonspeech auditory stimuli have a positive effect on memory retrieval. Auditory stimuli are typically embedded around key concepts in instructional videos, auditory story clips, and computer-based lessons. During recall, auditory stimuli could serve as a memory anchor to retrieve content and evoke associated information (Bajaj, 2015; Calvert & Scott, 1987, 1989; Hativa, 1987;

Mann, 1979). Second, the use of nonspeech auditory stimuli affects the way learning information is processed and retained. A systematic application of auditory stimuli directs learners' attention to specific information, emphasizes key concepts, and organizes learning information (Bishop, 2000; Hativa, 1987; Calvert & Scott, 1987). If nonspeech sound is used to build information structures, learners are able to transfer knowledge to new learning situations more effectively (Bishop, 2000). Third, nonspeech sound, and environmental sounds, in particular, add a sense of immersion to learning experiences. For narrative audio clips and instructional videos, associating environmental sound with critical content helps to visualize the message and keep learners motivated during the learning process (Bishop, 2000; Psotka, 1995).

The proper use of different types of sound as stimuli is essential for the effective use of nonspeech sound. It is well known that environmental sound is associated with the environment. Therefore, when presented together with other information representations such as text, graphics, and narrations, the environmental sound is effective in cueing the related instructional message. On the other hand, a careful design is required for computer-generated tones to be effective to cue the critical information in the instruction. Since musical notes are not naturally relevant to the presented information, selected computer-generated notes can be effective enforcers of critical information when regularly patterned in the instruction (Bajaj, 2015; Hativa, 1987; Hupp & Allen, 2005). If learners fail to understand the connection between the musical notes and the content, these musical notes could become irrelevant and even distracting (Boltz et al., 1991).

Background Music to Regulate Emotions

Another way of using nonspeech sound is to embed it as a background that regulates emotions in order to enhance the quality of the learning experience (Chou, 2010; Fumham & Bradley, 1997; Grice & Hughes, 2009; Perham & Currie, 2014; Perham & Vizard, 2011). Instrumental music is mainly used to regulate emotions by providing a relaxed atmosphere that allows learners to study in a state of the optimum emotional climate (Bishop & Sonnenschein, 2012; Schäfer, Sedlmeier, Städtler, & Huron, 2013). In the typical computer-based learning modules, background music is best used to create an atmosphere during the introduction, major content transitions, or at the end of a learning experience. By embedding background music in the transitional areas, it creates a "cinematic style" (Bishop & Sonnenschein, 2012) that motivates learners to explore the lessons actively (Digelidis, Karageorghis, Papapavlou, &

Papaioannou, 2014; White, 2007). For example, in one of the background sound designs in Bishop's computer-based lesson, while the lesson's title "Thinking Zone" was scrolling across the screen, a piece of the dramatic orchestral theme music was playing as background.

However, background music could have a distracting effect that overloads the learners' information processing capacities and negatively affects the performance of other cognitive tasks, particularly when music is irrelevant to the content of the instructional message (Perham & Currie, 2014; Perham & Vizard, 2011). Therefore, all styles of background music should be used with caution when learners are required to perform cognitive-related tasks.

Convey Information

Nonspeech sound can be used to convey information (Ferati, Pfaff, Mannheimer, & Bolchini, 2012; Lunney & Morrison, 1990; Pfeiffer, 2008; Vickers & Alty, 2002). Sound is a longitudinal wave that can be described through characteristics such as timbre, amplitude, and frequency resolution (Hermann, Hunt, & Neuhoff, 2011). Given that sound has such attributes, a variety of information can be conveyed by sound as an alternative or complement to visual representations. (Hermann et al., 2011; Lunney & Morrison, 1990). Computer-generated tones usually are created to convey information. For example, in Pfeiffer's study (2008), he examined whether or not the use of computer-generated sound helped participants better understand designated concepts and improved students' online learning experience. He used computer-generated sound to complement visual graphics, such as a buzzy sound with a curved line represented sheep, a piercing sound with a straight line referred to rodents, and an "ooo" sound with a dotted line pointed to coyotes.

Although results indicated no significant difference in test scores of concept understanding between the visual graphics group and the sonified graphics group, the use of musical notes did have a positive effect on the online learning experience. In Vickers' study (Vickers & Alty, 2002), computer-generated tones were designed to represent different computer programming concepts. For instance, the sound of a fog-horn represented the concept of IF and IF . . . ELSE, and the sound of a plagal cadence represented WHILE. Nonspeech sound is found to be effective for visually impaired learners in recognizing and understanding information delivered through sound. Compared to visually impaired students, benefits are less clear for learners with normal vision. This difference might be due to the ways in which visually impaired learners and normal vision learners perceive sound (Pfeiffer, 2008). In addition, when using nonspeech sound to convey information, it certainly requires training to help learners recognize patterns in the information presented by sound (Pfeiffer, 2008; Vickers & Alty, 2002).

Summary

Although studies focused on nonspeech sound are limited, these studies still help to build an understanding of how nonspeech sound is being used in education. Different types of sound are integrated into various learning materials such as instructional videos, auditory clips, and computer-based learning modules. Moreover, nonspeech sound is mainly implemented as the auditory stimuli to direct learners' attention to important content in the learning materials. When integrating nonspeech auditory stimuli, the general design process is to identify the important learning concepts, select a nonspeech sound that is associated with the concept, and determine if sound is being used as pre-cue or post-cue. Such design rationale stems from the film industry, where sound plays a critical role in directing the audience's attention to a specific scene in fast-paced movies (Bajaj, 2015). Similar to how sound helps to captivate the audience in a movie, nonspeech auditory stimuli help to engage learners in the learning process (Bishop & Sonnenschein, 2012; Hupp & Allen, 2005), thereby potentially improving learners' performance on information retrieval and content comprehension (Bajaj, 2015; Calvert & Scott, 1987, 1989; Hativa, 1987; Mann, 1979).

INTEGRATING NONSPEECH SOUND IN INTERACTION PROCESS

In addition to the aforementioned benefits, nonspeech sound has the potential to play an active role in the process of knowledge construction. In the existing literature, nonspeech sound conveys information in a relatively static way. Learners only listen to the auditory information to identify the specific concept associated with the sound, yet learners have limited interaction with the learning interface. In a highly interactive environment, learners can use nonspeech sound to guide their movement and modify their actions by detecting subtle changes in sound throughout the interaction process. A well-known example is the use of nonspeech sound in video games. Game players heavily rely on nonspeech sound to monitor the game environment and make appropriate decisions (Jørgensen, 2009). Such interaction between learners and learning interface has made it possible for the nonspeech sound to play an important role in the learning process. In this section, we attempt to explore the possibilities of integrating nonspeech sound into the interaction process to facilitate active learning.

The integration of nonspeech sound in the interaction process is guided from the perspective of human-computer interaction. When we take a granular view of one interaction process in a learning task (see Figure 6.1), it starts with a trigger, is followed by the learner's actions, and ends with the completion of the interaction.

In the process of each interaction, nonspeech sound can be implemented by itself or together with other input formats to function as a stimulus to trigger an action (Aleksy, Bronmark, & Mahate, 2016; Brewster, 1997; Buxton, 1989). And then, the learner responds to the stimulus by acting on the interactive learning environment (Learner Action). Nonspeech sound can guide the learner's movement and provide real-time auditory feedback that ensures the learner's movement is on track (real-time feedback). Real-time auditory feedback can be used alone or co-present with other input formats to modify and guide the learner's action until the correct response is received from the programmed learning interface. At last, when the learner's action is considered to be a correct response, nonspeech audio can be used alone or co-present with other input formats to confirm the learner's correct action (Feedback).

The functions served by nonspeech audio in the interaction process can be summarized in the following three broad categories: (1) Alert: Notifying learners to pay immediate attention to something that occurred

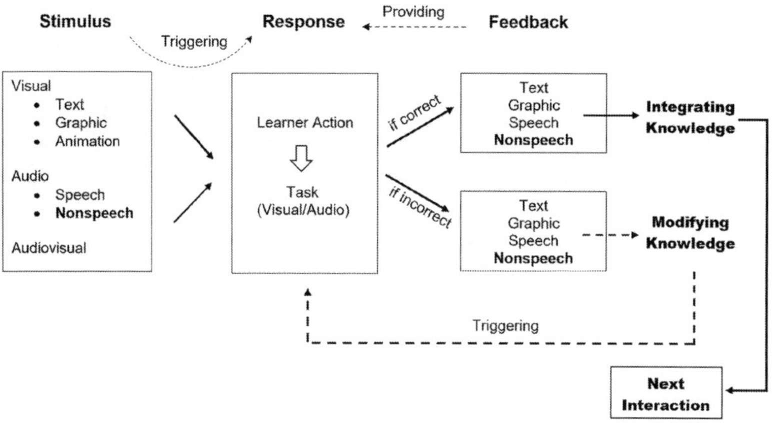

Figure 6.1 One Interaction Process Embedded With Nonspeech Audio

in the learning environment. The alert sound usually doesn't contain many details of the event or task but directs the learner's attention to the designated task (Buxton, 1989). For example, a beep simply indicates that a problem is detected and requires immediate attention. The basic beep sound does not indicate the nature or the cause of the problem. Examples of such sounds include a fire alarm that has a distinct sound when the battery is low and needs to be replaced, the sound from a cell phone when it receives an "Amber alert," and the tone that calls an airline attendant to assist a passenger on a plane; (2) Confirm: Notifying learners that their actions have been completed. Getting an action confirmed is a type of expectation that comes naturally from the learner's real-life experience. Learners expect to receive confirmations from the learning interface on actions while they perform learning activities (Brown, Newsome, & Glinert, 1989). In addition to confirming that their action has been executed, learners expect to know the result of their actions, whether they respond to the input correctly or not. The nonspeech sound sends the learners positive or negative feedback that enables them to recognize the result of their actions (Kramer et al., 1999). For example, if you want to download an app in the Apple Store, a "ding" sound combined with a visual checkmark indicates the successful installation of the app after the user selects the "Get" button, and when filling up your car with gas, you get a "ding" sound when the tank is full; (3) Guide: Sending real-time auditory feedback that provides a helpful constraint on actions or a directive to guide learners' ongoing movement. Learners can detect subtle changes in real-time auditory feedback to understand whether their movements are on the right learning path. If they are out of the designed task track, sound can guide them back on the right learning path. For example, continuous auditory signals sent by the car radar help you to avoid nearby objects that might be outside of your view and guide you to pull the car into a safe spot.

Rapid Prototyping Design Demo

To make the idea of using nonspeech sound tangible, a rapid prototype of a writing activity was implemented to explore how nonspeech sound could be integrated into the interaction process to facilitate learning. The writing activity selected for this demo design was to compose Chinese characters on a web-based canvas using a mouse, which required learners to deploy a specific strategy such as planning, formulation, and revision to write the character in the correct order (Gánem-Gutiérrez & Gilmore, 2018; Hacker, Keener, & Kircher, 2017). Nonspeech sound could be used to guide learners' movement and to facilitate their construction on knowledge of Chinese stroke order throughout their writing process. Eight entry-level Chinese characters with different writing rules were designed on a custom-designed website and nonspeech sound was programmed on the website to facilitate the learners' writing process. We used the character 山 (Mountain) in this section as an example to describe how we embedded nonspeech sound into learner-interface interaction. The character 山 (Mountain) has three strokes (see Figure 6.2). First, the center vertical stroke is drawn from the top downward (1,2). Then, the left-wing is drawn from the top downward before turning to continue from left to right (3,4). Finally, the right-wing is drawn from the top downwards (5,6).

Audio file size and latency were two significant challenges in the design phase. Initially, pre-recorded nonspeech audio files were considered in the design to facilitate learner-interface interaction. However, the audio files required for this writing task were too large and made the website heavy and slow to load. Loading large audio files in a web browser can prevent the page from loading at all, and the amount of time spent waiting for the audio files to load would hurt learners' experience. What's worse is that a serious flaw with pre-recorded audio files is the high latency issue. Synchronizing sound to learner actions plays a crucial role in connecting learners' perceptions of learner-interface interaction.

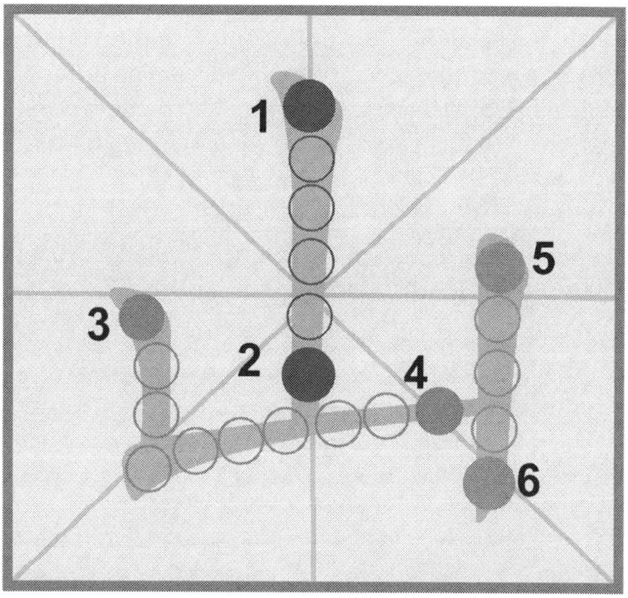

Figure 6.2 Stroke Order of 山 (Mountain)

With good synchronization, learners can gauge their performance, process sound-related cues in a timely manner, and complete the writing task based on real-time auditory feedback. When sound and actions are not synced, it can disturb a learner's actions, convey misleading information, and prevent a learner from being able to perform the writing task properly.

To address these issues, we used the Web Audio Application Programming Interface (Web Audio API) to generate all four types of nonspeech sound in our design. Web Audio API allowed processing, mixing, and filtering audio within a web application through the internet. For example, a programmed nonspeech sound used in our design to indicate the incorrect direction of the writing movement was coded (see Figure 6.3) as *playSound ('square', 240.0, 0.09, false)* along with *playSound ('sawtooth', 60.13, 0, 0.12, false)*.

When nonspeech sound was created with JavaScript, it eliminated the problems such as large file sizes and long wait time for files to load. In addition, Web Audio API had a precise timing model that allowed a fast auditory response to learners' actions during the interaction process, which alleviated the latency problem. More examples of Web Audio API-generated sound can be reviewed on Finch's website (2019).

As part of the interactions, nonspeech sound was designed to better teach learners to construct their understanding of Chinese stroke order in the writing process. During the interaction analysis phase, the following

```
{
    //playSound('square',240,0,0.09,false);
    //playSound('sawtooth',60.13,0,0.12);
    var prevLength = checkapp.length;
    //clearLine(samples);
    checkapp.splice(0, checkapp.length);
    for(var i = 0; i < prevLength - 2; ++i)
        checkapp.push(cordname[i]);

    right = false;
    // this indicates when you have made the wrong line
    playSound('square',240,0,0.09,false);
    playSound('sawtooth',60.13, 0, 0.12,false);
    //alert('Incorrect Line. Try Again.');
    visque("Incorrect! Try Again.");
    clearLine(samples);

}
```

Figure 6.3 An Example of Web Audio API

questions guided the decision-making process about where nonspeech sound should be implemented:

1. What is the goal of an interaction?
2. What are the possible actions or reactions that might be expected from the learners when they are presented with a specific type of information?
3. What are the possible roles that nonspeech sound can play in a particular interaction, stimulus, or feedback?
4. Is nonspeech sound the best format to serve the stimulus or feedback role?

Four types of nonspeech audio were embedded to guide learners' writing through dynamic interactions with the digital canvas (see Figure 6.4). Nonspeech sound S1 confirmed the learner's movement so that she/he knows to continue to write the next stroke. For example, the learner would hear a short and low-pitched "ding" sound if the mouse dropped on circle 1 (see Figure 6.2). Nonspeech sound S2 indicated the learner recognizes the negative results of the movement.

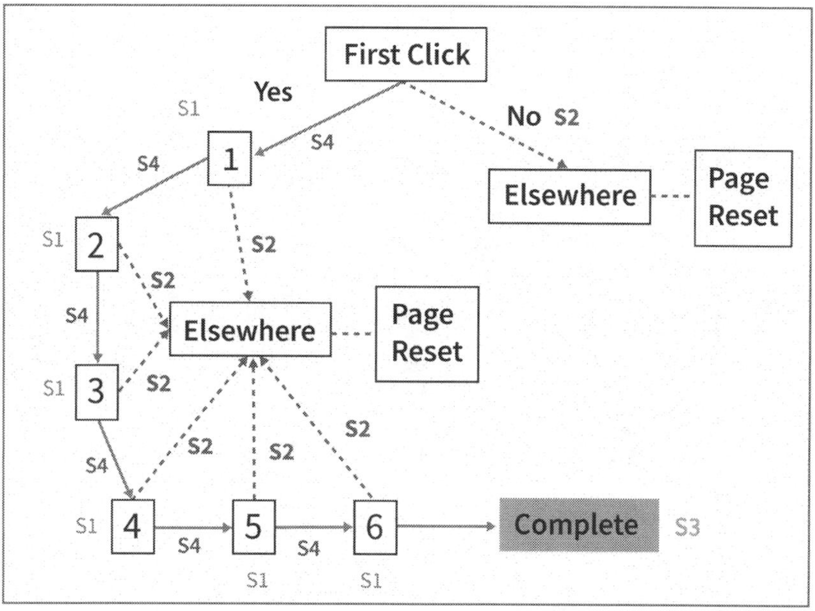

Figure 6.4 The Implementation of Nonspeech Audio in the Interaction Process

For instance, if the first step was to write the center vertical stroke, the learner would be notified by a short but heavy "dur" sound if the learner started with any other strokes. Nonspeech audio S3 implied that the learner has completed the character in the correct stroke order. The learner would hear a prolonged high-pitched "ding" sound when the character was complete and all strokes were written in the correct order. Nonspeech audio S4 was the continuous sound to guide the learner to stay on track when writing a specific stroke. For instance, if the center vertical stroke was drawn from top to bottom. The learner would hear continuously rising "ding . . . Ding . . . DIng . . . DINg . . . DING" (the circles marked in Figure 6.2) sounds while drawing the stroke from the top to the bottom. If drawing the strokes in the incorrect order, the learner would hear the "dur" sound to guide him/her back to the stroke.

Overall, our rapid prototyping demo design is relatively simple. Moreover, due to the time and resource constraints, the writing task designed in this chapter doesn't involve the use of nonspeech sound as the stimuli to trigger attention in the interaction process. However, this demo takes an initial step to explore the possibilities of adding nonspeech sound in the interaction process.

CONCLUSION

We have reviewed in this chapter the existing research to understand how nonspeech sound is currently being used for learning purposes and attempted to explore the possibilities of adding nonspeech sound in the interaction process to facilitate the writing activity.

As revealed in the available literature, only a few studies have investigated the effect of nonspeech audio on learning. Despite the general immaturity of nonspeech audio as a field of study in education, conclusions drawn from the existing studies provide guidelines and recommendations for designers when they consider incorporating nonspeech sound in learning materials. The major findings revealed in the available literature include careful planning and guidelines for the effective use of auditory cues, concerns about the appropriate use of background music, and the use of nonspeech audio to communicate information and evoke emotion. In the existing literature, nonspeech sound is embedded as the static media; limited interaction between learners and the learning interface is required. Although nonspeech sound and learners' actions seem to be associated when learners are directed to locate and click on critical content by the auditory stimuli, the connection between sound and learners' actions are loose, with little involvement in the knowledge construction process.

As an important information provider that can give critical information about learning environments (Brewster, 1997), nonspeech sound can have a direct connection to learners' actions as a part of learner-interface interaction to facilitate the knowledge construction process. In our rapid prototyping design demo, a systematic application of nonspeech sound in the interaction process enables learners to perform the writing task using touch, sight, and hearing senses that simulate how we construct knowledge to accomplish the tasks in real-life. Today's emerging technologies, such as virtual reality and extended reality, allow for the development of interactive learning environments through which learners can interact with their surroundings in similar ways as they would in real life. The implementation of nonspeech sound in emerging technologies such as virtual reality makes the learning experience more authentic and engaging, which would also facilitate knowledge construction and retention. Although sonic interaction design in this chapter is relatively simple, the concept of integrating nonspeech sound in the interaction can be applied to other subjects and instructional programs to develop a further understanding of the circumstances in which nonspeech sound is being used to facilitate learning in the highly interactive multimodal environments.

The goal of this chapter was to draw attention to the growing importance of nonspeech sound in the highly interactive multimodal learning environments. Therefore, the future of this work is to test the effectiveness of nonspeech sound on enhancing learners' interactive experience. In addition to measuring how the sonically enhanced interaction could affect learner experience, tests should measure a deep understanding of how the use of nonspeech audio could influence factors that contribute to effective learning, such as learners' attention, short-term memory, and long-term memory in the interactive multimodal learning environments.

REFERENCES

Aleksy, M., Bronmark, J., & Mahate, S. (2016, March). Microinteractions in mobile and wearable computing. In *Advanced information networking and applications (AINA), 2016 IEEE 30th international conference on* (pp. 495–500). Crans-Montana, Switzerland: IEEE.

Bajaj, J., Harlalka, A., Kumar, A., Punekar, R. M., Sorathia, K., Deshmukh, O., & Yadav, K. (2015). Audio cues: Can sound be worth a hundred words? In *Learning and collaboration technologies* (pp. 14–23). Cham: Springer.

Bishop, M. J. (2000). The systematic use of sound in multimedia instruction to enhance learning. *Dissertation Abstracts International*, *61*, 07.

Bishop, M. J., & Sonnenschein, D. (2012). Designing with sound to enhance learning: Four recommendations from the film industry. *Journal of Applied Instructional Design, 2*(1), 5–15.

Boltz, M., Schulkind, M., & Kantra, S. (1991). Effects of background music on the remembering of filmed events. *Memory & Cognition, 19*(6), 593–606.

Brewster, S. A. (1997). Using non-speech sound to overcome information overload. *Displays, 17*(3–4), 179–189.

Brown, M. L., Newsome, S. L., & Glinert, E. P. (1989, March). An experiment into the use of auditory cues to reduce visual workload. In *ACM SIGCHI bulletin* (Vol. 20, No. SI, pp. 339–346). New York, NY: ACM. https://doi.org/10.1145/67450.67515

Buxton, W. (1989). Introduction to this special issue on non-speech audio. *Human-Computer Interaction, 4*, 1–9.

Calvert, S. L., & Scott, M. C. (1987). Sound effects for children's comprehension of variably-paced television programs. *Journal of Applied Developmental Psychology, 8*, pp. 363–375.

Calvert, S. L., & Scott, M. C. (1989). Sound effects for children's temporal integration of fast-paced television content. *Journal of Broadcasting & Electronic Media, 33*(3), 233–246.

Chou, P. T. M. (2010). Attention drainage effect: How background music effects concentration in Taiwanese college students. *Journal of the Scholarship of Teaching and Learning, 10*(1), 36–46.

Csapó, Á., & Wersényi, G. (2013). Overview of auditory representations in human-machine interfaces. *ACM Computing Surveys (CSUR), 46*(2), 19. http://doi.org/10.1145/2543581.2543586

Digelidis, N., Karageorghis, C., Papapavlou, A., & Papaioannou, A. G. (2014). Effects of asynchronous music on students' lesson satisfaction and motivation at the situational level. *Journal of Teaching in Physical Education, 33*(3), 326–341.

Ferati, M., Pfaff, M. S., Mannheimer, S., & Bolchini, D. (2012). Audemes at work: Investigating features of non-speech sounds to maximize content recognition. *International Journal of Human-Computer Studies, 70*(12), 936–966. https://doi.org/10.1016/j.ijhcs.2012.09.003

Finch, S. (Host). (2019). *Wave + Frequency Chart/sine: Octave scale* [Interactive Non-speech Audio]. Retrieved from https://shermanfinch.com/wordpress/?page_id=2714

Fumham, A., & Bradley, A. (1997). Music while you work: The differential distraction of background music on the cognitive test performance of introverts and extraverts. *Applied Cognitive Psychology, 11*(5), 445–455.

Gánem-Gutiérrez, G. A., & Gilmore, A. (2018). Tracking the real-time evolution of a writing event: Second language writers at different proficiency levels. *Language Learning, 68*(2), 469–506. https://doi.org/10.1111/lang.12280

Grice, S., & Hughes, J. (2009). Can music and animation improve the flow and attainment in online learning? *Journal of Educational Multimedia and Hypermedia, 18*(4), 385.

Hacker, D. J., Keener, M. C., & Kircher, J. C. (2017). TRAKTEXT: Investigating writing processes using eye-tracking technology. *Methodological Innovations, 10*(2), 2059799116689574.

Hativa, N., & Reingold, A. (1987). Effects of audiovisual stimuli on learning through microcomputer-based class presentation. *Instructional Science, 16*(3), 287–306.

Hermann, T., Hunt, A., & Neuhoff, J. G. (2011). *The sonification handbook* (pp. 399–425). Berlin: Logos Verlag.

Hupp, S. D., & Allen, K. D. (2005). Using an audio cueing procedure to increase rate of parental attention during parent training. *Child & family behavior therapy, 27*(2), 43–49.

Jørgensen, K. (2009). *A comprehensive study of sound in computer games: How audio affects player action*. Lewiston: Edwin Mellen Press.

Kramer, G., Walker, B. N., Bonebright, T., Cook, P., Flowciers, J., Miner, N., & Evreinov, G. (1999). The sonification report: Status of the field and research agenda. *Report prepared for the national science foundation by members of the international community for auditory display*. Santa Fe, NM: International Community for Auditory Display (ICAD).

Lunney, D., & Morrison, R. C. (1990, August). Auditory presentation of experimental data. In *Extracting meaning from complex data: Processing, display, interaction* (Vol. 1259, pp. 140–147). Santa Clara, CA: International Society for Optics and Photonics.

Mann, R. E. (1979). *The effect of music and sound effects on the listening comprehension of fourth grade students* [Doctoral Dissertation], North Texas State University. *Dissertation Abstracts International, 1979, 40*, 1220A. University Microfilms No. 7919733.

Mayer, R. E. (2002). Multimedia learning. In *Psychology of Learning and Motivation* (Vol. 41, pp. 85–139). Cambridge, MA: Academic Press.

Mayer, R. E. (2005). Cognitive theory of multimedia learning. *The Cambridge Handbook of Multimedia Learning, 41*, 31–48.

Mayer, R. E., Heiser, J., & Lonn, S. (2001). Cognitive constraints on multimedia learning: When presenting more material results in less understanding. *Journal of Educational Psychology, 93*(1), 187. https://doi.org/10.1037//0022-0663.93.1.187

Mayer, R. E., & Moreno, R. (2003). Nine ways to reduce cognitive load in multimedia learning. *Educational Psychologist, 38*(1), 43–52. https://doi.org/10.1207/S15326985EP3801_6

Moreno, R., & Mayer, R. (2007). Interactive multimodal learning environments. *Educational Psychology Review, 19*(3), 309–326. https://doi.org/10.1007/s10648-007-9047-2

Perham, N., & Currie, H. (2014). Does listening to preferred music improve reading comprehension performance? *Applied Cognitive Psychology, 28*(2), 279–284.

Perham, N., & Vizard, J. (2011). Can preference for background music mediate the irrelevant sound effect? *Applied Cognitive Psychology, 25*(4), 625–631. https://doi.org/10.1002/acp.1731

Pfeiffer, D. G. (2008). Listen and learn: An investigation of sonification as an instructional variable to improve understanding of complex environments. *Computers in Human Behavior, 24*(2), 475–485.

Psotka, J. (1995). Immersive training systems: Virtual reality and education and training. *Instructional Science, 23*(5), 405–431.

Schäfer, T., Sedlmeier, P., Städtler, C., & Huron, D. (2013). The psychological functions of music listening. *Frontiers in Psychology, 4*, 511.

Sweller, J. (1999). *Instructional design in technical areas*. Melbourne, Australia: ACER Press.

Vickers, P., & Alty, J. L. (2002). Using music to communicate computing information. *Interacting with Computers, 14*(5), 435–456. https://doi.org/10.1016/S0953-5438(02)00003-6

Wersényi, G. (2010). Auditory representations of a graphical user interface for a better human-computer interaction. In *Auditory display* (pp. 80–102). Berlin, Heidelberg: Springer.

White, K. N. (2007). The effects of background music in the classroom on the productivity, motivation, and behavior of fourth grade students. *Online Submission*. Columbia College Press.

CHAPTER 7

From Online Interaction to Social Learning Analytics and Community Building

A Learning Engineering Perspective

Chih-Hsiung Tu, Cherng-Jyh Yen, Emrah Emre Ozkeskin, and Laura E. Sujo-Montes

INTRODUCTION

The 2020 pandemic has accelerated students' and educators' understanding on the vital role of network learning in an online learning environment (Hodges, Moore, Lockee, Trust, & Bond, 2020) from K–12 education to graduate and postgraduate studies. Focusing on the cognitive learning process encourages educators to review their thinking about how important online learning is to integrating social interactivity that demonstrates how humans interconnect and learn. Although many students are well familiar with social networking for informal learning, in a formal learning environment, both educators and students just marched into a new uncharted territory. It is paramount to create effective and meaningful online learning, social interaction, interconnection, and a learning community that is grounded in social network theory.

The purpose of this chapter, designed in a social interconnectivity framework, is to discuss the importance of social interactivity in online learning from the perspectives of learning engineering and social learning analytics. In addition, it directs researchers and educators to explore how social network learning may be integrated to forge effective learning networks to build a learning community. Furthermore, data-informed instructions and learning are discussed to support practitioners to apply

DOI: 10.4324/9781003089704-10

social network analysis to benefit students' learning experiences and behaviors directly.

Learning engineering leverages network and interconnecting data to obtain a better understanding of interconnectivity. Online learning empowers learners to create, to share, to connect, and to comment, facilitating interconnectivity for the learning network and learning community. Social network platforms, such as social network sites, chats, feeds, and discussion boards with network features, embrace advanced social and technological infrastructures to augment learners' connecting and networking experiences (Hansen, Shneiderman, & Smith, 2011). By integrating learning engineering with a social network platform, educators can obtain better understanding of online social learning.

Researchers channeled their efforts to explore the knowledge in human interactivity that is related to social learning and is grounded in the patterns of social connections, relationships, and structures. The further sought to learn how this knowledge may impact social connection, collaboration, and community building. Alhajj and Rokne (2014) noted that the knowledge obtained from examining learning network structures would support educators in understanding and visualizing how knowledge is created, shared, and distributed within networks. Furthermore, it helps to dissect how networks and communities evolve between and among students and teachers (Galikyan & Admiraal, 2019) and how they practice their social and emotional learning in an environment.

Social Network Analysis (SNA) is a process employed to understand the quality and the connections of social interactions and the roles each individual plays in networks and communities (Hansen et al., 2011). With social and technical infrastructure available, these dynamic interactivities can be unraveled by mapping them in sociograms in conjunctions with network metrics to identify core connections, the key persons based on the network metrics and the locations they occupied (Yen, Bozkurt, Tu, Sujo-Montes, & Rodas, 2019a). Research in online learning community has provided educators with vital measures to understand students' and teachers' perceptions, attitudes, attributes, and their messages exchange based on self-reported data, learning outcomes, and content analyses. Human relational behavior was rarely examined comprehensively. Studying relational behaviors in the online learning community would add additional knowledge to design and would foster organic and effective learning networks. Wagner (2019) suggested network learning research would bridge the gaps between self-reported and relational behavior data. The knowledge gained from social network learning research would lead instructional designers, teachers, students, and administrators to different layers of understanding of how people connect, how influential their social roles are, how knowledge is distributed, how learning networks emerge, and how a learning community evolves. These insights would stimulate the innovation in social learning (Borgatti, Everett, & Johnson, 2018).

Advanced social learning analytics does not stop at a point-in-time activity or a snapshot analysis at the end of learning. Social learning analytics should be expanded to detect temporal movement within a learning community. Wise and Vytasek (2017) clearly indicated that multiple layers of formative measurements should be applied to temporal and digital spatial changes in a learning environment, such as examining different interactions, connections, and networks or cluster evolving. Exploring aggregated and progressive movements of a learning community offers multiple dimensions of insights in determining effective instructional detections, remediation, facilitations, predictions, and prescriptions. These innovative research practices should grow from the comprehensions of hindsight and insights to foresights. Researchers and practitioners would be able to apply social learning analytics to drive their instructional designs, called data-driven or data-informed instructions and learning.

FROM INTERACTION TO INTERCONNECTIVITY

Online communication, conducted on discussion boards, chats, feeds, or social network sites, is one of the effective learning activities in online instruction. From the perspective of socio-constructivism, online discussions are integrated into the curriculum to bolster learning engagements, critical thinking, social interactions, higher-order thinking, cognitive engagements, knowledge and community building, academic achievements, and so on (Darabi, Liang, Suryavanshi, & Yurekli, 2013; Johnson et al., 2017; Klisc, McGill, & Hobbs, 2017; Msonde & Van Aalst, 2017; Sun, Lin, Wu, Zhou, & Luo, 2018; Tirado, Hernando, & Aguaded, 2015; Zhu, 2006).

With more advanced technology of social learning analytics available, researchers go beyond studying a student's or an instructor's interaction with students. They do this by examining how students and teachers connect with students and how they engage in many-to-many interconnectivities that shed light on developments of social networks and learning communities. The values of interconnectivity values are beyond frequency or numbers, of three types of interactions (learner-learner, learner-content, and learner-instructor interactions) (Moore,

1989). Studying interconnectivity and social networks would comprehend social interconnections, social roles, social relationships, clusters, and social structures of learning communities (Yen et al., 2019a).

For instance, the threaded conversation, either initiated by students or teachers on a discussion board or social media, is a structure built on a directed link between individuals. The structure is created when one person replies to another person's message. The threaded conversation provides an ideal basis for conducting social learning analytics. With the power of data mining that harvests rivers of information from learning systems or social network systems, each individual interaction in online discussion interactions can be captured and analyzed to detect the development of networks. Such detection occurs through temporal perspectives, such as participation patterns, individual progression of peripheral to core position, transitional phenomenon, and the change of network structural characteristics. Different network indices can be utilized to understand diversified interaction roles, behaviors, patterns, achievements, and discussion moderation activities. Sun et al. (2018) investigated knowledge construction processes in online discussion activities and discerned that students mainly deployed egocentric elaborations, followed by allocation elaborations, information sharing, and applications to construct knowledge.

SOCIAL NETWORK THEORY

Social interconnectivity concerns the connections and relationships which are derived from network or social network theories, which are emergent frameworks for describing and analyzing the connections and relationships among different entities (Wasserman & Faust, 1994). Researchers foresee the value of network theory and apply it to comprehend interconnectivity in online learning contexts (Yen et al., 2019a). Since interactions could be seen as a collection of interconnected pieces, the quality of interconnectivity becomes critical and can be determined by how strategically one connects and with whom one connects. Network-based research complements the traditional social sciences that value individual attributes and interaction products. Hansen et al. (2011) distinctly pointed out that despite the focus on the quality of interconnectivity, network theory does not exclude the quality or abilities of each individual. This adds additional values to address the complex interdependencies of interactive network phenomena in social interactions. This transformation in focus from "attribute" data to "relational" data dramatically affects how interaction data are collected, measured, analyzed, observed, and represented.

Relationships, imputed from social connections, are the building blocks to network theory. Each set of relationships combine to create emerging patterns of connections among people, groups, and different entities. Humans and their social exchanges are primordial. They rely on social networks to navigate through life and to develop community through social networks formed by language, exchange, and collaboration. Six degrees of separation investigated by Milgram (1967) pointed out the importance of how people connected through networks. Relationships create relational data that record information about who knows/interacts with whom, who are friends with whom, and who share similar interests (Borgatti et al., 2018). These relational data provide a wealth of opportunities to understand and improve social network learning.

SOCIAL NETWORK ANALYSIS

Social network analysis (SNA), as a subarea of social learning analytics, holds potential to deepen knowledge of behavioral patterns of learning interconnectivity and community building in online learning (Aguilar, Buendia, Pinto, & Gutiérrez, 2019; Jo, Park, & Lee, 2017).

Metrics, Visualizations, and Structural Models

Network metrics, visualizations, and structural models are the core constituents of SNA (Hansen et al., 2011). Network metrics are used to quantify connections to discover important vertices, edges, and structural features, such as cliques, chains, and missing connections. Community metrics range from reciprocated edges and vertices to network densities, geodesic distances, modularities, clusters, and so on. Network visualizations are constituted by people, nodes, or vertices connected by lines, ties, or edges that diagram these structures into the shapes, sizes, densities, subregions, positions, and locations. Instructional innovators, using information visualization features of emerging digital tools, are able to discover key participants, network patterns, trends, gaps, outliers, and communities in complex networks. Combining and cross-referencing network metrics and visualizations, observing the aggregated large data to reveal the emergent network structures and identify structural models, become attainable (see Figure 7.1).

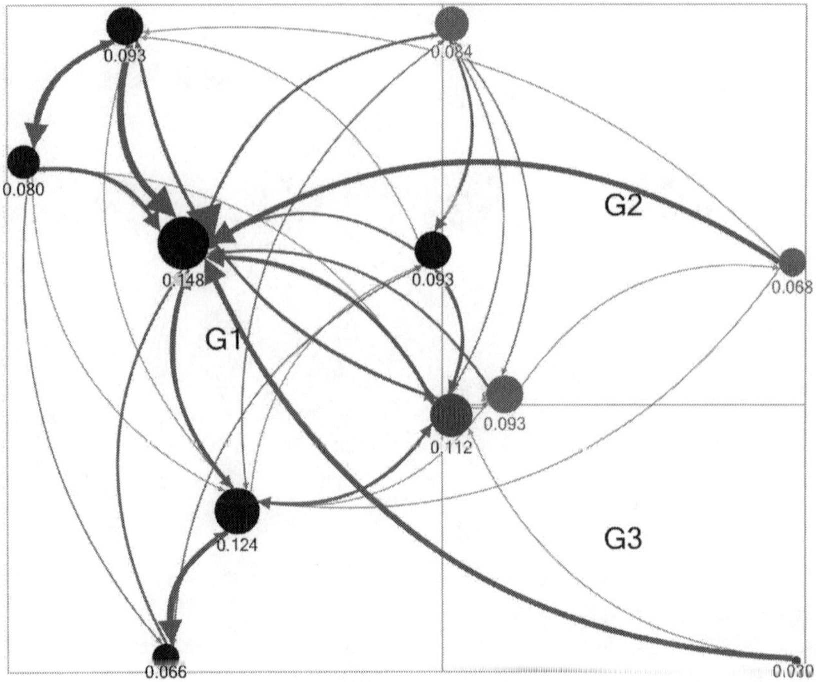

Figure 7.1 Aggregated Social Network Diagram

Centralities

As connection metrics, centrality is a measurement of each individual (vertex or nodes) situated in a social network based on the extent and with whom they interact (edge or ties) (Wasserman & Faust, 1994). Different centralities denote the levels and types of connection structures presented. These social network indices are in-degree, out-degree, betweenness, closeness, eigenvector centralities, and PageRank. For example, in Figure 7.2, V1 and V5 are situated in strategical positions with higher centrality scores which demonstrated their connections are more influential and prominent. In-degree and out-degree, similar to frequency, analyze the numbers of communications each individual posted, and the numbers of messages received. Betweenness centrality is a measure of the degree that a person is strategically situated between different networks. It indicates the potential influence of the information flow between networks through both direct and indirect pathways (Friedkin, 1993). Individuals who demonstrate a higher betweenness hold stronger roles

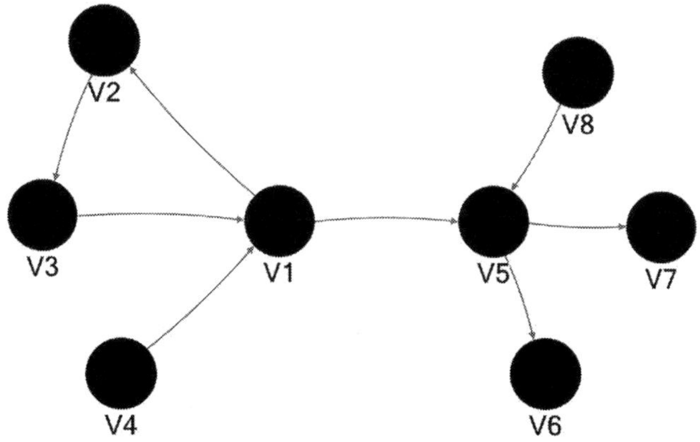

Figure 7.2 The Indirect and Binary Social Network Diagram of Relationships Among Members

as a gatekeepers, bridges, or facilitators who control the two-way information flow between networks.

Network flow is the key act in social interaction, whereas closeness centrality observes the distance of connection. Closeness centrality gauges the shortest paths to reach others more efficiently. Higher closeness is displayed by individuals who apply fewer connections to access others and demonstrates their ability to obtain resources more efficiently (Otte & Rousseau, 2002). These roles are situated to disseminate information quickly and are also referred to as broadcasters or transmitters. Eigenvector centrality detects the quality and level of how individuals connect to other more active and strategically connected members. While betweenness and closeness may value the numbers of connection types, eigenvector accentuates the quality of connection given to more active members. Those who interact with more active and interactive participants, such as those with higher closeness or PageRank, would obtain higher eigenvector scores and are perceived as more prominent. PageRank is the value to which a participant is connected with inbound replies by other active participants (higher eigenvector) (de Keyser, 2012).

Visualized Sociograms

Visualized sociograms or network visualizations map different centrality scores in a figure format (see Figure 7.1) to enhance the understanding of connections and networks. Individuals who hold conspicuous roles are placed in more central locations in the graphs. Connected symbols and calculated sizes, shapes, and densities of the network serve as representations for information paths, patterns detection, inferences, and manipulations (Card, Mackinlay, & Shneiderman, 1999). Stevens (2016) believes sociograms can be deployed to examine online discussion activities to support instructors' discernment and diagnosis of how interactions adapt, whereas Goggins, Gallagher, and Laffey (2011) utilized sociograms to examine the development of networks and online learning communities.

The visualization power of sociograms can facilitate a deeper understanding of social interaction behaviors and patterns that may not be easily observed in different centrality scores, such as betweenness, closeness, or eigenvector centralities. Huang, Hong, and Eades (2007) revealed that visual representations support the ability of people to understand network structures, progression, and how information flows and is exchanged in networks. These complex sets of social relationships among members and networks could be effectively unfolded in sociograms to support instructors in making crucial instructional decisions (Sobieski & Dell'Angelo, 2016). Liu and Tsai (2008) employed sociograms to analyze how knowledge was distributed in networks and to identify potential hindrances experienced by certain individuals during knowledge exchanges. By identifying disconnected students, patterns of student communication, and teacher positioning within the network, Macfadyen and Dawson (2010) applied similar sociogram strategies to identify the students at risk in online social interaction activities in order to avoid dropouts or failures. Furthermore, this technique can be extended to indicate whether students build denser networks in gamification-based instructional activities (Huang, Hwang, Hew, & Warning, 2019).

Social Roles

Based on different centrality scores and visualized sociograms, researchers have been determining and identifying different social roles that participants play in a learning community. To create an effective learning community, it is vital to facilitate diversified social roles in learning networks. Each role is attributed to a wide and multifaceted set of culturally shared values, meanings, goals, and expectations directed toward other distinctive role holders (Suthers, 2017). Although social roles may not be as explicitly recognized by the participants, they have the ability to identify content as well as behavioral, and structural features. Yen, Tu, Sujo-Montes, Harati, and Rodas (2019b; Yen et al., 2019c) named betweenness, closeness, eigenvector, and PageRank centralities as facilitators, transmitters, prominent roles, and prestigious roles, respectively.

Both Feng (2016) and Adalat, Niazi, and Vasilakos (2018), using subgraphs and creating composite metrics, explored different emerging high-value or unique contributors, such as conversation starters, influencers, active engagers, network builders, and information bridges.

Kim, Wang, and Ketenci (2020) identified three leadership roles as full facilitator, transactional facilitator, and attractive facilitator, based on the attributes of advantageous positions in discussion networks due to popularity, influence, mediation, and interaction frequency. The results concluded that these roles are assumed to be associated with learners' levels of engagement in behavior, cognition, and emotions. Furthermore, Ouyang and Scharber (2017) were able to categorize the instructor's interaction behavior evolved from a facilitator, an observer, to a collaborator. Such observations were innovative to support instructors to design and to strategize effective network learning environments. This knowledge of social roles offers insights on identifying topical experts, facilitators, and information transmitters, and roles that may benefit from connecting with other roles, how participants may absorb multiple roles in different networks, and how they manage the reality of multiple and shifting memberships.

Each individual rarely plays one single role in a learning community; therefore, researchers go beyond the status quo of SNA and employ inter-SNA metrics to detect the interconnections in an online discussion context. In-degree centrality is highly correlated with out-degree (Tirado et al., 2015), while Chen and Huang (2019) had the same findings that high in-degree participants received more responses and maintained stronger and better-quality connections. Both studies continued a series of inter-SNA metric investigations. Tirado et al. (2015) discovered higher betweenness was correlated with higher in-degree and out-degree, and they applied both centralities to identify network coordinators. In addition, Chen and Huang (2019) observed that higher in-degree was located in a more influential position (closeness and eigenvector centralities) but not facilitating role (betweenness). They suggested further that lower in-degree participants intended to interact with higher in-degree participants, but lower reciprocation was found.

With emerging interaction and connection patterns, it is valuable to deepen the examinations of social roles, tasks, network formations, instructors' feedback, and meaningful postings. Rook (2018) found high-authority students who demonstrated a higher in-degree centrality and inclination to interact with other authority participants. Both betweenness and in-degree centralities could serve as indices to identify network facilitators. da Silva, Barbosa, and Gomes (2019) called these students stimulators because they strengthen the interaction and engagements in flow of information. Network density and interaction cliques also can serve as a means of how collaboration tasks and structures are carried out. Msonde and Van Aalst (2017) found stronger interaction cliques would lead to more collaboration activities. Lee and Lee (2016) probed how closeness centrality is related to instructors' feedback and meaningful posts; they concluded that the levels of closeness centrality could allow instructors to promote effective and interactive participation. Ghadirian, Salehi, and Ayub (2019) extended the examinations to student moderation behaviors and their effects and concluded that peer moderators exhibited a higher degree of interaction quantity and patterns; their facilitations also led to higher network density interaction.

Community Development

Social learning analytics with SNA are used to understand the development of the learning community. Through the lens of detecting network interconnective structures (Khalil, Ardoin, & Wojcik, 2017), the analytics expanded investigations to the development, cohesion, and resilience of the online learning community and the community of practice. Community metrics, geodesic distance, density, and modalities with sociograms can reveal and diagnose the vigor of a learning community. Balfour and Alter (2016) advocated using SNA to comprehend effective collaboration in order to improve and stimulate innovation that supports community growth. Turkkila, Lommi, and Koponen (2019) integrated predictive analysis to envisage community connections and identified characteristic structural features for both initial knowledge and network analysis of discussion. They concluded the structure and extension of students' initial knowledge cannot explain community activity and their role in online discussions.

Yen et al. (2019b, 2019c) went beyond a snapshot study and applied SNA to study the evolvements of an online learning community through multiple points in time. They found the students' closeness centrality changed and increased over time. In addition, the increasing of closeness centrality was observed at all levels of self-regulated learning (SRL) and social presence. Through online discussion activities, students developed a learning community, and networks became a community of learners over time.

Sentiment Analysis

Gunawardena, Flor, Gómez, and Sánchez (2016) made the seminal claim that learning is not purely a cognitive process but is also emotionally loaded and situated within a social context. With the advanced technology of social learning analytics, sentiment analysis, as an extension of SNA, can be applied to understand learners' affective status through analyzing their digital shared text messages. Batrinca and Treleaven (2015) defined sentiment analysis as "the application of natural language processing, computational linguistics, and text analytics to identify and extract subjective information in source materials" (p. 90). Liu (2012) indicated that sentiment analysis uses a set of lexicons with automatic mechanisms to systematically identify, quantify, and compute a list of positive (good, wonderful, fantastic, etc.) and negative words (bad, awful, terrible, etc.). Liu and Zhang (2012) indicated that sentiment analysis is designed to discover and to detect implicit and subjective information of messages. Unlike traditional content analysis by human coding, with network analysis application, sentiment analysis is able to analyze all posting content without random sampling postings and without human coding errors. Despite the widely used in the customers' review on online shopping, sentiment analysis poses potentials to understand online learners' affective status, such as social and emotional learning in online community development.

Lexicons

Lexicons are the theoretical foundation for sentiment analysis to determine levels and degrees of sentiment orientation (Feldman, 2013). Different sets of lexicons measure different affective statuses, such as positive, negative (Liu, 2012), or social presence (Gunawardena et al., 2016). Harris, Zheng, Kumar, and Kinshuk (2014) categorized textual data into six areas, positive, negative, neutral, insightful, angry and joke in order to understand students' affective status in online discussions and collaboration. Conducted on social network software, such as NodeXL Pro, Gephi, sentiment analysis conducts content analysis on the transcripts by calculating the positive, negative, or social presence words.

Social and Emotional Status

Researchers start supervising sentiment analysis to diagonalize students' social and emotional learning status in an online learning environment. Ortigosa, Martín, and Carro (2014) noted sentiment in Facebook postings returned high accuracy of students' social and emotional status. They extended their findings and recommended that sentiment analysis should be used for adaptive learning to facilitate a personalized learning environment that suggests effective learning activities.

Sentiment analysis could empower teachers and designers to support the online learning community through facilitating effective teaching presence and social presence to drive cognitive presence more meaningfully. Gunawardena et al. (2016) applied sentiment analysis to identify key students' affective status and their participation phases in online discussion activities. However, students' sentiment status is related to the trends of upward and downward. They concluded that positive sentiment may be the indices of the knowledge co-construction process. Using sentiment analysis to detect potential dropout is an additional aspect, so it supports students. Alencar et al. (2020) analyzed students' discussion postings to detect their learning obstacles, frustrations, and discouragement. They indicated these findings should be applied to data-driven decisions to drive future teaching and learning enhancement. In fact, Elia, Solazzo, Lorenzo, and Passiante (2019) proposed a model that utilized students' posting contributions in real time in online learning activities to detect their learning satisfaction and online collaboration progress. Such knowledge would provide teachers with insights of each student's emotional status and provide just-in-time support in order to adjust instructions to meet instructional needs. This adaptive practice is particularly powerful where face-to-face instructional contact is less frequent, such as remote learning amid the 2020 pandemic.

Due to the high enrollment and large data set available, sentiment analysis is also administered to understand Massive Open Online Courses (MOOCs) students' learning experiences. Such learning analytics were not available in the past. Shapiro et al. (2017) noted the students from Africa and Asia were less critical compared to their counterparts of America white male students. They also tended to be more positive than their female counterparts based on the shared textual comments. Hew, Hu, Qiao, and Tang (2020) employed a machine-learning algorithm to conduct sentiment analysis to understand students' learning satisfaction in multiple MOOCs and found instructors, learning assessment, and course schedule as strong predictors of learning satisfaction.

DATA-DRIVEN INSTRUCTION

By obtaining knowledge about social interconnectivity, educators can feasibly integrate data-driven instruction into the curriculum to improve social learning and community building. Educational data are becoming the predominant driver in decision-making for teaching, learning, instructions, and education, and such data will increase demand for educators who can understand and utilize the power of data-driven processes. Data collected during social learning activities are effective sources of information for the diagnosis of student engagement, feedback, and learning experience.

Normally, educators adopt summative assessment items as a benchmark to measure the learning community and make pedagogical improvements. By applying real-time or near-real-time social learning analytics, educational professionals can employ effective instructional strategies, such as facilitating self-regulated learning or social presence skills, in order to efficiently integrate these socio-technological options into courses, modules, and instructional activities. Kaliisa, Mørch, and Kluge (2019) promoted the thought that teachers should use social learning analytics as a proxy to understand learning and instructional processes and to support students in making informed pedagogical decisions to improve course instruction.

DATA-INFORMED LEARNING

The results of social learning analytics should not stop at the implications for teachers, administrators, and researchers. It can be integrated as the index to guide the practices of data-driven instructions or data-driven decision-making for teaching and learning.

Data-Informed Learning (DIL), evolving from data-driven decision-making, can support instructors and students in making responsive adjustments to their teaching and learning in the moment and lead to iterative improvements in learning designs (Wise, 2016). Maybee and Zilinski (2015) defined DIL as an approach to information literacy that purposefully addresses contextual concerns by suggesting pedagogic strategies (constructive formative feedback) that enable students to use information in ways that support discipline-focused learning outcomes. With computational thinking, DIL investigates a learning phenomenon to gain a better understanding of learning data. DIL "emphasizes learning as an outcome of engaging with information" (Maybee & Zilinski, 2015, p. 3). Research has applied DIL to support students, teachers, and educators in instruction planning, learning improvements, and reflections. By providing network metrics, and visualizations to students, DIL can evoke and strengthen effective students' self-reflections on their learning interaction and network connections.

Self-Reflection

Data-informed learning (DIL) can be perceived as the regulatory process of individual behaviors that can positively impact group performance

(Xie, Hensley, Law, & Sun, 2019). Gaul and Kim (2020) proffered that DIL is a type of feedback that constitutes self-reflection, uses visualizations generated from social learning activity logs, and promotes social interaction behaviors with meaningful postings. Instructors could share the social learning analytics based on their prior interaction activities with each individual student. In addition, DIL would serve as recommendations and to prompt active self-reflection to improve their upcoming social interaction.

Network Visualization

Individualized person-level metrics and network visualization (see Figure 7.3) facilitate insights on rapid progress of a student's interconnectivity performances within the learning network, helping instructors to understand and identify important or "central" roles. Network visualizations provide an objective representation of one's interaction performance, encouraging self-reflection and providing a guide to social

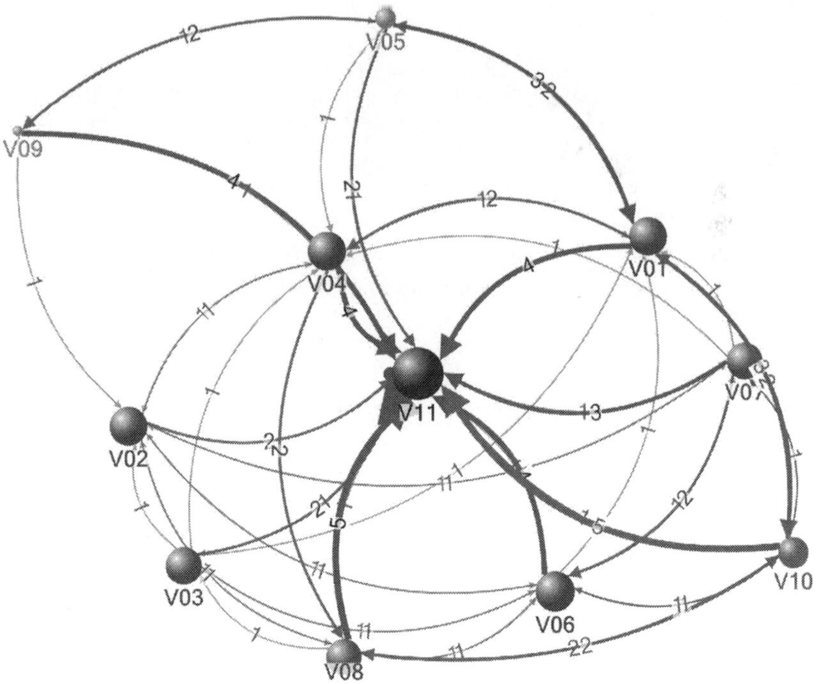

Figure 7.3 Subgraph for Aggregated Social Network Diagram

hygiene in a social learning environment. Based on the network visualizations, students can analyze their critical, unappreciated, or forgotten social interaction and relationships with their peers. By engaging in such critical reflection progress, students can adjust and modify their interaction behavior. Furthermore, such design would enhance or rekindle students' community learning to become a better collaborator in a group or a class.

The self-reflecting process leads students to actionable insights by assuming critical roles that facilitate more cross-fertilization, helping others get an overview of the social structure in which they participate, evaluating the effectiveness of a new community of practice initiative, and much more. Menekse (2019) found the students, who engaged in reflection with DIL, performed significantly better than the control condition. In addition, reflection analysis showed that both quality and quantity of reflections were significantly associated with exam performance. Teachers have integrated data to inform their instruction choices effectively (Wardrip & Herman, 2018), while Datnow, Choi, Park, and John (2018) found teachers used DIL to achieve collective action in instructional planning, deliberation, and practices. Furthermore, Shen, Gao, and Xia (2017) observed significant associations between data-informed improvement efforts at the school and the classroom levels.

Wiljer et al. (2018) integrated DIL to support medical professionals' continued professional development as a lifelong learning process. They found DIL supports learners to master their adaptive learning by constantly reviewing learning goals. Furthermore, lifelong learners deepen their thinking and learning in professional environments and cultural realities. In the past, students relied on their memory to recall their community learning performance. Memories, however, are prone to biases such as weighing recent events more or remembering things they have initiated more than those initiated by others.

DATA-INFORMED LEARNING DESIGN MODEL

Simply providing students with the data and results of social learning analytics does not promote positive learning experiences in data-informed learning. Wise's (2016) proposed a DIL Design Model to formulate an effective instructional design. The model includes four dimensions: principles of integration, agency, reference frame, and dialogue. The principles of integration are to make sure students are grounded in how the learning analytics relate to the learning activities while agency gives students the opportunity to interpret and act on their own analytics. Reference frame provides one or more comparison points for interpreting the analytics. Dialogue offers feedback and support to students as needed.

Data-informed learning must embrace changes by providing an environment that allows students to explore and experiment with data, offers unique experiences enabling new perspectives, and provides opportunities to collaborate with others for their learning. The rapid advancement of digital learning has generated a rising demand for the community to understand and make sense of data.

Current research and practices in DIL are burgeoning. Future research should direct its energies to query the understanding of the effective and efficient utilization of DIL in the development of teaching and learning. The findings from research will encourage educators to not only set high expectations for all students but also provide appropriate personal and social analytics as instructional support to enable learners to regulate and navigate through social network learning. In the conjoining adaptive learning environment, just-in-time personalization guidance can be delivered at any point in discussion activities.

Data Literacy

In a pilot study, Harati and Tu (2019) concluded that students lacked data literacy to interpret the information provided in the personalized recommendation of DIL. The students felt DIL was critical but not beneficial to their social learning because they were unable to digest network metrics and network visualizations. Ridsdale et al. (2015) state: "Data literacy is the ability to collect, manage, evaluate, and apply data, in a critical manner" (p. 2). Future research should examine how educators might teach, improve, and enhance students' digital data literacy.

Participants in the pilot study recommended several strategies for social learning analytics as monitoring, reflecting, and adjusting their social interactivity performances (Harati & Tu, 2019). These strategies are meaningful context, clear instructions, clean social graphs, expressive communication, and personalized recommendation. DIL should provide meaningful context on what social learning analytics are for and how DIL may improve learning. The clear instructions should be delivered with social learning analytics, allowing a complete understanding of different social roles (Liaison, Transmitter, Prominent, and Prestigious roles). Video tutorials would be effective. Clean social graphs should be provided for easily identifiable social roles in network visualizations with clean line and edge connections. Furthermore, expressive communication should be provided to inform students to adjust their interactivity for the upcoming instructional activities. Lastly, personalization is paramount to allowing students to download data that is easily accessible from different types of devices and that is in formats that allow students to "play" and investigate both simple and static exercises as well as dynamic, real-time, more complex, and sophisticated phenomena.

DESCRIPTIVE, DIAGNOSTIC, PREDICTIVE, AND PRESCRIPTIVE

Research in social learning analytics should migrate from hindsight, to insight, and address foresight in the future. In other words, it should evolve from descriptive analytics and diagnostic analytics to predictive and prescriptive analytics (HR Future, 2016). Research in educational technology has extensively explored the understanding of what happened in the social learning process based on perceptions, attitude, self-reported data, and content analysis. This descriptive and diagnostic research has provided rich hindsight and insight of social learning. Reactive learning analytics lead to the consumption and presentation of data without any processing being applied. They allow understanding of the past and, based on historical data, influence the future (IAD Learning, 2018). Descriptive analytics monitor how social learning behaviors unfold but may not foresee what learning interactivity and what effective strategies will advance ideal social interconnectivity.

With the knowledge in descriptive analytics, researchers and teachers synthesize various data sources to diagnose social learning behavior to gain the insights. Ideally, all stakeholders of learning analytics should apply the insights to predict social learning behavior and to prescribe effective strategies to facilitate ideal social learning behaviors. More proactive research analytics, such as predictive and prescriptive research, influence the present and, therefore, improve ongoing learning processes (IAD Learning, 2018).

Certainly, based on students' learning competencies and previous social learning behaviors, teachers can foresee and predict how each individual student may exhibit possible interaction behaviors and prescribe and provide just-in-time support to reach more effective learning. From a learning engineering standpoint, it is not sufficient to obtain the intelligence on descriptions and diagnoses of social learning. It is necessary to foresee what may happen in a learning community before the interactivity occurs.

Researchers were able to use students' perceptions of self-regulated learning (SRL) and social presence (SP), based on self-reported data, to predict students' social interaction behaviors in online discussion board activities before the discussion activities took place. Yen et al. (2019b) applied the perception data to predict students' behavior to social interconnectivity. They found that learners who perceived greater SRL skills play more influential social roles in online discussion networks. Learners with higher SRL skills tend to connect to others based on flow and distance of the social network connections. Their further study found the predictive utility of online social presence based on self-reported data for all social network interaction (Yen et al., 2019c). Learners, who perceive with higher social presence, play more active, intermediate, central, prominent, and prestigious roles in a learning community. In addition, Jo et al. (2017) identified students' in-degree and out-degree centralities in online discussions served as predictors of their final grades. Furthermore, higher-degree centralities lead to better learner engagements and achievements, as validated by Lai, Lin, Lin, and Tho's conclusions (2019).

FINAL WORDS

The prospect of viewing learning as science and engineering must embrace changes by providing an environment that allows: students to explore and experiment with data; offering unique experiences enabling new perspectives and providing opportunities to collaborate with others for their learning. Simply engaging in social interaction may not be sufficient for dynamic digital social network learning. Social network interconnectivity that values how learners connect, with whom they connect, and how they collaborate to create and to distribute knowledge is the main focus for the next level of social learning research. This chapter pointed out the importance of online interconnection instructions supporting the development of a collegial community in which peers and teachers are viewed as allies that are essential for greater engagement and learning effectiveness. Gaining the knowledge in social learning analytics assists educators to set high expectations for all students while providing appropriate social and instructional support to develop a model that provides personalized guidance and support for learners to navigate through the learning network and community. The rapid advancement of digital learning has generated a rising demand for the community to understand and make sense of data. Researchers should investigate further in conjoining social learning analytics and adaptive learning systems that potentially collect real-time social network interaction data. Such advanced instruction would engage students with just-in-time personalization guidance at any point in social interactive activities.

REFERENCES

Adalat, M., Niazi, M. A., & Vasilakos, A. V. (2018). Variations in power of opinion leaders in online communication networks. *Royal Society Open Science, 5*(10). https://doi.org/10.1098/rsos.180642

Aguilar, J., Buendia, O., Pinto, A., & Gutiérrez, J. (2019). Social learning analytics for determining learning styles in a smart classroom. *Interactive Learning Environments*, 1–17. https://doi.org/10.1080/10494820.2019.1651745

Alencar, M., & Netto, J. F. (2020). Measuring student emotions in an online learning environment. *Conference: 12th International Conference on Agents and Artificial Intelligence, 2*, 563–569. http://doi.org/10.5220/0008956505630569

Alhajj, R., & Rokne, J. (Eds.). (2014). *Encyclopedia of social network analysis and mining*. Springer-Verlag. Retrieved from www.springer.com/gp/book/9781461461692

Balfour, B., & Alter, T. R. (2016). Mapping community innovation: Using social network analysis to map the interactional field, identify facilitators, and foster community development. *Community Development, 47*(4), 431–448. https://doi.org/10.1080/15575330.2016.1153493

Batrinca, B., & Treleaven, P. C. (2015). Social media analytics: A survey of techniques, tools and platforms. *AI & Society, 30*(1), 89–116. https://doi.org/10.1007/s00146-014-0549-4

Borgatti, S. P., Everett, M. G., & Johnson, J. C. (2018). *Analyzing social networks* (2nd ed.). Sage. Retrieved from https://us.sagepub.com/en-us/nam/analyzing-social-networks/book255068

Card, S. K., Mackinlay, J. D., & Shneiderman, B. (1999). *Readings in information visualization: Using vision to think*. San Francisco, CA: Morgan Kaufmann.

Chen, B., & Huang, T. (2019). It is about timing: Network prestige in asynchronous online discussions. *Journal of Computer Assisted Learning, 35*(4), 503–515. https://doi.org/10.1111/jcal.12355

Darabi, A., Liang, X., Suryavanshi, R., & Yurekli, H. (2013). Effectiveness of online discussion strategies: A meta-analysis. *American Journal of Distance Education, 27*(4), 228–241. https://doi.org/10.1080/08923647.2013.837651

da Silva, L. F. C., Barbosa, M. W., & Gomes, R. R. (2019). Measuring participation in distance education online discussion forums using social network analysis. *Journal of the Association for Information Science and Technology, 70*(2), 140–150. https://doi.org/10.1002/asi.24080

Datnow, A., Choi, B., Park, V., & John, E. S. (2018). Teacher talk about student ability and achievement in the era of data-driven decision making. *Teachers College Record, 120*(4).

de Keyser, P. (2012). *Indexing: From thesauri to the semantic web*. Oxford, UK: Chandos Publishing.

Elia, G., Solazzo, G., Lorenzo, G., & Passiante, G. (2019). Assessing learners' satisfaction in collaborative online courses through a big data approach. *Computers in Human Behavior, 92*, 589–599. https://doi.org/10.1016/j.chb.2018.04.033

Feldman, R. (2013). Techniques and applications for sentiment analysis. *Communications of the ACM, 56*, 82–89. http://doi.org/10.1145/2436256.2436274

Feng, Y. (2016). Are you connected? Evaluating information cascades in online discussion about the #RaceTogether campaign. *Computers in Human Behavior, 54*, 43–53. https://doi.org/10.1016/j.chb.2015.07.052

Friedkin, N. E. (1993). Structural bases of interpersonal influence in groups: A longitudinal case study. *American Sociological Review, 58*(6), 861–872. http://doi.org/10.2307/2095955

Galikyan, I., & Admiraal, W. (2019). Students' engagement in asynchronous online discussion: The relationship between cognitive presence, learner prominence, and academic performance. *Internet and Higher Education, 43*. https://doi.org/10.1016/j.iheduc.2019.100692

Gaul, C., & Kim, M. K. (2020). Learner participation regulation supported by long-term peer moderation and participation feedback during asynchronous discussions. *Journal of Computers in Education*, 7, 295–331. https://doi.org/10.1007/s40692-020-00158-5

Ghadirian, H., Salehi, K., & Ayub, A. F. M. (2019). Assessing the effectiveness of role assignment on improving students' asynchronous online discussion participation. *International Journal of Distance Education Technologies, 17*(1), 31–51. https://doi.org/10.4018/IJDET.2019010103

Goggins, S. P., Gallagher, M., & Laffey, J. (2011). Completely online group formation and development: Small groups as socio-technical systems. *Information Technology & People, 24*(2), 104–133. https://doi.org/10.1108/09593841111137322

Gunawardena, C. N., Flor, N., Gómez, D., & Sánchez, D. (2016). Analyzing social construction of knowledge online by employing interaction analysis, learning analytics, and social network analysis. *Quarterly Review of Distance Education, 17*(3), 35.

Hansen, D., Shneiderman, B., & Smith, M. (2011). *Analyzing social media networks with NodeXL*. Elsevier. Retrieved from www.elsevier.com/books/analyzing-social-media-networks-with-nodexl/hansen/978-0-12-382229-1

Harati, H., & Tu, C.-H. (2019). Social network analysis in data-informed learning environment. *Environment. Presented at the ICEM panel discussion in the annual meeting of the association for educational communications technology (AECT)*, October 21–25, 2019, Las Vegas, Nevada.

Harris, S. C., Zheng, L., Kumar, V., & Kinshuk. (2014). Multi-dimensional sentiment classification in online learning environment. *IEEE*, 172–175. https://doi.org/10.1109/T4E.2014.50

Hew, K. F., Hu, X., Qiao, C., & Tang, Y. (2020). What predicts student satisfaction with MOOCs: A gradient boosting trees supervised machine learning and sentiment analysis approach. *Computers and Education, 145*. https://doi.org/10.1016/j.compedu.2019.103724

Hodges, C., Moore, S., Lockee, B., Trust, T., & Bond, A. (2020). The difference between emergency remote teaching and online learning. *EDUCAUSE Review*. Retrieved from https://er.educause.edu/articles/2020/3/the-difference-between-emergency-remote-teaching-and-online-learning

HR Future. (2016, June 17). *Cognitive analytics – From hindsight, to insight, to foresight*. HR Future. Retrieved from www.hrfuture.net/news-1/cognitive-analytics-from-hindsight-to-insight-to-foresight-21449/

Huang, B., Hwang, G.-J., Hew, K. F., & Warning, P. (2019). Effects of gamification on students' online interactive patterns and peer-feedback. *Distance Education, 40*(3), 350–379. https://doi.org/10.1080/01587919.2019.1632168

Huang, W., Hong, S.-H., & Eades, P. (2007). Effects of sociogram drawing conventions and edge crossings in social network visualization. *Journal of Graph Algorithms and Applications, 11*(2), 397–429. https://doi.org/10.7155/jgaa.00152

IAD Learning. (2018, February 9). Learning analytics 2018 – An updated perspective. *IADLearning*. Retrieved from www.iadlearning.com/learning-analytics-2018/

Jo, I., Park, Y., & Lee, H. (2017). Three interaction patterns on asynchronous online discussion behaviours: A methodological comparison. *Journal of Computer Assisted Learning, 33*(2), 106–122. https://doi.org/10.1111/jcal.12168

Johnson, C., Hill, L., Lock, J., Altowairiki, N., Ostrowski, C., da Rosa dos Santos, L., & Liu, Y. (2017). Using design-based research to develop meaningful online discussions in undergraduate field experience courses. *International Review of Research in Open and Distributed Learning, 18*(6), 36–53. http://doi.org/10.19173/irrodl.v18i6.2901

Kaliisa, R., Mørch, A. I., & Kluge, A. (2019). Exploring social learning analytics to support teaching and learning decisions in online learning environments. *Lecture notes in computer science (Including Subseries Lecture Notes in Artificial Intelligence and Lecture Notes in Bioinformatics), 11722 LNCS* (pp. 187–198). Cham, Switzerland: Springer. https://doi.org/10.1007/978-3-030-29736-7_14

Khalil, K., Ardoin, N. M., & Wojcik, D. (2017). Social learning within a community of practice: Investigating interactions about evaluation among zoo education professionals. *Evaluation and Program Planning, 61*, 45–54. https://doi.org/10.1016/j.evalprogplan.2016.12.001

Kim, M. K., Wang, Y., & Ketenci, T. (2020). Who are online learning leaders? Piloting a leader identification method (LIM). *Computers in Human Behavior, 105*. https://doi.org/10.1016/j.chb.2019.106205

Klisc, C., McGill, T., & Hobbs, V. (2017). Use of a post-asynchronous online discussion assessment to enhance student critical thinking. *Australasian Journal of Educational Technology, 33*(5), 63–76. https://doi.org/10.14742/ajet.3030

Lai, C.-H., Lin, H.-W., Lin, R.-M., & Tho, P. D. (2019). Effect of peer interaction among online learning community on learning engagement and achievement. *International Journal of Distance Education Technologies, 17*(1), 66–77. https://doi.org/10.4018/IJDET.2019010105

Lee, H. Y., & Lee, H. W. (2016). Comparing social network analysis of posts with counting of posts as a measurement of learners' participation in Facebook discussions. *Turkish Online Journal of Educational Technology, 15*(1), 11–19. Retrieved from www.tojet.net/articles/v15i1/1512.pdf

Liu, B. (2012). *Sentiment analysis and opinion mining*. San Rafael, CA: Morgan & Claypool Publishers. http://doi.org/10.1007/978-3-642-19460-3_11

Liu, B., & Zhang, L. (2012). A survey of opinion mining and sentiment analysis. In C. C. Aggarwal & C. Zhai (Eds.), *Mining text data* (pp. 415–463). Boston, MA: Springer. https://doi.org/10.1007/978-1-4614-3223-4_13

Liu, P., & Tsai, C. (2008). Using analytic network process to construct evaluation indicators of knowledge sharing effectiveness in Taiwan's high-tech industries. *Asian Journal on Quality, 9*(2), 99–117. https://doi.org/10.1108/15982688200800020

Macfadyen, L. P., & Dawson, S. (2010). Mining LMS data to develop an "early warning system" for educators: A proof of concept. *Computers & Education, 54*(2), 588–599. https://doi.org/10.1016/j.compedu.2009.09.008

Maybee, C., & Zilinski, L. (2015). Data informed learning: A next phase data literacy framework for higher education. *Proceedings of the Association for Information Science and Technology, 52*(1), 1–4. http://doi.org/10.1002/pra2.2015.1450520100108

Menekse, M. (2019). The reflection-informed learning and instruction to improve students' academic success in undergraduate classrooms. *Journal of Experimental Education*, *88*(2), 183–199. https://doi.org/10.1080/00220973.2019.1620159

Milgram, S. (1967). The small world problem. *Psychology Today*, *2*(1), 60–67.

Moore, M. G. (1989). Three types of interaction. *The American Journal of Distance Education*, *3*(2), 1–6.

Msonde, S. E., & Van Aalst, J. (2017). Designing for interaction, thinking and academic achievement in a Tanzanian undergraduate chemistry course. *Educational Technology Research and Development*, *65*(5), 1389–1413. https://doi.org/10.1007/s11423-017-9531-4

Ortigosa, A., Martín, J. M., & Carro, R. M. (2014). Sentiment analysis in Facebook and its application to e-learning. *Computers in Human Behavior*, *31*(1), 527–541. https://doi.org/10.1016/j.chb.2013.05.024

Otte, E., & Rousseau, R. (2002). Social network analysis: A powerful strategy, also for the information sciences. *Journal of Information Science*, *28*(6), 441–453. http://doi.org/10.1177/016555150202800601

Ouyang, F., & Scharber, C. (2017). The influences of an experienced instructor's discussion design and facilitation on an online learning community development: A social network analysis study. *Internet and Higher Education*, *35*, 34–47. https://doi.org/10.1016/j.iheduc.2017.07.002

Ridsdale, C., Rothwell, J., Smit, M., Ali-Hassan, H., Bliemel, M., Irvine, D., . . . & Wuetherick, B. (2015). *Strategies and best practices for data literacy education: Knowledge synthesis report* [Report]. Halifax, Canada: Dalhousie University. https://doi.org/info:doi/10.13140/RG.2.1.1922.5044

Rook, M. M. (2018). Identifying the help givers in a community of learners: Using peer reporting and social network analysis as strategies for participant selection. *TechTrends: Linking Research and Practice to Improve Learning*, *62*(1), 71–76. https://doi.org/10.1007/s11528-017-0200-6

Shapiro, H. B., Lee, C. H., Wyman Roth, N. E., Li, K., Çetinkaya-Rundel, M., & Canelas, D. A. (2017). Understanding the massive open online course (MOOC) student experience: An examination of attitudes, motivations, and barriers. *Computers and Education*, *110*, 35–50. https://doi.org/10.1016/j.compedu.2017.03.003

Shen, J., Gao, X., & Xia, J. (2017). School as a loosely coupled organization? An empirical examination using national SASS 2003–04 data. *Educational Management Administration and Leadership*, *45*(4), 657–681. https://doi.org/10.1177/1741143216628533

Sobieski, C., & Dell'Angelo, T. (2016). Sociograms as a tool for teaching and learning: Discoveries from a teacher research study. *Educational Forum*, *80*(4), 417–429. https://doi.org/10.1080/00131725.2016.1207734

Stevens, T. L. (2016). I "see" what you are saying: The analytical work of diagrams in online discussions. *Australasian Journal of Educational Technology*, *42*(4), 50–67. https://doi.org/10.14742/ajet.2757

Sun, Z., Lin, C.-H., Wu, M., Zhou, J., & Luo, L. (2018). A tale of two communication tools: Discussion-forum and mobile instant-messaging apps in collaborative learning. *British Journal of Educational Technology*, *49*(2), 248–261. https://doi.org/10.1111/bjet.12571

Suthers, D. D. (2017). Multilevel analysis of activity and actors in heterogeneous networked learning environments. In C. Lang, G. Siemens, A. Wise, & D. Gašević (Eds.), *Handbook of learning analytics* (pp. 189–197). Beaumont, AB, Canada: Society for Learning Analytics Research. Retrieved from www.solaresearch.org/hla-17/. https://doi.org/10.18608/hla17

Tirado, R., Hernando, Á., & Aguaded, J. I. (2015). The effect of centralization and cohesion on the social construction of knowledge in discussion forums. *Interactive Learning Environments*, *23*(3), 293–316. http://doi.org/10.1080/10494820.2012.745437

Turkkila, M., Lommi, H., & Koponen, I. (2019). Initial knowledge and the intensity of online discussion. In K. Lund, G. P. Niccolai, E. Lavoue, C. Hmelo-Silver, G. Gweon, & M. Baker (Eds.), *Computer-supported collaborative learning conference, CSCL. ISLS international society of the learning sciences, international conference on computer supported collaborative learning*, *2* (pp. 837–838). Lyon, France. http://hdl.handle.net/10138/321358

Wagner, E. (2019). *Learning engineering: A primer* (Community & Resources for ELearning Professionals). eLearning Guild. Retrieved from www.elearningguild.com/showfile.cfm?id=6302

Wardrip, P. S., & Herman, P. (2018). "We're keeping on top of the students": Making sense of test data with more informal data in a grade-level instructional team. *Teacher Development*, *22*(1), 31–50. https://doi.org/10.1080/13664530.2017.1308428

Wasserman, S., & Faust, K. (1994). *Social network analysis methods and applications*. Cambridge: Cambridge University Press. https://doi.org/10.1017/CBO9780511815478

Wiljer, D., Tavares, W., Mylopoulos, M., Campbell, C., Charow, R., Davis, D., . . . & Sockalingam, S. (2018). Data and lifelong learning protocol: Understanding cultural barriers and facilitators to using clinical performance data to support continuing professional development. *Journal of Continuing Education in the Health Professions*, *38*(4), 293–298. https://doi.org/10.1097/CEH.0000000000000223

Wise, A. (2016). Data-informed learning environments. *EDUCAUSE Review*. Retrieved from https://er.educause.edu/articles/2016/10/data-informed-learning-environments

Wise, A., & Vytasek, J. (2017). Learning analytics implementation design. In C. Lang, G. Siemens, A. Wise, & D. Gašević (Eds.), *Handbook of learning analytics* (pp. 151–160). Society for Learning Analytics Research. Retrieved from www.solaresearch.org/hla-17/. https://doi.org/10.18608/hla17

Xie, K., Hensley, L. C., Law, V., & Sun, Z. (2019). Self-regulation as a function of perceived leadership and cohesion in small group online collaborative learning. *British Journal of Educational Technology*, *50*(1), 456–468. https://doi.org/10.1111/bjet.12594

Yen, C.-J., Bozkurt, A., Tu, C. H., Sujo-Montes, L., & Rodas, C. (2019a). A predictive study of students' self-regulated learning skills and their roles in the social network interaction of online discussion board. *Journal of Educational Technology Development and Exchange*, *11*(1), Article 2. http://doi.org/10.18785/jetde.1101.02

Yen, C.-J., Tu, C.-H., Sujo-Montes, L., Harati, H., & Rodas, C. (2019b). Social network interaction and self-regulated learning skills in online discussion. *Paper presented at annual meeting of American educational research association (AERA)*, April 5–9, 2019. Toronto, Canada.

Yen, C.-J., Tu, C.-H., Sujo-Montes, L., Rodas, C., Harati, H., & Armfield, S. (2019c). Community development in social network Interaction and social presence in online discussion. *Paper presented at annual meeting of American educational research association (AERA)*, April 5–9, 2019. Toronto, Canada.

Zhu, E. (2006). Interaction and cognitive engagement: An analysis of four asynchronous online discussions. *Instructional Science: An International Journal of Learning and Cognition, 34*(6), 451–480. https://doi.org/10.1007/s11251-006-0004-0

UNIT III

Revamping Professionalism

CHAPTER 8

Virtual Reality as Participant

Instructional Design Considerations for an Introduction to Flying Course

Kim A. Hosler

INTRODUCTION

It is easy to get caught up in the immersive experiences offered by virtual reality (VR), especially as the technology to provide high-fidelity virtual experiences has become less expensive and easier to use (Coburn, Freeman, & Salmon, 2017). VR can be found in many applications today, and according to Cipresso, Giglioli, Raya, and Riva (2018), low-cost VR technologies may be "the next largest stepping stone in technological innovation" (p. 1).

The advancement of VR and its use in training future pilots is of special interest to the United States Air Force. Virtual reality flight training better prepares United States Air Force Academy cadets for undergraduate pilot training by allowing them to further develop memorization skills and by providing them more realistic rehearsal and preparation opportunities (Spradlin, 2019). Additionally, the use of VR trains Airmen better and faster while fostering deeper learning as the Air Force "looks for ways to streamline the training pipeline and graduate more aviators each year" (Losey, 2018). Notably, the United States Air Force ended 2019 with roughly 1 in 10 bomber, fighter, and special operations pilot positions vacant (Losey, 2020).

Cadets at the United States Air Force Academy are using virtual reality systems to learn how to fly. While these systems do not replace actual flying time, they give cadets the opportunity to explore aviation as a possible career while honing basic maneuverability skills such as level flight, maintaining a constant air speed, and setting pitch, power,

DOI: 10.4324/9781003089704-12

and trim to maintain control. According to Ellis (2019), "Virtual reality is about to change the way students are taught at pilot training schools, in what is set to be more than just a breakthrough for technology" (para 1). The use of virtual reality pilot training systems has the potential to significantly lower flight training costs while decreasing Air Force budgets (Ellis, 2019).

In a learning environment where immersive VR experiences are central to the course, what are key considerations for the instructional design of said course or lesson? How should an immersive VR course be designed when the technology directly interacts with and responds to learners, a perspective where the technology is viewed as a participant in the learning experience? Should key features or characteristics of virtual reality inform the design of such a course or lesson? What follows offers instructional design considerations for immersive virtual reality lessons or courses using key features of VR, a technology as participant perspective, and the analyze, design, develop, implement, and evaluate (ADDIE) procedural model.

VIRTUAL REALITY

According to the Franklin Institute (n.d.), the idea of virtual reality (VR) dates to the 1800s, most notably when the first stereoscope (twin mirrors used to project a single image) was invented in 1838. Over time that invention led to the creation of the View-Master, patented in 1939. The more mainstream version of VR was introduced in 1987 by Jaron Lanier who began developing the devices (goggles, gloves) needed to experience what he called virtual reality (Franklin Institute, n.d.). Tom Furness, another VR pioneer, built the first helmet-mounted displays and visually coupled systems for the United States Air Force, which led to the creation of the Super Cockpit in the 1980s (Voices of VR, 2015). From 1986 to 1989, Furness directed the Air Force's Super Cockpit program, where the capacity of human pilots to handle spatial information depended on data being "portrayed in a way that takes advantage of the human's natural perceptual mechanisms" (Lowood, 2020).

In 1994, Franchi described virtual reality as "[a] computer-created sensory experience that completely immerses a participant to believe and barely distinguish a 'virtual' experience from a real one. It is the use of computer graphics, sounds and images to reproduce an electronic version of real-life situations" (p. 23). Mandal (2013) added the notion of user interaction, explaining VR as a "technology which allows a user to interact with a computer-simulated environment, whether that environment is a simulation of the real world or an imaginary world" (p. 304). He noted that virtual reality offers users a computer-generated virtual environment that may be moved through and manipulated by a user in real time. Mandal further described the equipment used in a virtual reality setting to include "a head mounted display, a computer monitor, or a large projection screen. Head and hand tracking systems . . . to enable the user to observe, move around, and manipulate the virtual environment" (p. 305).

Another perspective on virtual reality comes from the Virtual Reality Society (2017). They defined VR by parsing out the two words – virtual and reality:

> The definition of "virtual" is near, and reality is what we experience as human beings. So the term "virtual reality" basically means "near-reality." This could, of course, mean anything but it usually refers to a specific type of reality emulation.
>
> (Virtual Reality Society, 2017, para 1)

Like Mandal's explanation, the Virtual Reality Society also noted that the three-dimensional, computer-generated environment VR affords is explored and interacted with by a person. "That person becomes part of this virtual world or is immersed within this environment and whilst there, is able to manipulate objects or perform a series of actions" (Virtual Reality Society, 2017, para 2).

Martin-Gutierrez, Mora, Anorbe-Diaz, and Gonzalez-Marrero (2017), found that virtual worlds encourage students to be active learners, while promoting decision making when they interact with the virtual environment. These virtual interactions permit autonomous exploration and create new experiences. The authors noted that "real-time interaction permits visualizing results instantly, so students are able to make decisions based on these results to reach their learning goals, increasing their learning performance and cognitive skills" (p. 479).

Cipresso et al. (2018) identified three essential characteristics of virtual reality systems: "immersion, perception to be present in an environment, and interaction with that environment" (p. 2). Likewise, Radianti, Majchrzak, Fromm, and Wohlgenannt (2020) stated that immersion, presence, and interactivity are regarded as the core characteristics of VR technologies. Mutterlein (2018) postulated that presence as well as interactivity contributes to immersion, and that interactivity contributes to presence and thus these three characteristics influence the participants' perception of VR.

Immersion is the sensation of being present in an environment rather than observing an environment from the outside. It indicates the participant loses or becomes disconnected from their awareness of time and the outside world, "thus providing a sense of 'being' in the task environment instead" (Radianti et al., 2020, p. 147).

According to Brey (2014), "Interactivity includes the ability to navigate virtual worlds and to interact with objects, characters, and places" (p. 2). He noted that interaction refers to the responsiveness of the virtual world to user actions. Keeping these descriptions of VR in mind, along with the three primary characteristics of VR (immersion, presence, interactivity), we begin to see how virtual reality can be perceived as a participant in tandem with the learner.

VIRTUAL REALITY AS AN INTERACTIVE PARTICIPANT

The Merriam Webster dictionary (n.d.), holds that "participant" refers to a person who is involved in an activity or an event. Applying this simple definition to a technology (technology as participant) would mean that the technology becomes an actor or an entity that is involved in an activity or an event. That is not to ascribe anthropomorphism (attributing human characteristics such as emotions and intentions to something non-human) to the concept of VR; however, in order to understand it as a participative, interactive technology, this consideration is invited.

Designing good interaction techniques for a virtual reality environment is not a trivial endeavor (Kjeldskov, 2001). According to the Interaction Design Foundation (n.d.), it is vital to design VR experiences with a first-person perspective. They noted that interactivity necessitates intuitive design and the elimination of interference from outside of the virtual world. They found that how users interact with the virtual environment needs to match what they would actually be doing in a real situation.

Hillman, Willis, and Gunawardena (1994) labeled interaction that occurred between the learner and the technologies used to deliver instruction as learner-interface interaction. Thus, learner-interface interaction describes the interaction between the learner and the tools needed to perform a task. In the case of this discussion, the task is flying a single-engine airplane encapsulated in a virtual reality interface. Hillman et al. (1994) posited that learner-interface interaction necessitates that the learner interacts with the technological medium in support of other interactions such as those with the instructor, content, or other learners.

Coupling these explanations of virtual reality and interaction with the term participant indicates that technology as participant is about how the technology responds to and engages with the learner in a participant to participant manner, and how the technology responds to the actions of the learner in a "type of reality emulation" (Virtual Reality Society, 2017, para 1). Oden (2013) recognized that back in 1854, Henry David Thoreau said, "But lo! Men have become the tools of their tools," which in today's world raises the notion that technology tools "are more than mere objects; they are integral implements that interact with people to facilitate achievement of goals" (Oden, 2013, p. 73). Thus, virtual reality as a course participant engages learners and their senses, while creating a realistic and experiential environment. Therefore, purposeful instructional design is necessary if the VR experience is to be optimized.

INSTRUCTIONAL DESIGN AND VR

Instructional design (ID) has been defined in a variety of ways, generally highlighting the process of creating effective and efficient instruction. Reiser (2001) defined the field of instructional design as encompassing "the analysis of learning and performance problems, and the design, development, implementation, evaluation and management of instructional and noninstructional processes and resources intended to improve learning and performance in a variety of settings, particularly educational institutions and the workplace" (p. 57). Smith and Ragan (2004) explained ID as something distinct "from other forms of instructional planning by the level of precision, care, and expertise that is employed in planning, development, and evaluation processes" (p. 6). Richey, Klein, and Tracey (2011) described instructional design as the "science and art of creating detailed specifications for the development, evaluation, and maintenance of situations which facilitate learning and performance" (p. 3). In sum, instructional design is a complex process which promotes creativity during development, resulting in instruction that is effective and appealing to learners (Branch & Dousay, 2015).

The instructional design process is instantiated through various models that offer a representation of reality in a bounded and orderly way. These models provide systematic approaches that limit and set parameters within which course content can be created. Branch and Kopcha (2014) offered that ID models provide "conceptual tools to visualize, direct, and manage processes for creating high-quality teaching and learning materials. The proper selection of instructional design models assists us in appropriately matching the right process with the right situation" (p. 77). These models are "typically idealized and simplified versions of reality" (Richey et al., 2011, p. 8). Gustafson and Branch (2002) explained that models support our ability to conceptualize representations of reality. Models allow us to represent complex forms, processes, and functions of physical ideas or phenomena in a simplified manner. The authors further explain that models "visually communicate their associated processes to stakeholders by illustrating the procedures that make it possible to produce instruction" (p. 2). In short, an instructional design model is a systematic tool that assists designers "in understanding related instructional variables and/or guides them through the process of analyzing, designing, developing, implementing and evaluating instructional products" (Lee & Jang, 2014, p. 744). According to Reiser, while the:

> specific combination of procedures often varies from one instructional design model to the next, most of the models include the analysis of instructional problems, and the design, development, implementation and evaluation of instructional procedures and materials intended to solve those problems.
>
> (Reiser, 2001, p. 58)

Emerging from these procedures is a well-known model for instructional design labeled ADDIE, an acronym for Analyze, Design, Develop, Implement, and Evaluate. Notably, Molenda (2003), found that the ADDIE model "is merely a colloquial term used to describe a systematic approach to instructional development. . . . The label seems not to have a single author, but rather to have evolved informally through oral tradition" (p. 35). Richey et al. (2011) put forth that the elements of the ADDIE model are general enough to be applied to program design and the design of instructional materials and that these elements can be used with any type of content or delivery method.

The phases or elements within the ADDIE model inform each other and do not necessarily progress in a sequential or linear order. Instead, the phases can be used in an iterative manner before a final unit of instruction is completed and then used again after the lesson or course is evaluated.

According to Lee and Wong (2008), to use VR as a learning tool, "an appropriate instructional design that guides the development of a VR-based learning environment is imperative" (p. 236). Merchant (2012) wrote that "it is critical that instructional designers make careful decisions in the design and development of instructional materials utilizing virtual reality technologies" (p. 32). As with most instructional design endeavors, learning outcomes for the VR experience, (e.g., the course and/or the lesson) must be determined first, with additional content, learning experiences, and assessments following in an aligned manner.

Fowler (2015) posited that while VR holds great promise for learning, it has its challenges. Among those is "understanding the pedagogical underpinning that should inform the design and use of these VR systems"

(p. 412). He believed we need to go beyond technological affordances to include pedagogical requirements that inform the design of the learning experience. Pedagogical or learning requirements, according to Fowler, offer a holistic approach to the design of the course and include objectives based on Bloom, Englehart, Furst, Hill, and Krathwohl's (1956) taxonomy as well as learning activities. Combining the pedagogical underpinnings grounded in instructional design with the perspective of virtual reality, (the technology) as participant offers course designers and instructors a new way to think about and create a course that is virtual reality-based.

When considering the design for a course that consists of virtual-reality experiences, such as the United States Air Force Academy's Aviation 100 (AV100) course, it is reasonable to give the technology as participant its own pedagogical consideration. Technology, according to Girvan (2018), "needs to take into account the activities and practices when using it, as well as the social arrangements and organizational forms surrounding its use" (p. 1088). Is it possible to separate the technology from the pedagogy? No, not when the technology is participating in the learner's experience.

Technology is generally viewed as a pedagogical support tool and thus is not considered a participant that directly interacts with users and changes the way the user constructs knowledge. Creating objectives, learning activities, assignments, and assessments for learners are standard fare in course design work, but what considerations are given to the technology? Technology as participant is not meant to anthropomorphize the technology. However, in the case of virtual reality, it is critical to identify the purpose and the role that VR technology plays within the course. Instructional designers and course authors should consider the application of a procedural model such as ADDIE to a technology treated as a participant in their course design. ADDIE can provide the necessary boundaries and guidance that support the design of effective and efficient courses.

AVIATION 100

In a desire to give the USAFA cadets more opportunities to experience flying, and to create a larger, more informed diverse pool of graduates who are prepared to excel in rated career fields, the Airmanship Next program was launched in the fall of 2018. One objective of the program was to "reach cadets who may have been excluded in the past due to scheduling conflicts" (Spradlin, 2019). Losey (2019) reported that cadets interested in becoming pilots can use a combination of virtual reality and artificial intelligence to learn flying skills.

"Using VR does not replace flying time in an actual airplane but augments it so students have more time to hone their knowledge and maneuvers" (Losey, 2019, para 1).

Aviation 100, (AV100 - Introduction to Powered Flight Operations) is a key part of Airmanship Next. The course has nine single-period (53 minutes) classes in a virtual reality lab housed at the United States Air Force Academy. This course introduces cadets to the fundamentals of aircraft control in a single-engine aircraft. The virtual reality lab provides cadets a low-stress, hands-on, high-tech environment in which they gain knowledge and experience that may help them decide if a career in aviation is right for them. AV100 uses readings, video demonstrations, and VR to introduce the fundamentals of aircraft control, aerodynamics, airmanship, and airmindedness. Participating in this course is voluntary, and no course credit or academic grade is awarded for course completion. The stated learning objectives for AV100 are:

- Demonstrate the knowledge and skills required for basic aircraft control in a single-seat, single-engine aircraft.
- Using the Airmanship Experience Model, describe the aviation-related opportunities at USAFA and submit preferences for future enrollment consideration.
- List from memory the four rated career fields: Air Battle Manager [ABM], Remote Pilot Aircraft [RPA], Combat Systems Officer [CSO], Pilot.
- Using AFI 36–2605, *Air Force Military Personnel Testing System*, explain the Air Force Officer Qualifying Test (AFOQT) and Pilot Candidate Selector Method (PCSM) eligibility requirements for these career fields (Aviation 100 Syllabus, March 2020).

The course consists of online training modules or tutorials (with self-check quizzes) specifically developed for the Air Force Academy. These computer-based tutorials are completed independently by cadets and before class begins. Class time starts with a short introduction to relevant content, including what students will be practicing in class. Once this overview is completed, cadets are ready to practice flying. The virtual reality flying environment is proprietary software purchased for use by the Air Force Academy and is a fully immersive system. According to Mandal (2013), in a fully immersive system the learner is "immersed in a computer generated world with the help of Head Mounted Display (HMD) that supports a stereoscopic view of the scene according to the user's position and orientation. These systems may be enhanced by audio, haptic and sensory interfaces" (p. 307). Fully immersive systems depict a virtual world presented in full scale, and they relate properly to the size of human beings. These systems use special hardware where learners are isolated from the physical world outside, thus fully engrossed in the virtual environment. The learner has a stereoscopic view of the virtual world generated according to the user's head position and orientation (Mandal, 2013).

VR AND THE ADDIE MODEL

When designing a course that employs immersive virtual reality, it is important to consider key features of virtual reality systems such as those put forth by Cipresso et al. (2018) and Mutterlein (2018). Cipresso et al. (2018) found immersion perception to be present in an environment and interaction with that environment to be common features among many descriptions of VR. When considering the immersion characteristic of VR, does the VR experience cause the learner to disconnect from their awareness of time while offering an experience of being there? Does the VR experience provide interactivity such that it participates with and responds to the learner in an authentic, engaging manner?

The perception of being present refers to the learner feeling a sense of belonging or being in the virtual environment. Immersive virtual reality provides "a complex psychological feeling of being there in VR that involves the sensation and perception of physical presence, as well as the possibility to interact and react as in the real world" (Cipresso et al., 2018, p. 3). The authors describe immersion as a "complete simulated experience due to the support of several sensory outputs [*sic*] devices" [e.g., head-mounted displays] (p. 2). As such, does the VR experience provide an authentic representation that induces a feeling of physically being in the virtual environment? Is the learner participating with virtual reality at a cognitive, emotional, and physical level?

Virtual reality interaction provides users with the same feeling as the real world through feedback. Sutcliffe and Gault (2004) stated that intuitive interaction should approach the users' expectations of interaction in the real world as far as possible, something they labeled natural engagement (p. 833). Natural or intuitive interaction is a strong motivator for engagement (Huang, Rauch, & Liaw, 2010). For example, the interactions with the virtual reality environment should be the same as the interactions the learner would encounter in the real world: interactions that are natural.

Each phase of the ADDIE model could be considered and informed by one or more of the three VR characteristics when designing a VR course. In the *analyze* phase the learning needs, tasks, and audience for immersive VR are identified. During this phase, course designers and instructors should be mindful of the immersion aspect of VR and the amount of senses stimulated by the VR experience. Preliminary instructional design questions to consider during this phase are:

- What physical, cognitive, and emotional constraints does a simulated, immersive environment place on the learner?
- What considerations are needed regarding immersion and interaction during the task analysis performed during this phase?
- How can instructors or course designers prepare the learner, based on learner characteristics, for an immersive VR experience? For example, should they be warned about simulator sickness? (a sensorial conflict between virtual and real stimuli, especially between visual feedback indicating motion and kinesthetic cuing).

(Alexander, Westhoven, & Conradi, 2016, p. 27)

The *design* phase of an immersive VR course or lesson necessitates conceiving the learning objectives, learning strategies, aligned learning activities, interactions, and assessments. Sequencing of the content is also a consideration in this phase. During the design phase, all three common features of VR should be considered: immersion, perception to be present, and interaction with that environment. When planning for VR instruction and engagement in the *design* phase, important questions are:

- Do the learning objectives clearly articulate the desired outcomes from a virtual reality-based lesson or course?
- Do the objectives incorporate the key characteristics of VR, which may enrich the learning as attention is focused on the complex psychological feeling of being there (perception of being present)?
- Should there be an objective that focuses on the congruency of the learner's VR experience with their reality expectations (i.e., the simulated environment is rich enough that the learner feels immersed and unaware they are in a simulated situation)?
- Is the lesson or course structured such that tasks and activities are explained or demonstrated before learners enter the VR environment?
- Do the activities and tasks to be performed in the VR environment allow for meaningful interaction that replicates what the learner would do in the real world?
- What are the tasks that need to be executed successfully to virtually fly?

- How will learners be assessed on their proficiencies regarding flying in a virtual environment?
- What instructional strategies are effective for preparing students to learn and work in a virtual environment?

During the *design* phase, instructors and course designers should purposefully map virtual tasks and learning experiences not only to objectives but also to real-world activities. For example, the primary objective for the AV100 course was broad (demonstrate the knowledge and skills required for basic aircraft control in a single-seat, single-engine aircraft) and there were no measurable or observable lesson objectives specified. To improve upon this design, specific skills and skill levels should be articulated and mapped to the real-life activities students perform while in the virtual flying environment. This mapping would make transparent the path to achieving the broader course objective. According to Cipresso et al. (2018), the higher the degree of reality of interactions within the virtual environment, the more enhanced is the VR experience resulting in the perception of a real experience.

When considering learning objectives during the design phase that attend to the perceptions of being present and immersed in the virtual environment, course designers and instructors may draw from Simpson's (1966) psycho-motor domain taxonomy. This taxonomy offers suggestions for measuring and observing sensory cues to guide motor activities, manipulation, responses, readiness to act, and adaptation. For example, what is the learner's visual sensitivity to cues found in the Cessna's virtual control panel regarding color, spatial relations, motion, light, or shade?

The *development* phase is when content, learning activities, and assessments are created. This is the process of authoring and producing the materials conceived in the analyze and design phases. The purpose of this phase is to generate the instructional strategies, lesson materials, assignments, and assessments. During development, as in the design phase, attention should be paid to the interactions occurring within the virtual environment. In the context of the AV100 course, learner interactions include reading and understanding performance instruments, flying straight and level, and performing level turns. These pilot training activities provide meaningful, authentic interactions. The content created in the development phase should have appropriate sequencing and scaffolding of tasks to minimize cognitive load and to replicate the steps one would follow when preparing to fly a single-engine plane. Developing materials for VR-based learning is generally informed by plans detailed in the design phase; however, there are recurrent iterations between the two phases as development progresses. Other questions to consider during the development phase are:

- Are there or should there be introductory materials or content that will help learners get started with the VR environment and understand the framework for the course?
- What instructions and explanations are necessary for students to safely begin using the VR equipment (e.g., how to position and wear the head-mounted display correctly)?
- If a student experiences simulation sickness, are alternative activities planned until the student acclimates or adapts to the simulated environment?

The *implement* phase is the process of launching the course in context (plans into action). This phase refers to the actual delivery of the instruction that was created in the *development* phase. The purpose of this phase is the effective and efficient delivery of instruction. This rollout phase needs to promote the students' understanding of the material, to support the students' mastery of objectives, and to ensure the students' knowledge and skills are transferable to the workplace. In the case of virtual reality flying lessons, preflight materials, such as introductory content, step-by-step getting started instructions, and clearly identified tasks to be performed need to be presented before learners situate themselves in the VR cockpit.

The *evaluate* phase is the process of determining the adequacy of the instruction, including the materials presented, learning activities and tasks, and assessments. In other words, this phase measures the effectiveness and efficiency of the instruction. Richey et al. (2011) offered that this phase is a "try-out of courseware with learner population, diagnosis of learning and courseware failures" and making necessary revisions based on the findings (p. 21). In the VR environment, it is important not only to ask for student feedback about the experience but to also ask about their perception of being present, immersed, and interactive within that environment. When evaluating the instruction and overall virtual reality experience, design questions to consider are:

- How well did learners perform against the stated learning objectives? For example, was the learner able to perform VR flying maneuvers as specified by lesson objectives?
- How did learners rate (or describe) their perception of being present in a virtual cockpit and feeling like they were actually piloting the plane? Did they perceive their interactions as real?

- Did the classroom-based instructional materials and computer-based tutorials increase their knowledge and confidence levels before beginning virtual reality flying tasks?
- Was the course organized (appropriately scaffolded) in a manner that helped them fly virtually?

The ADDIE model, as a procedural and iterative model for planning, developing, and implementing a course for immersive VR, offers critical guidance to course design. Applying this model, while considering key characteristics of a virtual reality environment, produces a VR-focused framework from which to design a course or lessons and from which to view virtual reality as a participant. The ADDIE model informs the design process by supporting a more pedagogically enriched learning experience.

APPLYING THE FRAMEWORK

To apply this framework along with the key characteristics of a virtual reality environment, the first lesson of the AV100 course, along with a primary objective for the course, will be examined in this section, and a lesson redesign will be proposed. The primary objective for this course, broadly stated, is: At the completion of this course, students will be able to: Demonstrate the knowledge and skills required for basic aircraft control in a single-seat, single-engine aircraft.

This objective is supported by nine classroom-based lessons and seven computer-based training modules or tutorials which are completed before each class lesson. Lesson one of the computer-based tutorials starts with aircraft familiarization, followed by level flight, straight flight, and then a combination of level and straight flight explanations. Within this computer-based tutorial are short readings, a series of videos that offer overviews and introductory information designed for individuals with little or no piloting experience. The videos in the tutorials for lesson one show simulated flying using the Cessna and include realistic sounds. These videos resemble the simulations one might see in video games. The lesson concludes with a short quiz that students can take multiple times. Currently, the lessons in the computer-based tutorials and the classroom preflight briefs (short lecture accompanied by PowerPoint slides) have no stated objectives. Instead, each presents topics that students will be learning about and practicing in virtual reality.

Applying the *analyze* phase of the ADDIE model to the first lesson (classroom activities and the computer-based tutorial) means understanding that the student participant is a novice who seeks to learn more about flying as a potential Air Force career. By design, the course and the lessons offer a low-stress approach to learning about flying and experiencing flying in virtual reality. Considering the characteristic of immersion in this example, means considering the constraints placed on the novice learner and the types of interaction being considered. For example, class scheduling, ability to log into the computer-based tutorials, malfunctioning VR equipment, and simulator sickness may constrain the learner from a fluid, immersive experience or even from getting started.

Revising lesson one during the *design* and *development* phases involves reworking the learning objectives, activities, and assessments. For AV100, the primary objective is broken down into more detailed sub-objectives that support the knowledge and skills learners are to acquire during lesson one. For example, at the completion of classroom-based lesson one, students should be able to:

- Log into the computer-based tutorial and locate the readings, videos, and quizzes for lesson one.
- Identify the parts of the joystick (elevator trim, pause button, seat management switch, heading bug, paddle switch parking brake).
- Demonstrate the correct use of the brake pedals and seat adjustment.
- Correctly position, adjust, and secure the head-mounted display.
- Start the simulator and begin practicing level flight.

Additionally, the assigned tasks and assessment for successfully completing this module should align with the objectives. These serve as precursors to starting the VR software in the lab that will allow students to begin practicing level flight and straight flight, which they learned about in the computer-based tutorial. During the *design* and *development* phases, learning objectives and activities need to incorporate the key features of VR, which may enhance the learning when attention is focused on the complex psychological feeling of being there and flying in the virtual environment. The perception of being present and performing tasks (interacting) in the virtual environment can be observed and focused on with psychomotor objectives. Verbs such as calibrates, differentiates by touch, operates, guided by sensory cues, reacts can be used to inform psychomotor objectives. For example, at the completion of this lesson, students should be able to fly the Cessna straight and level using sight, sound, and tactile responses from the simulator. To measure the perception of being there, an objective might be, at the completion of this lesson, students should be able to describe their feelings of immersion while flying.

The *implementation* of lesson one provides an opportunity to investigate whether including aspects of the three key characteristics of VR supported an enhanced learning experience and created a sense that the technology was acting as a participant. Implementation leads into the *evaluation* of the completed lesson. Here, formative and summative assessment of student learning takes place, as well as questions about the effectiveness of the redesigned lesson. From a course design perspective, questions to be considered include:

- Did inclusion of the key VR characteristics in the lesson result in a more immersive perception of presence and a more interactive learning experience?
- Did inclusion of the key characteristics support consideration of VR as a technology participant?

This brief example and accompanying instructional design questions elucidate the concept of integrating key features of VR into the design of an immersive virtual reality course. The point is to demonstrate that fundamental features of virtual reality should be attended to in course and lesson design because immersive VR can act as a technology participant in student learning. Learners interact with the virtual environment, and that environment responds to the interactions of the learner. The virtual environment can be programmed to initiate interaction and provoke feelings, responses, and actions from the learner.

By exploring the application of the ADDIE process model, informed by immersion, perception to be present, and interaction, we can begin contemplation of virtual reality as a technology participant. But as Radianti et al. insightfully pointed out (2020), "For the inclusion of VR in curricula, much more work is needed on the role of the design elements and the design of learning contents for VR" (p. 23). Indeed, the questions and ideas presented in this chapter necessitate further investigation, application, and evaluation when immersive virtual reality plays a key role in a course. These questions and ideas offer practitioners a starting point and a way forward when considering VR as a technology participant throughout the instructional design process.

The views expressed in Chapter 8 are those of the author and do not necessarily reflect the official policy or position of the United States Air Force Academy, the Air Force, the Department of Defense or the USAFA Government. PA#: USAFA-DF-2020–269

REFERENCES

Alexander, T., Westhoven, M., & Conradi, J. (2016). Virtual environments for competency-oriented education and training. In J. Kantola, T. Barath, S. Nazir, & T. Andre (Eds.), *Advances in human factors, business management, training and education: Advances in intelligent systems and computing* (pp. 23–29). *Proceedings of the AHFE 2016 International Conference on Human Factors*. Business Management and Society, Walt Disney World®, Florida, July 27–31, 2016. https://doi.org/10.1007/978-3-319-42070-7_3

Bloom, B. S., Englehart, M. D., Furst, E. J., Hill, W. H., & Krathwohl, D. R. (1956). *The taxonomy of educational objectives, handbook I: The Cognitive domain*. New York: David McKay Co., Inc.

Branch, R. M., & Dousay, T. A. (2015). *Survey of instructional development models* (5th ed.). Association for Educational Communications and Technology. Retrieved from https://aect.org/docs/SurveyofInstructionalDesignModels.pdf?pdf=SurveyofInstructionalDesignModels

Branch, R. M., & Kopcha, T. J. (2014). Instructional design models. In J. Spector, M. Merrill, J. Elen, & M. Bishop (Eds.), *Handbook of research on educational communications and technology* (pp. 77–87). New York, NY: Springer.

Brey, P. (2014). Virtual reality and computer simulation. In R. L. Sandler (Ed.), *Ethics and emerging technologies*. London, UK: Palgrave Macmillan. https://doi.org/10.1057/9781137349088_21

Cipresso, P., Giglioli, I. A. C., Raya, M. A., & Riva, G. (2018). The past, present, and future of virtual and augmented reality research: A network and cluster analysis of the literature. *Frontiers in Psychology*, *9*(2086), 1–20. https://doi.org/10.3389/fpsyg.2018.02086

Coburn, J. Q., Freeman, I., & Salmon, J. L. (2017, July 18). A review of the capabilities of current low-cost virtual reality technology and its potential to enhance the design process. *Journal of Computing and Information Science in Engineering*, *17*(3). https://doi.org/10.1115/1.4036921

Ellis, C. (2019). *Are VR flight simulators the future of pilot training*? Air Charter Service. Retrieved August 22, 2020, from www.aircharterservice.com/about-us/news-features/blog/are-vr-flight-simulators-the-future-of-pilot-training

Fowler, C. (2015). Virtual reality and learning: Where is the pedagogy? *British Journal of Educational Technology*, *46*(2), 412–422. https://doi.org/10.1111/bjet.12135

Franchi, J. (1994). Virtual reality: An overview. *Tech Trends*, 23–26.

Franklin Institute. (n.d.). *History of virtual reality*. Retrieved June 22, 2020, from www.fi.edu/virtual-reality/history-of-virtual-reality

Girvan, C. (2018). What is a virtual world? Definition and classification. *Educational Technology Research & Development*, *66*, 1087–1100. https://doi.org/10.1007/s11423-018-9577-y

Gustafson, K. L., & Branch, R. M. (2002). *Survey of instructional development models* (4th ed.). (ERIC Document Reproduction Service No. ED 477517). Retrieved from https://eric.ed.gov/?id=ED477517.

Hillman, D. C. A., Willis, D. J., & Gunawardena, C. N. (1994). Learner-interface interaction in distance education: An extension of contemporary models and strategies for practitioners. *American Journal of Distance Education*, *8*(2), 30–42. https://doi.org/10.1080/08923649409526853

Huang, H., Rauch, U., & Liaw, S. (2010). Investigating learners' attitudes toward virtual reality learning environments: Based on a constructivist approach. *Computers & Education, 55*(3), 1171–1182. https://doi.org/10.1016/j.compedu.2010.05.014

Interaction Design Foundation. (n.d.). *Virtual reality*. Retrieved from www.interaction-design.org/literature/topics/virtual-reality

Kjeldskov, J. (2001). Combining interaction techniques and display types for virtual reality. In *Proceedings of OzCHI 2001:Annual conference of the Australian computer-human interaction special interest group* (pp. 77–83). Edith Cowan University Press.

Lee, E. A., & Wong, K.W. (2008). A review of using virtual reality for learning. In Z. Pan, A.D. Cheok, W. Müller,& A. El Rhalibi (Eds.), *Transactions on edutainment I:Lecture notes in computer science* (pp. 231–241). Springer. https://doi.org/10.1007/978-3-540-69744-2_18

Lee, J.,& Jang, S. (2014). A methodological framework for instructional design model development: Critical dimensions and synthesized procedures. *Education Technology Research and Development,62*, 743–765. https://doi.org/10.1007/s11423-014-9352-7

Losey, S. (2018). The Air Force is revolutionizing the way airmen learn to be aviators. *AirForceTimes*. Retrieved from www.airforcetimes.com/news/your-air-force/2018/09/30/the-air-force-is-revolutionizing-the-way-airmen-learn-to-be-aviators/

Losey, S. (2019). Academy brings VR pilot training to cadets.*AirForceTimes*. Retrieved from www.airforcetimes.com/news/your-air-force/2019/10/08/academy-brings-vr-pilot-training-to-cadets/

Losey, S. (2020). Here's where the Air Force's pilot shortfall is the worst. *AirForceTimes*. Retrieved from www.airforcetimes.com/news/your-air-force/2020/07/07/heres-where-the-air-forces-pilot-shortfall-is-the-worst/

Lowood, H. E. (2020). Virtual reality. *Britannica*. Retrieved from www.britannica.com/technology/virtual-reality

Mandal, S. (2013). Brief introduction of virtual reality & its challenges. *International Journal of Scientific & Engineering Research,4*(4), 304–309.

Martin-Gutierrez, J., Mora, C. E., Anorbe-Diaz, B.,& Gonzalez-Marrero, A. (2017). Virtual technologies trends in education. *EURASIA Journal of Mathematics Science and Technology Education, 13*(2), 469–486. https://doi.org/10.12973/eurasia.2017.00626a

Merchant, Z. H. (2012). *The impact of virtual reality-based learning environment design features on students' academic achievements*[Doctoral Dissertation], Texas A&M University. Retrieved electronically from http://hdl.handle.net/1969.1/148077

Merriam-Webster. (n.d.). Participant. In *Merriam-Webster.com dictionary*.Retrieved from www.merriam-webster.com/dictionary/participant

Molenda, M. (2003). In search of the elusive ADDIE model. *Performance Improvement,45*(5), 34–36. Retrieved May 12, 2020, from https://writertech.com/files/MolendaADDIEModelOriginsUnknown.pdf

Mutterlein, J. (2018). The three pillars of virtual reality? Investigating the roles of immersion, presence, and interactivity. In *Proceedings of the 51st Hawaii international conference on system sciences*. Retrieved from https://scholarspace.manoa.hawaii.edu/bitstream/10125/50061/paper0174.pdf

Oden, K. (2013). Augmenting instructional design with state-based assessment. In D.D. Schmorrow & C.M. Fidopiastis (Eds.), *Foundations of augmented cognition:Lecture notes in computer science* (pp. 70–79). Springer. https://doi.org/10.1007/978-3-642-39454-6_8

Radianti, J., Majchrzak, T. M., Fromm, J., & Wohlgenannt, I. (2020). A systematic review of immersive virtual reality applications for higher education: Design elements, lessons learned, and research agenda. *Computers & Education, 147*,1–29. https://doi.org/10.1016/j.compedu.2019.103778

Reiser, R.A. (2001). A history of instructional design and technology, part II: A history of instructional design. *Educational Technology Research and Development, 49*(2),57–67. ERIC Document Reproduction Service No. EJ 629 874.

Richey, R., Klein, J., &Tracey, M. (2011). *The instructional design knowledge base.* Routledge.

Simpson, E. (1966). *The classification of educational objectives, psychomotor domain.* Eric doc 010 368 010. Retrieved from https://files.eric.ed.gov/fulltext/ED010368.pdf

Spradlin, J. (2019). *Air Force academy launches new airmanship next program.* Retrieved from www.usafa.af.mil/News/Article/1982775/air-force-academy-launches-new-airmanship-next-program/

Sutcliffe, A.,& Gault, B. (2004). Heuristic evaluation of virtual reality applications. *Interacting with Computers, 16*(4), 831–849. https://doi.org/10.1016/j.intcom.2004.05.001

Virtual Reality Society. (2017). *What is virtual reality*? Retrieved from www.vrs.org.uk/virtual-reality/what-is-virtual-reality.html

Voices of VR Podcast. (2015). *#245:50 years of VR with Tom Furness: The super cockpit, virtual retinal display, HIT lab, & virtual world society.* Retrieved July 21, 2020, from http://voicesofvr.com/245-50-years-of-vr-with-tom-furness-the-super-cockpit-virtual-retinal-display-hit-lab-virtual-world-society/

CHAPTER 9

Learning Technology in the Secondary Classroom

Chastity Rohan and Corey Duzan

TECHNOLOGY IN THE SECONDARY CLASSROOM

March 2020 began a new era for everyone throughout the world due to the COVID-19 pandemic. The thread of society and culture was drastically changed in how people interacted with one another in every aspect of their typical daily lives. The interaction that people had with those around them was buffered through the use of materials like acrylic fiber, if it was a physical interaction, or through video. The education system and classrooms were obviously not immune to these changes and guidelines from government officials. Educators and administrators had to quickly reformulate how they were going to deliver materials and instruction in the most efficient and safe way as possible. Like many businesses and companies, schools and universities began to implement technology that could provide live online learning or pre-recorded lessons to students. Many traditional teachers had to learn and adopt methods of teaching that they had never used or experienced before. While this scenario was not ideal and proved to be challenging, it forced all educational professionals to embrace technological tools that replicated and resembled traditional practices but used a different vehicle or platform. This chapter highlights the successes and struggles of two highly technical educators who taught engineering, technology, and robotics for years prior to the pandemic. Their experiences reveal the impact that virtual and hybrid learning has had on technology-efficient educators working in a K–12 world that was not prepared for full online immersion. The discussions that ensue can provide insight into new ways technology can be used to promote positive interactions among teachers and learners and the role technology can play in the future of K–12 education.

DOI: 10.4324/9781003089704-13

During the initial stages of the pandemic, many educators were able to find success through trial and error with new forms of content delivery, but at the end of the modified school year, many teachers would agree that this new look of education was not the gold standard that education should take while moving forward. Even though the lessons learned while implementing technology were valuable, successful face-to-face teaching and learning environments cannot be replaced with digital classrooms or technology alone. For many students, they need the structure of the classroom and the encouragement from an adult. For some students who were not self-motivated or who did not have a positive learning environment at home, a complete online learning experience was challenging. Once those students were back in the classroom, they were able to connect with their teachers and classmates.

Face-to-face teaching and learning environments can be enhanced with digital and technological tools to create an environment that is more balanced and wholesome to meet the needs of all stakeholders. Prior to the pandemic, students and teachers spent hours working face-to-face with each other, and technology was mostly a tool in the classroom. Recently, the interaction between teachers and students has changed as technology has become the only means of communication. Many students had not previously been taught how to advocate for themselves via online learning formats. Students were used to raising their hand in class to ask for help, but getting on a Google Meet during open office hours or tutoring time was a foreign and intimidating concept. Once the students grasped the concepts, they started improving. As teachers became more comfortable with the available technology tools, they were able to try to replicate some of the normal classroom interactions. For example, using videoconferencing software to create breakout groups where students can work together in smaller settings and check in with each other on their learning, mimics traditional classroom interactions. Creating a comfortable and familiar learning environment, despite the restrictions of virtual learning, can help students find success regardless of whether they're using in-person or virtual learning.

As professional educators, we can use a system of traditional practices and technology to achieve goals in four scenarios: to help teachers teach students, students teach students, parents teach students, and teachers teach teachers. All four of these scenarios recognize the student as the direct or indirect party for receiving instruction or experiences to help them learn and achieve. The formula that teachers use to achieve these goals can be quite complex because of the system variables that they choose to implement and considering the vast array of traditional teaching strategies and technology that have been created over time.

Often you will hear teachers refer to their toolbox of resources for teaching that include strategies of how to build relationships with students, how to manage a classroom, how to develop a classroom culture, and how to utilize technology in the classroom. Many of the aspects that contribute to a comprehensive classroom that were previously mentioned require the presence of the human element found within a physical teaching/learning environment. What the pandemic has taught us as educators is that once teachers go back to physical classrooms, the way they teach cannot be the same as it was prior to the COVID-19 pandemic. We have seen the benefits of technology, and we have witnessed the positive and negative impacts technology has on communication and interaction. Therefore, it is important to learn from this experience and accept and adapt to new teaching standards where technology is commonplace among various interactions.

Students in a physical classroom learn from each other when teachers use collaborative learning strategies. Students share in the work and create discourse among each other, and those interactions can lead to deeper, more meaningful learning. Rusli, Degeng, Setyosari, and Sulton (2020) state that these methods increase students' learning and their participation in lectures. While teachers can attempt to replace the in-person interactions using technology, they can never fully deliver the same effects of in-person interactions through the use of technology alone. Instead, teachers can shore up traditional methods used to achieve these goals with new methods rooted in technology and come away as a classroom that incorporates technology into myriad facets of interactions to promote learner engagement and critical thinking.

Educators Using Technology to Teach Students

Educators, particularly those teaching technology classes where the focus of the class is on learning new technologies with a focus on engineering, have seen the benefits of teaching software and hardware to students. These technology classes require the students to not just attain knowledge but to apply that knowledge. Students apply that new knowledge to new situations, demonstrating complex analytical thinking. In many of these technology classrooms, there is collaboration among students where they interact and learn from each other. The curriculum requires an essential use of different software, for example CAD software, programming software, and circuitry design software, to build a foundation for students. For example, in engineering, software platforms can span an array of disciplines, including civil, electrical, mechanical, and industrial. Autodesk Inventor, a 3D modeling software, can be used to design anything from a new pencil sharpener to a valve replacement for a human heart. A similar software is Autodesk Revit, which is a 3D modeling software for architecture and site planning. Students can use various software applications to design different projects and then have the opportunity to use 3D printers, laser engravers, and CNC machines to make those designs come to life. As students learn to design in these software applications, they interact with the technology in real and applicable ways.

Using technology for the purpose of building learner-to-technology interaction is a way to design curriculum aimed at allowing students to use technology and apply what they have learned. For example, students can use Multisim, software used to design electrical circuits, to test out ideas and see if they work before building a circuit on a breadboard. Students are able to take their knowledge of circuit design and apply it within the software to test their design for functionality. In a similar fashion to 3D printing, students can utilize these designs to create prototypes when paired with programmable logic controllers (PLC) and breadboards. Teachers can also use these tools to have a pre-setup circuit where students can perform different tasks and come to conclusions on what the circuit is designed to do or how it works. Using the software first to test their ideas saves them time and makes the students accountable for their learning. If the circuit or prototype doesn't work, then the students have to figure out what went wrong. This type of interaction with technology provides students with immediate feedback, and they are able to troubleshoot and learn from issues that arise. As students troubleshoot, they recognize errors, which leads to deeper understanding. Without these software and hardware elements, teaching technological concepts would not lead to learner growth and learner engagement. If the students did not have the software and hardware elements, they would just be learning about technology and would not be able to describe how the circuit works or be able to fix a problem in real life. Planning curriculum according to learner-to-technology interaction encourages learning in a real, tactile fashion, enabling both long-term retention and an engaging curriculum.

Expanding Learner-to-Technology Interaction

Even though the previously mentioned examples are heavily based in engineering, the software discussed can also be used to help other classrooms. For instance, a biomedical sciences class could have a project where the students need to create a medical device. The biomedical students can create the medical device on the 3D software and then 3D print the prototype. Students find value in the interaction, especially when it is related to solving a real-world problem.

Video lessons can be used as a way to accommodate students who need additional time with content or material. Students can actually interact with video by pausing, replaying, and fast-forwarding information. For some students who speak English as their second language or are hearing impaired, closed captioning can be a tool to help them better understand the teacher's notes.

Teachers can also use these types of videos for flipped classrooms. A flipped classroom is when the student watches the video and takes notes (lecture) for homework, and then class time is used for answering questions and developing students' deeper understanding. According to Altemueller and Lindquist (2017), a flipped classroom showed benefits for students such as increased motivation and engagement. Students not only interact with the video, but they interact with the content when they apply their learning in class. Flipped classroom practices allow teachers and students to utilize the majority of their classroom time for class engagement, investigation, and troubleshooting rather than just theory and concept analysis. This is another way teachers can differentiate their instruction, which is important to maximizing students' learning.

Video interaction can also be used as an instructional tool when a physical classroom is not an option. Teachers can use screen-capturing software to demonstrate how to make a part on a program like Autodesk Inventor, because there are typically many steps that can get complicated. If students have access to the video, they can interact with the tutorial and then use class time to work through an idea at their own pace.

The use of an online learning management system became crucial during the Non-Traditional Instruction (NTI) days. The students were used to using it in regular classrooms to turn in assignments, but it now became a communication hub. As noted by Capone, Donizzetti, and Petrillo (2018), students need a sense of belonging in the classroom and to feel part of a community. Google Classroom gave teachers and students that opportunity to interact with each other in discussion boards where students could comment back and forth on their thoughts or their work and receive input from the teacher. In some classrooms, having this in place before the pandemic, made the transition to online learning easier for students. According to Capone et al., students who have positive relationships with their teachers will interact with others as well as engage in their learning. Some students who did not do all of their classwork would at least do their weekly survey to keep in touch. Kids need to know teachers care about them even if they are utilizing technology to reach out to them.

Giving feedback to students can be an obstacle and is an important part of the interaction/communication piece of educating students. Learning Management Systems (LMS) like Canvas and Google Classroom can help educators provide timely feedback with which students can interact and improve. Through LMSs, discussion boards can be used to distribute questions that may require a learner-to-learner debate. Students can see each other's answers and comment back and forth. This can lead to great discussion where students will even ask each other deeper questions and defend their ideas with excellent arguments. Student discourse can lead to deeper understanding of the content, and discussion boards give students that opportunity when face-to-face conversations are no longer available.

Creating multiple versions of a test takes time, but teachers can use learning management systems to help create and maintain multiple versions. Having different versions of a test in math is a common practice among math teachers, where numbers are changed but the basic idea of the question is not. The setup takes just a little longer than typing up a test by hand but in certain LMSs teachers can even set up formulas for math where it will change the number values so each student gets a different question with different answers. The time it takes to set this up is worth it for teachers who teach the same course multiple times. Teachers can also reorder the questions and set up quiz questions based on a specific learning target and tell the system to pull one question from that set. Students can see their scores immediately, which is a form of instant feedback that students can use to inform their learning.

Using an LMS to teach and assess students helps students to start taking ownership of their own learning. Peranginangin, Saragih, and Siagian (2019) assert that self-efficacy is important to student learning outcomes because it is based on their confidence in their ability to learn the material. Peranginangin et al. also mention that students sometimes are afraid to present in a classroom; using an LMS system gives them the opportunity to get feedback without judgment from peers. Teachers can set up rubrics in the systems where students can interact with the rubric and determine their score before submitting an assignment. This also encourages students to recognize what assignments they need to improve on.

In the classroom, students can use peer-to-peer interaction as a way of learning. Using cooperative learning strategies in a traditional classroom promotes face-to-face learning, and this is a great teaching strategy that can be difficult to replicate online, but through the use of videoconferencing and Google Documents, students can still interact with each other and achieve similar goals. By giving feedback in a program like a Google Document, students engage in peer-to-peer interaction through technology and use critical thinking skills to improve each other's and their own learning. This instant feedback in electronic form lets students reflect on their learning at a more efficient rate.

Addressing Peer-to-Peer Communication Problems

According to van Laar, van Deursen, van Dijk, and de Haan (2020), communication and collaboration are two of the essential skills for 21st century learning. Using technology to enhance this form of interaction is a challenge educators must undertake on a daily basis during the pandemic as they navigate their way through online and hybrid learning. But this form of interaction does not begin and end with the classroom; in our ever-changing world that tends to rely on technology more and more, we have to teach students not only how to interact in person but also virtually.

To exemplify students overcoming obstacles to engage in peer-to-peer interaction, Project Lead The Way (PLTW) created a problem called the virtual project where students work together in teams in order to solve a problem. PLTW teachers collaborated over a two-week period using Google Drive to share information back and forth between two teams. Like any good project, there were hours of planning spent ahead of time to think about which students we would pair up and how we would address issues; such issues would include anything from how students would communicate to what we would do if students were being inappropriate with their messaging.

Students would have to interact with each other through different means of communication. Once the project was opened, the students were excited to "meet" their teammates. Skype was used to project both classrooms so students could interact with each other. The students were used to using things like FaceTime and other social media platforms, so they quickly took it upon themselves to find new ways to interact. PLTW teachers were not expecting students to take ownership of their interactions, but it shows that when communication is important, students can find ways around roadblocks because they live in a time where there are a plethora of communication tools, and the value of peer-to-peer interaction is something that students need. As students were able to determine what communication outlet worked best for their team, they were learning how to problem solve and also how to collaborate with others. Students took ownership of the project, assigned roles, built Gantt Charts (schedules), and created 3D objects. Teachers set the ground rules and gave students the resources; from there, students took ownership. Students collaborated in a team format that was very similar to a lot of work cultures today. The students had to use critical thinking and creativity to solve the problem given to them. As students mastered 3D software to create the projects and became proficient with editing software like Google Documents, they also honed technology literacy skills and established the importance of peer-to-peer interaction.

Similar to video recordings, LMS enhancements such as community groups, chat, blogs, and video sharing give students the ability to use materials and guidance from their peers to overcome challenges not typically present in a physical classroom. Video Chat technology like Zoom, Skype, Google Hangouts, and Microsoft Teams gives teachers and students the tools for teacher-to-learner and learner-to-learner interactions. Using online resources to enhance interaction not only teaches students the designed curriculum but also immerses them in the importance interaction plays in education and the real world. This type of learning is crucial to today's ideology of instant gratification. Many students want to know right away how they are doing, and technology provides them that opportunity.

As educators, it is understandable to sometimes feel that technology is replacing the need for a real-life teacher, but if the pandemic and virtual learning has taught us anything, it is that technology is not replacing teachers. Technology is enhancing teachers' curriculum and opening doors to new ways of interaction, and in many cases, technology allows for students to interact with their own learning, a feat that is sometimes not attainable in in-person classes.

Students Using Technology to Teach Students

For the past decade we have seen a new trend in education that acknowledges that all stakeholders make up an education system, not just teachers and students. Stakeholders can include, but are not limited to, teachers, students, parents, school support staff, community members, businesses, and school board members. A valuable and resourceful subgroup found within this group are the students themselves and the role they play in their own education and the education of their peers. When the idea of students teaching students first gained traction in education, it was approached with cautious optimism (Rusli et al., 2020). Most traditional methods in education were often mapped out with rigid guidelines and boundaries that placed the teacher in a role to send out information and the student to receive the information (Hirsch, 2011). In many past educational settings, history classes were more geared toward questions regarding who, what, and when and emphasizing less about the why. Business classes at one time were geared more toward business models and systems instead of marketing to the consumer. Later, when learner-to-learner strategies were implemented, many teachers saw students using a language and approach that were unique and beneficial to them and their classmates. Students were given an opportunity to take on a role that instilled purpose and a sense of belonging in the classroom. The classroom was no longer viewed as just as a classroom, it was now their classroom.

New technology has been invented that presents innovative methods for learner-to-learner interaction, where students teach students. A good example of this is when students are learning software like CAD programs. The traditional approach of teaching CAD software would see the teacher placed in front of a CAD workstation that would be projected onto a screen. The teacher would be going step-by-step to complete an exercise with the students following along. This method took a considerable amount of time due to student comprehension, lack of teacher monitoring, and student questioning. While this approach could still be successful, it takes time to keep the class together as a group, and it keeps the student in the role of only receiving information instead of researching and delivering information according to their findings.

One way for learner-to-learner interaction to work in a technology classroom where students teach students is for the teacher to use screencasting technology as a tool for students to guide their own learning. The teacher can pair students up to research the function of a particular CAD feature, investigate and explore the feature firsthand, and then create a video tutorial using the screencast to explain what the feature is, how it works, and how it can be used. The library of video tutorials could then be accessed by students for future projects or assignments. Students can utilize their peers' work at their own pace, which is a version of learner-to-learner interaction through technology.

Creating a library of student-led tutorials checks many boxes, from student ownership, learner interaction, innovative technology use, and learner engagement. In my classroom, the student interaction that happened after developing a library of student-led tutorials was much different than the way content was taught in the past. With the library of tutorials accessible, students sought out conversation, dialogue, and interaction with students who created certain tutorials and were now viewed as experts on the topic. Students developed a trust in each other because of their ability to learn new concepts from what their peers produced. The teacher's role in all of this has changed from being the content knowledge expert and classroom manager to a facilitator and manager.

The teacher is now free to move about the room and help students who may be having problems and then focus on releasing the polished product. In my classroom, the amount of questions decreased because students were more focused on one problem rather than a list of problems. This scenario gives students a sense of control and ownership of the class content and the ability to explain the content using language and a process that is unique to other people of their own age group, which according to Conley and French (2013) is an important component to mastery of a concept. Using learner-to-learner interaction to guide students teaching students gives students the ability to use the work of their peers at the pace that they feel best fits their needs and feel more comfortable with their own learning.

Parents Using Technology to Teach Students

Parents and guardians can play an important role in the learning process that goes beyond monitoring their child's grades (Rubie-Davies, Peterson, Irving, Widdowson, & Dixon, 2010). Parents and guardians have a valuable wealth of experiences and knowledge that can inform and engage students. Technology can give classes the ability to call on that knowledge from home and use it as part of the learning process. A program like FlipGrid can be implemented to allow and encourage parents and guardians to engage in course content. An example from my class of parents interacting with students using technology allowed parents to become the teacher. Using FlipGrid, students went home to find a tool, gadget, or object at their house that their parents used but that the student did not have much experience with. Some students chose power tools, other students selected kitchen appliances, and some students identified dated items like rotary phones, VCRs, and old video games. The students used FlipGrid to post a video about how they thought the item was used based on a visual inspection. In a Tech Ed or Pre-Engineering course, this assignment would be geared toward research and Visual/Functional/Structural Analysis of an object. The second part of the FlipGrid assignment required a second video prompt where students had to find someone at home (parent or guardian) who knew what the gadget/tool/object did and then explained or demonstrated what it does. The scenario prompts students to investigate all aspects of visual, functional, and structural analysis to form a hypothesis and then present their hypothesis according to their observations. The scenario then prompts the student to call on the knowledge and experience of somebody at home to help teach them something that they do not understand. The scenario finally prompts students to document the entire process using presentation skills. Once again, the teacher has taken on the role of a facilitator. Several teachers in the technology program found that after completing the assignment, they were surprised to find that students who were less likely to talk in a classroom setting were so willing to communicate using a different means of communication like a video captured from a phone or computer. Teachers were also surprised at the amount of positive feedback that they received from parents during and after the assignment. Parents truly enjoyed the opportunity to teach their child something in the kitchen, garage, or house. The videos also showed that their children enjoyed it as well when they were working alongside their parent or guardian during the activity.

After this activity was over some teachers realized how they could use this type of interaction as an effective tool with their students. Teachers realized that they could give students the ability to communicate with them indirectly if they gave them a video response prompt that could not be visible by other students. Students could use FlipGrid or video responses as a communication route to explain any problems that they were having without having to approach teachers directly during class. In addition, some teachers found that this could also be another effective way to approach exit slips.

Teachers Using Technology to Teach Teachers

Like new teaching methods, Professional Learning Communities (PLC) have also become part of the norm within many schools and content departments. A professional learning community is a group of teachers who teach similar content and work together to develop activities, assessments, or resources to teach their classes. In my past experiences as an educator, I came to realize that many educators were simply focused on their own classroom and students and never found time or reason to get away to see what other educators were doing in their own classrooms. The absence of the colleague dialogue, especially within the same department or content area, allowed for curriculum and content overlap/deficiency, the inability to share teaching methods and ideas, and the inability to develop as a professional and person. The establishment of PLCs within schools and departments have countered those trends but only within that school. As discussed by Lieberman and Miller (2011), these meetings are ongoing and meant for growth by the community. Many teachers have the opportunity to grow professionally at state and regional conferences or regional institute, but few opportunities exist within their own buildings. The concept of teachers teaching teachers is not a new concept by any means but has been much more difficult to address due to distance and the availability of networking opportunities. However, the introduction of social media has given educators the tools and ability to remedy these problems.

Burbules (2016) describes the behaviors on social media and includes how collaboration toward a goal is a way social media can be used in professional development. Social media platforms like Facebook and Twitter with the help of YouTube can be used in a way to communicate all the great things that are happening in a teacher's classroom to the world. Many educators have even adopted the philosophy that if others do not see what they are doing in their classroom then it is not happening. Blogs, especially Video Blogs (Vlogs) are a great way for educators to share their ideas with other educators. Through the use of screencast software, slideshows, or written tutorials, educators can begin creating these resources to share using short daily or weekly "shows" for others to reference or to use as resources. Software or projects that require a process are great ways to share ideas with other educators to help them in their own classroom or to give them ideas to build off of. The exponential growth that can happen in social media due to sharing and posting can link educators throughout the world. The number of ideas and information that educators can use from social media can be used in their own school's PLC groups as an added resource. Some educators are now saying that most of the ideas that they are getting for their classrooms are not coming from textbooks or conversations but from social media alone.

Taking a chance to learn something new, especially when it comes to technology, can improve teaching and students' learning (Nawzad, Rahim, & Said, 2018). Taking developmental risks can be challenging at times, but the risk is worth the reward. Teachers are preparing a new generation of learners who use technology on a regular basis and in innovative ways. If students are using their own technology, teachers need to challenge themselves to find new ways to create interaction with those technologies and with all stakeholders. Technology opens avenues for bringing learning and classrooms to the rest of the world, whether it's to other students, parents, community members, or administrators. Interactions with technology gives educators the opportunity to see what is going on in individual classes and leads to important opportunities for collaboration and learning.

REFERENCES

Altemueller, L., & Lindquist, C. (2017). Flipped classroom instruction for inclusive learning. *British Journal of Special Education, 44*(3), 341–358.

Burbules, N. C. (2016). How we use and are used by social media in education. *Educational Theory, 66*(4), 551–565.

Capone, V., Donizzetti, A. R., & Petrillo, G. (2018). Classroom relationships, sense of community, perceptions of justice, and collective efficacy for students' social well-being. *Journal of Community Psychology, 46*(3), 374–382.

Conley, D. T., & French, E. (2013). Student ownership of learning as a key component of college readiness. *American Behavioral Scientist, 58*(8), 1018–1034.

Hirsch, E. D. (2011). Beyond comprehension: We have yet to adopt a common core curriculum that builds knowledge grade by grade – But we need to. *American Educator, 34*(4), 30–36.

Lieberman, A., & Miller, L. (2011). The starting point of professional learning is in schools and classrooms. *Learning Communities, 32*(4), 16–20.

Nawzad, L., Rahim, D., & Said, K. W. (2018). The effectiveness of technology for improving the teaching of natural science subjects. *Indonesian Journal of Curriculum and Educational Technology Studies, 6*(1), 15–21.

Peranginangin, S. A., Saragih, S., & Siagian, P. (2019). Development of learning materials through PBL with karo culture context to improve students' problem solving ability and self-efficacy. *International Electronic Journal of Mathematics Education, 14*(2), 265–274.

Rubie-Davies, C. M., Peterson, E., Irving, E., Widdowson, D., & Dixon, R. (2010). Expectations of achievement: Student, teacher and parent perceptions. *Research in Education, 83*(1), 36–53. https://doi.org/10.7227/rie.83.4

Rusli, M., Degeng, N. S., Setyosari, P., & Sulton. (2020). Peer teaching: Students teaching students to increase academic performance. *Teaching Theology and Religion, 21*(19), 1–11. https://doi.org/10.1111/teth.12549

van Laar, E., van Deursen, A. J. A. M., van Dijk, J. A. G. M., & de Haan, J. (2020). Determinants of 21st-century skills and 21st-century digital skills for workers: A systematic literature review. *SAGE Open*. https://doi.org/10.1177/2158244019900176

CHAPTER 10

Remote Learning and the Democratization of the Student-Teacher Relationship

Larissa Pahomov

INTRODUCTION

For schoolteachers, our work lives in our classrooms. As a result, our practice has traditionally been defined by the spaces and systems that exist in the physical world. Worksheets, gradebooks, daily schedules, and the layout of our classrooms – they all speak volumes about what we want students to learn and how we expect them to move through school and the world. In many cases, teachers are active designers of these elements. At other times, they are provided or mandated by school administrators. And in some cases, the elements are so deeply ingrained in the paradigm of school that they are universally practiced without question.

The past decade has seen an explosion in learning technology being added to the teacher's toolkit. Access to these technologies requires a physical device but then offers a wide range of virtual tools that have an equally wide range of implications for classroom practice. Many of those programs seek to augment or even eliminate tasks completed by a live instructor, through videos that can teach a student math (Khan Academy), plug-ins that correct their writing (Grammarly), and programs that can assess the quality of their accent in a foreign language (Rosetta Stone). However, the learning technologies that have been most widely adopted are designed to help teachers transfer their own practices into the online realm, as opposed to fundamentally transforming how teaching and learning happens. The pop-up opening screen for Google Classroom declares that the program "helps classes communicate, save time, and stay organized" – working as a hybrid of an assignment book for students

DOI: 10.4324/9781003089704-14

and a gradebook for teachers. There are apps for multiple-choice quizzes and other testing assessments and ones that allow teachers to turn their paper worksheets into digital ones.

While these learning-facilitation technologies do not promise a transformation of learning the way others do, their adoption can still fundamentally change how teachers and students operate. This chapter seeks to explore how learning technology design alters teacher interactions with students, with a special focus on whether these interactions become egalitarian and democratized. My original plan for this research was to focus exclusively on Science Leadership Academy, a public high school in Philadelphia which has had a 1:1 laptop program since opening its doors in 2006, and where teachers carefully integrate online learning technologies into a primarily in-person learning environment. However, the sudden catastrophic outbreak of COVID-19 has forced teachers nationwide to adapt to teaching exclusively online – so later research also included educators who were unexpectedly thrown into using learning-facilitation technologies that they had not actively chosen. This revolution can be adequately described as "future shock," which occurs "when you are confronted by the fact that the world you were educated to believe in doesn't exist" (Postman & Weingarten, 1969, p. 14). In addition to the ideological shock of a world brought to its knees by COVID-19, virtual learning was a novel development for almost all high school teachers – suddenly the entirety of their practice had to be contained by online tools, instead of just playing a supporting role. To explore the contrasts effectively, I looked at both synchronous and asynchronous interactions and the different technologies that teachers had to use as replacement venues for these exchanges.

TRADITIONAL SYNCHRONOUS STUDENT-TEACHER INTERACTION

In order to effectively assess how learning technologies may have transformed interactions when schools adopted remote learning, we must first consider what came before. Traditionally, teachers had two media through which they could interact with their students: verbally or via analog writing. For synchronous interactions – instruction in a physical classroom – diagrams can help illustrate the most common flows of communication.

If a teacher is participating in a lecture format, content is being pushed out to every student – although that act is not an interaction in and of itself. Lectures are typically paired with question and answer

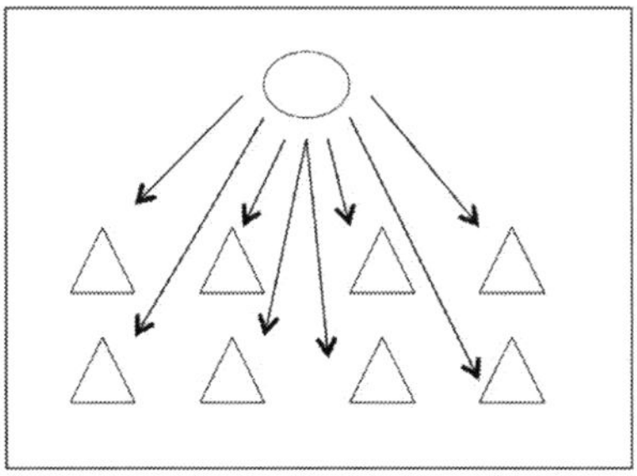

Figure 10.1 Lecture Format

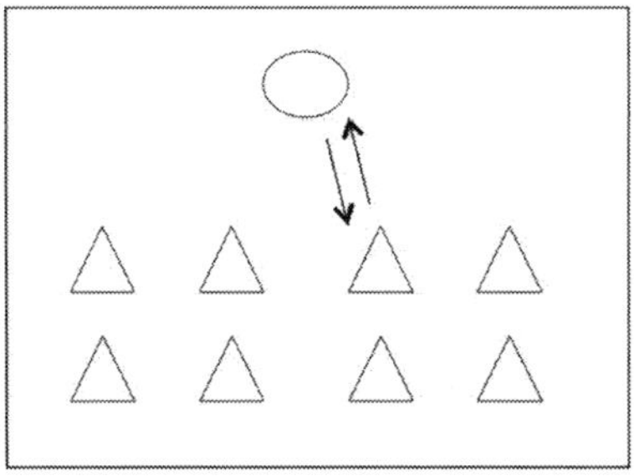

Figure 10.2 Question and Answer

sessions – one student can direct their query to the teacher, and the teacher can respond, with other students as passive observers. Visualizations of these two formats are provided in Figures 10.1 and 10.2.

A seminar setup gives students easy access to all faces and voices in the room. The teacher can either be a floating presence or situate themselves into the setup. This physical arrangement awards each speaker the same level of prominence, a visual suggestion that the actors in the room are more equal (which may or may not be confirmed by what the teacher says or does). Figures 10.3 and 10.4 illustrate the variations in these two arrangements.

A small group setup allows for a greater variety of interactions. The teacher can still push out information from the front of the room, but the design also allows for students to interact with each other and makes physical space for there to be more organic and free-flowing interactions between the teacher and students. Like the seminar, it assumes that the learning is centered with the students. Figure 10.5 illustrates the physical impact of this setup.

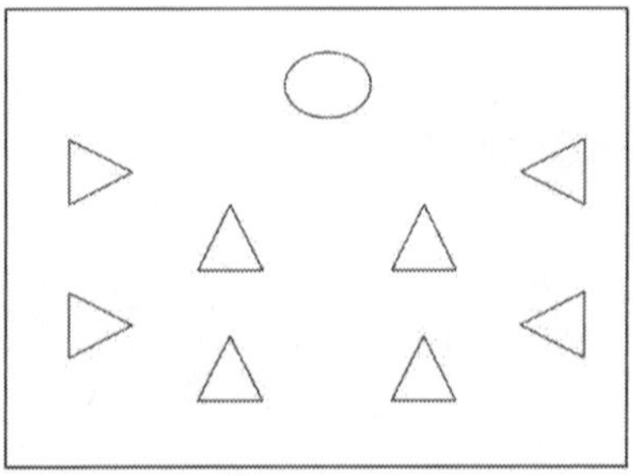

Figure 10.3 U-Shaped Seminar

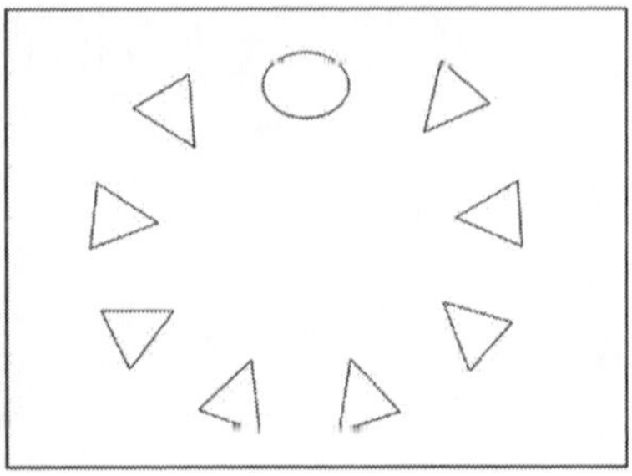

Figure 10.4 Seminar in the Round

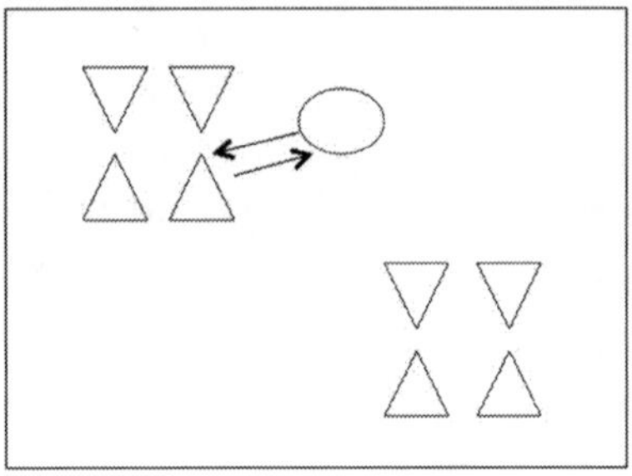

Figure 10.5 Small Group Setup

For the most part, students are expected to remain stationary in a classroom setting, with the teacher coming to them as necessary. Exceptions are when the teacher invites students to approach their desk or other meeting station for consultation, or when students are entering or leaving the room. Teachers may leverage these moments of transition

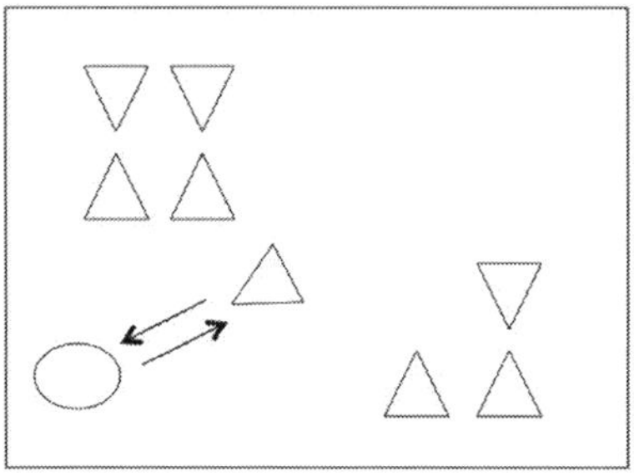

Figure 10.6 Classroom Consultation

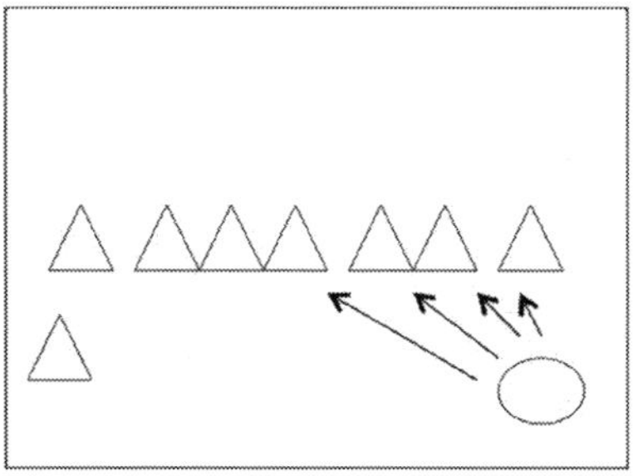

Figure 10.7 Check-Ins at the Door

by greeting students at the door individually, or requesting an "exit slip" or some other kind of checkout function as students leave. These two scenarios are depicted in Figures 10.6 and 10.7.

TRADITIONS OF ASYNCHRONOUS STUDENT-TEACHER INTERACTION

The most common reason for interaction between students and teachers outside of the physical classroom is via the review of student work. After students hand in materials, there are a number of ways that the teacher may interact with that work:

- By providing free-form written feedback.
- By assessing it based on a predetermined rubric.
- By assigning a numerical or letter grade.

If and when work is returned to students, there are also a number of ways that it may be handled:

- The work is collected in a folder or portfolio.
- The work is publicly displayed in the classroom.
- No system is provided for what happens.

Before online media existed, these moments almost always happened within the same routine – students complete work, and then teachers comment on it. Like the question and answer portion of a lecture, this format at its most minimal is not truly a dialogue. The student presents a question or work, and the teacher acts as authority in responding. Should the student want to continue that dialogue, they must take the initiative and make a successful bid for the teacher's time and attention. As anyone knows who has watched a teacher hand back an exam or essay and then be inundated with questions from their students, getting the teacher's attention can be quite difficult! Conscientious teachers will set up avenues for these dialogues to continue and encourage students to engage; teachers seeking to defend their authority will do the opposite.

As in a physical classroom, asynchronous communication directly between students can be engineered but requires a baseline of both accessibility and interest on the part of those students. As the assessor and assigner of grades, teachers will always be approached by their students. The teacher must create equally urgent reasons for students to communicate with each other – either through intrinsic or extrinsic motivations – in order for students to turn their attention away from their individual achievement and towards each other.

DEMOCRATIZATION AND THE INTERNET

As mentioned in the introduction to this chapter, the term "learning technology" refers to a wide range of apps, websites, and programs that all seek to interface with – and in some cases, transform or supplant – the physical world of schools.

However, these learning technologies only facilitate a tiny fraction of learning on the internet. Users can instantly access any facts or figures they want to know – thus decreasing the necessity for memorization. John Dewey (1990) saw this shift even 100 years ago: "Knowledge is no longer an immobile solid; it has been liquefied. It is actively moving in all the currents of society itself" (p. 25). Online audio and video expand that to include discrete skills, from how to play a musical instrument to learning a foreign language. Likewise, the all-access mindset of social media and online forums allows for communication where every voice is given equal volume or equal space on a discussion thread. As a result, many of the skills and activities that were once seen as the exclusive domain of a classroom teacher can be pursued in online venues with complete autonomy on the part of the learner.

Some of these democratizing effects have been embraced by traditional learning institutions and incorporated into their practices, at least in part. Many large universities have developed Massive Online Open Courses and made some of their most popular content available to online users for free. However, there are other elements of traditional education that remain closely guarded by their practitioners. Part of this refusal to transform reflects schools seeking to protect their status from being cheapened by universal access. Even Harvard University has established MOOCs, but credits earned from these courses cannot be counted toward actual degrees from the school. It also reflects a belief that education directly benefits from greater quantity and quality of interaction with a teacher, a mindset confirmed by a recent study of the completion rates of university MOOCs (Kizilcec et al., 2020).

Prior to the COVID-19 shutdown, students and teachers all had some experience with autonomous, online learning and may have attempted to bring those benefits into the classroom. However, the shift to remote learning forced those two previously more separate worlds to combine in ways that had not previously been attempted.

TEACHER EXPERIENCES

Six teachers were interviewed for this research, five of whom teach in Philadelphia:

- Clarice Brazas, Humanities, The U School.
- Marita Fitzpatrick, Art, Bodine High School.
- Victor Hernandez, Math and Computer Science, Science Leadership Academy, Center City.
- Pearl Jonas, History, Science Leadership Academy, Center City.
- Amit Schwalb, Biology and Finance, Saul Agricultural High School.

And one in Los Angeles:

- Rabiya Kassam-Clay, History, John Marshall High School.

They reported major changes in how they interacted with students, both synchronously and asynchronously. Each of these areas provided opportunities for shifting their practice, as well as points of frustration when the technology limited what they hoped to achieve – all a reminder that the "social reality" in which we teach is neither created nor transformed by chance (Freire, 1970, p. 32).

Synchronous Student Teacher Interaction

While the amount required varied by school district, all teachers whose schools closed due to COVID-19 were expected to provide instruction via live video feed. A few design elements played a major role in how the classroom power dynamics shifted during this time. The visual layout of these programs replaced the layout of a physical classroom, which challenged how students and teachers should interact in a space. And the ability to toggle the audio and video functions on and off – as well contribute, or not, via text in the chat function – hands an unprecedented level of control to students.

Video Meetings

The layout of video meetings can be customized by each viewer – the screen of one participant can show one face or many. Both Zoom and Google Meet default to showing the current speaker on a majority of the screen, with a few additional images tiled along the margin. This arrangement places emphasis on the speaker but renders other participants invisible if the number of users goes beyond a handful, since they get pushed off screen.

Users can circumvent this setting by selecting a "gallery" or "tile" view, which displays most or all participant video feeds at once. Notably, Google Meet did not originally have this feature built into its program, and required users to download a "grid view" plugin to make it possible. This visual layout allows teachers and students to view each other in a way that can be even more egalitarian than a seminar format. Each participant is granted the same amount of space on the screen, and because the arrangement of the different feeds is randomized, no participant occupies a more central, powerful space than another.

Several teachers reported that the "grid view" option was essential to making remote live instruction resemble anything close to their regular classroom. Pearl Jonas used it from the beginning of her online teaching, and at her urging many of her students downloaded it as well. "Video instruction would have probably felt more out of my control if I hadn't planned for the platform," she admitted. Of course, the opportunity for human connection in this format depends on how many faces ended up on the screen. In Jonas's freshman classes, the fact that 35 or 40 students (from multiple sections of the course) attended each week, crowded out the possibility for spontaneous interaction via video or audio. As a result, the class "felt very teacher-centered" – a gallery of faces were present, but they were unable to build discussion. However, her senior courses had a lower attendance rate, which allowed them to interact without speaking over each other, thus making the course still feel student-centered.

Amit Schwalb found his students seeking a middle ground and turning on audio only during their online classes, effectively turning class into a conference call. He's not sure why they chose this particular medium for interaction, but a result was that his teaching "felt much more teacher-directed. It felt easier to go off script in your physical classroom. . . . In this version, I got less interaction out of the students."

Video Chat Functions

Schools with high levels of technology integration already use live chats during in-person instruction as a kind of back channel, with the intention of offering different modes that may appeal to different learning styles. The lower bar to entry, combined with the pressures of living life under lockdown, made this medium the preferred mode of communication for many, with teachers adjusting their communication methods accordingly.

Marita Fitzpatrick, an art teacher at Bodine High School in Philadelphia, reported that in the first days of the COVID-19 shutdown she tried to engage students in verbal conversation but that they had an overwhelming preference for communicating in the chat feature of Google Meet. When asked why they wouldn't turn on their cameras, some students reported that they did not look presentable for their peers – "We haven't been to the barber, we're still in our PJs" – while others stated they wanted the video off for privacy reasons or had heard they weren't supposed to show their faces in the first place. While the lack of visual connection was disorienting for Fitzpatrick at first, she quickly adapted, presenting her conversation prompts and then watching student responses in the chat, and reading them out loud so they would be captured in the live recording of the class, which she was required to post online for students who could not attend. In this way, Fitzpatrick was able to amplify and respond to student commentary – although she described this process as feeling "ADHD" because it required her both to read out content and questions from her own plan while reading and formulating responses to the constant thread of chat comments. This space is also one where students can wander from or actively disrupt the teacher's plan. While the off-topic discussion did not create an auditory disruption the way it would in a physical space, Fitzpatrick would still occasionally redirect students who began to tease each other in the chat and once kicked a student out of the Google Meet when he did not take the redirection.

While Fitzpatrick mostly regarded video instruction as inferior to her live classroom, she also observed upsides to the format. The kind of management she had to implement in a physical space melted away, making space for learners who had previously been in the background. She stated:

> I think some kids [they had] felt more access to me – when I'm in the classroom, it's so busy, kids are getting materials and walking around the classroom, I'm dealing with the boisterous kids. That all disappeared. I got to really engage with pretty much all the quiet kids, they really felt that I met a need that wasn't being met before. A couple of quiet kids would come to the [class] meeting first – they came every time – and we would have a little conversation before anybody joined. I would give them feedback and they would come back.

Pearl Jonas reported that her larger class – freshmen in African American history – also preferred the chat function, whereas seniors were more willing to use the audio and video features. While she encouraged all attendees to have their video on, many would only speak up when the activity required them to do so. However, the chat function was a place where an organic classroom culture did begin to grow. "Students could more freely comment on something from class using the chat," Jonas noted. "For example, the chat provided a space to celebrate Kahoot winners or vote on a question." The course was built around watching episodes of the civil rights documentary *Eyes on the Prize*, and Jonas noted that chat participation increased once students were asked to role play as members of the Student Non-Violent Coordinating Committee (SNCC) and vote on potential future actions.

Some video meeting programs also made it possible for teachers to replicate small group instruction by creating breakout rooms, where students could have more intimate conversations or complete other joint tasks. In this setup, the teacher also has the capacity to visit each room at will. Rabiya Kassam-Clay, a high school social studies teacher in Los Angeles, used this feature while teaching freshmen history during her school's COVID-19 shutdown. Her regular classroom setup included "conversation quartets," where groups of four would be expected to discuss as a group once or twice per class period. For remote learning, the practice "felt like a slightly less curated version than what I normally do" – groups were assigned more randomly, and then Kassam-Clay would visit each room one at a time as her students engaged with the prompt. "I think they did really well. . . . When I dropped into breakout groups, it sounded like it did in my classroom." This success was tempered somewhat by small design issues with the Zoom videoconferencing technology. "For students who didn't have . . . audio or video on the group call, we could get around that [in whole-class instruction] with the chat – but then because breakout groups didn't have their own dedicated chat spaces, that was a challenge to find ways to interact." This challenge would have been gladly welcomed by teachers in Philadelphia, where the district required that all online instruction take place on Google Meet, which did not offer small group breakouts at the time of the shutdown.

Of course, the video feed also gives more agency to participants by allowing them to shut off both their microphones or video feeds at will – and there's no easy way for teachers to re-engage these students the way they could in a physical space. Several teachers reported frustration with students who would log on but not give any visual or auditory sign that they were in fact listening in. Fitzpatrick reported: "That anonymity – you were kind of wondering, is anybody even out there?" This feature is arguably another example of how online learning handed more autonomy to the students and required teachers to reinvent their protocols for getting students to tune in. Clarice Brazas created flexible instruction for her students by pre-recording the instructions at the start of each week, and then also communicating the plan via a live session. She would then host "support sessions" on Wednesdays and Fridays, where "people could ask questions, but sometimes kids just came to hang out" and talk about how their day was going. This flexible setup provided different pathways for students to connect with her – and those that utilized the support sessions had the highest levels of assignment completion throughout the shutdown.

Ultimately, the way that video instruction operated depended on whether the teachers' or students' vision of interaction prevailed. All of the teachers interviewed pushed for video instruction to mimic a physical classroom space as closely as possible, with all faces visible and voices heard. However, based on their style of engagement, students may have seen this phase of school less like a virtual classroom and more like a live streaming event on social media – one that they would watch along with their peers as if through a two-way mirror, and possibly interact with via text. On one hand, the selective invisibility of students makes it harder for teachers to engineer authentic interaction between students – it effectively forces them into a lecture format. On the other hand, the power that students have to cloak themselves can be seen as its own form of democratization. By taking away the ability for teachers to demand a response face-to-face, students were able to opt in on their terms, forcing teachers to adapt accordingly.

Asynchronous Student-Teacher Interactions

Media theorist Douglas Rushkoff (2010) describes the "timeless" early qualities of online message boards and email exchanges as one that allowed "the kind of deliberation and contemplation that couldn't happen in the harried real world of jobs, kids, and automobiles" (p. 29). Rushkoff acknowledges that the quality of this exchange was bolstered by the fact that most of life was spent offline. Educators in the COVID-19 shutdown faced an inverse situation, where the *only* media they had for connection were virtual channels. All of the teachers I interviewed already used some kind of learning technology prior to the shutdown for communicating about student work, but this medium was always secondary to in-person interaction. With that avenue closed to them, they all recognized asynchronous interaction as the best opportunity for authentic dialogue with students – but to take advantage of that opportunity required a serious readjustment of how and when teachers sought to connect.

For Amit Schwalb, the expanded use of Google Classroom provided this space. A learning management system that can serve as both a home for curriculum and online gradebook, Schwalb already used the program to "occasionally" post assignments and educational resources. After the shutdown, it became the exclusive home for both content and assignments. As a result, the comments section of an assignment became a place where students could – and did – ask questions about a particular task, or respond to the grade or feedback they received once the work was turned in. This included students who did not attend Schwalb's live classes – often because they had conflicts with work schedules or taking care of siblings. "My main form of interacting with them became reading and looking at their work and leaving them comments. I definitely gave more written feedback than I normally do."

The proliferation of written dialogue drew Schwalb's attention to the fact that there was no natural space for it in his usual classroom setup. "I did all my grading externally, and then put it in SIS [the district's online gradebook], and use the comment bank . . . where I could state basic performance issues or celebration." That online gradebook, from which the school district pulls data for its quarterly report cards, offered no space for students to respond. For work handed back in person, "I would occasionally write comments on paper – and I guess a student could comment back – but it was very uncommon," Schwalb reported. When he was forced to adopt Google Classroom for all assignments, however, he also began using the comment bank feature, which meant students now had personalized feedback *and* a space to respond.

Fitzpatrick also reported that the necessary use of Google Classroom created a new and potentially more interactive space for dialogue with students. As an art teacher who was used to giving guidance as she physically observed work in progress, she was now more limited to commenting only on work when it was formally submitted. She reported:

> I typed out feedback that I would have previously shared in a discussion with students. It made me more aware of what I was saying. I also realized that I had to be cognizant of recognizing what students did well, in addition to telling them what they could have done better.

In her pre-shutdown classroom, there were also interactions around work, but primarily about scores, not content. "Previously, kids would come talk to me as soon as I posted a grade on SIS that they must have had notifications on. In that system, you can't write comments. That also isn't designed for art teachers." In Google Classroom, the benefit of the comments box was apparent. When Fitzpatrick provided feedback on a submitted assignment, "students replied most of the time. Sometimes they just said 'thank you.' Sometimes they asked follow up questions or justified the decisions that they made. It was nice; they could tell me their thoughts on something." By contrast, at the U School and the SLA – buildings where students already had a 1:1 laptop program and were used to electronic communication with their teachers – students continued to rely on email as their primary medium for communication about coursework.

This process of online communication also had its wrinkles. In a classroom setting, there are a limited number of times and places where the student can submit work. By contrast, students can upload an assignment to Google Classroom whenever they wish – but teachers do not automatically know it's happened the way they do when a paper is handed to them. Managing coursework can then fall into the same cycle of notifications and checking in that is commonly seen in email, text messaging, and other formats. Fitzpatrick turned on her Google Classroom notifications but would also selectively ignore her email until she was ready to devote time to actually reviewing work. This logistical practice supported her teaching philosophy. "Being in art, nothing's ever finished. Everything could always use more work. You want to turn it in again? I'll fix your grade. You can revise it four or five times with me." Rolling submissions made notifications all the more useful.

When leveraged correctly, teachers had an unprecedented level of connection with their students. However, the design of these learning management systems impeded other interactions. Schwalb noted that Google Classroom "doesn't allow students to answer questions with attachments, only text." In his biology classroom, he "wanted students to be able to see and respond to their peers' pictures of their natural environments, but it wasn't really possible." Because this particular learning technology had no place designed for student-to-student interaction, Schwalb ended up feeling like his online courses were much more "teacher-directed" than in his usual setup. "Students interacted with each other much less. There was no formalized 'think-pair-share' – no whiteboard stuff – no informal kids talking in class – all of that was happening less. There were so few kids, I didn't even go there." Like Kassam-Clay's small group breakouts, these technologies are not always designed for interactions that will take place *independent* of the main facilitator, in this case the teacher.

Likewise, Fitzpatrick could not easily engineer a way for her class to engage in student-centered critique of work. In her art room, she would have students hang works in progress around the room, with many simultaneous conversations happening at once. In a video classroom with no breakout room option, this kind of collaboration was difficult to organize. When students submitted artwork via Google Classroom, Fitzpatrick could access and share, but not more than one at a time – the turn-in feature was only accessible to the teacher on the back end of the technology. Because feedback in the formative stage of creation was so logistically difficult, students received less formative guidance while they worked. She stated:

> I do feel strongly that students can learn from each other – and kids are on all different levels in the art room. Some kids have had training since kindergarten and know how to do everything, and some kids have no experience, and if I sit them next to each other they will learn from each other.

It challenged and then transformed Fitzpatrick's understanding of her role as a teacher – when she polled students on what they wanted to learn, she then recorded drawing tutorials and posted them so students could access the instruction on their own time. The lack of peer feedback also compelled her to provide more commentary herself. "It has made me reevaluate what I do," she said. The idea of more feedback to kids is important now. I just never had time to give them all feedback. Now I feel like I have to."

With a learning technology designed to facilitate only private teacher-student interaction, teachers need a less specific tool if they want the dialogue to be more varied. Math teacher Victor Hernandez facilitates project work in his class by setting up a shared Google Doc where students are presented with vocabulary essential to the new unit. Then he leaves space for them to type responses to the prompts "I notice . . .", "I wonder . . .", and "what if . . ." so that Hernandez can assess where students stand. The more open system fits into his teaching philosophy, with some technological drawbacks:

> I want to know common patterns of misunderstanding and curiosity early and I want students to feel like they have access. The only pain is that Google Docs are hard to edit by multiple people at the same time, so there has to be some hand-holding so that previously entered text is not deleted.

Like the chat feature in Google Meet, typing in a shared document allows all participants to both share and absorb. This democratizes the learning process overall, according to Hernandez, because it "makes it possible for students to learn from each other's research and curiosity. . . . Students are more engaged in the initial ramp-up of a unit and don't have to rely on the teacher for context and introduction." This document also helps close the unit, where students can revisit and assess if their questions were answered.

Hernandez also relies on Desmos, an online math tool that allows him to assign specific problems or functions to an entire class. Then the tool provides him with a bird's-eye view of what each student has accomplished. Hernandez explained that this feature "lets me find patterns in understanding and misunderstanding in a convenient way that lets me base my decisions on how to continue on data from the whole class." Because these tools were already in use before the shutdown, they were easy to carry over to work that students were doing from home.

When schools closed and in-person meetings were made impossible, asynchronous interactions increased – in part because they had nothing to compete with. However, increased written exchange also reflected that, for many students, it feels easier to type than to say it out loud. At its best, the situation "fostered a depth of engagement and collaborative spirit" (Rushkoff, 2010, p. 30) that the pressures of live interaction can stifle. Just as with the chat function in video meetings, students who might not have had the courage to speak up in a noisy classroom or visit a teacher during office hours were now faced with an empty comments box that they could fill out from the comfort of their own home.

LIMITATIONS AND LESSONS

In no way can this chapter be taken as a comprehensive survey of how teachers fared during the shift to online teaching during COVID-19. Even during their individual interviews, teachers were quick to identify all of the mitigating factors that made it hard to assess why things played out the way they did. Students and teachers were thrown into these systems with little or no preparation. The global crisis created huge logistical and psychological barriers to learning, and many teachers were in districts that did not make this instruction count toward report card grades, effectively making attendance and assignment completion optional. In Philadelphia, schools closed with no advance notice, which meant that students went home without any materials for a longer absence from their regular learning environments. For Fitzpatrick, that meant that some students had zero art supplies to work with, leading her to make all of her assignments have an art research and appreciation option. For Schwalb, teaching biology at an agricultural high school with a working farm meant a curriculum which made active use of the outdoors impossible due to the shutdown.

In some cases, this decreased engagement made it harder for teachers and students to interact democratically. In other cases, it made more time and space for the students who *did* engage, and the lightened load felt liberating for teachers who could finally give the level of individual attention that their typical teaching schedule would never allow. As Schwalb reported about his classroom:

> I see more value in the process of feedback, revision, feedback, etc. But this is completely impossible given the structure of my school, the lackluster leadership of my current union leadership, and the criminal inequities in school funding. It would be so difficult to give meaningful, individualized feedback consistently and to give feedback on multiple revisions when I'm teaching 3 different subject areas and 200 students at a time.

All agreed that the many factors of the pandemic did nothing to improve learning outcomes for their students. And yet all teachers reported on how their instruction also felt more necessary, and more urgent, than it had ever felt before – for reasons that often had nothing to do with the assigned content and that managed to transcend the moments where online media felt otherwise limiting. In Fitzpatrick's art class, the discussion topics always touched on the state of the world, and students responded in kind. She said,

> I found that the students who, from the beginning, came . . . returned each time because the Meets met a need they had for something more than a place to make art, but a place to talk, ask questions, and get support.

According to Brazas, in the future, "Investing in student well-being will be more of a priority because I believe when students feel safe and welcome, they will actually produce more in class." Brazas reported that teaching during the pandemic affirmed her belief that her primary role as an educator is to "trust kids, give them tools, provide them with structure and interesting material and make sure they will be able to ask critical questions when they enter the world." The social tumult and movement for justice in the year of the pandemic only strengthened Brazas' commitment to these beliefs: "I think we need to be more involved in our students' home lives . . . and communities. Education doesn't stop at the school door where kids 'real lives' pick up; it should be ingrained in the way we are all living." And Kassam-Clay framed it as a glass half full: "Without each other, our pandemic experience would have been worse. So we needed each other, and that was a deepening of interaction, for communion and purpose and routine and reflection. Not just in terms of the day to day stuff – we talked about that fact too – the pandemic and the uprising, what it meant to experience that together, and how each of us were doing. And that deepened some of the emotional connections."

CONCLUSION

At the start of these interviews, I expected to produce a very specific, granular analysis of a handful of learning technologies and how they influenced student-teacher interaction in a "normal" learning environment. Instead, I found teachers reflecting on how the *entirety* of classroom interactions evolved when forced into online media. When we do not occupy a physical space together, we cannot compel each other to participate via the traditional methods we are accustomed to. Here, as in so many areas of life during the pandemic, educators were challenged to "break with the past and imagine their world anew" (Roy, 2020, para 52). When teachers were able to accept this decreased level of authority – both when students opted *out* of interacting, and also when they chose to opt *in* – they experienced refreshingly authentic connections with their students. Online learning programs were not designed to nudge participants toward this level of engagement – but moving forward, it is possible for teachers to encourage connection by continuing to embrace the many avenues that these technologies offer for students to speak up.

REFERENCES

Dewey, J. (1990). *The school and society*. Chicago, IL: University of Chicago Press.
Freire, P. (1970). *Pedagogy of the oppressed*. New York: Continuum.
Kizilcec, R. F., Reich, J., Yeomans, M., Dann, C., Brunskill, E., Lopez, G., . . . & Tingley, D. (2020). Scaling up behavior science interventions in online education. *Proceedings in the Natural Academy of Sciences of the United States of America, 117*(26). http://doi.org/10.1073/pnas.1921417117
Postman, N., & Weingarten, C. (1969). *Teaching as a subversive activity*. New York: Delta Books.
Roy, A. (2020, April 3). The pandemic is a portal. *Financial Times Online*. Retrieved from www.ft.com/content/10d8f5e8-74eb-11ea-95fe-fcd274e920ca
Rushkoff, D. (2010). *Program or be programmed*. Berkeley: Soft Skull Press.

Index

Made in the USA
Las Vegas, NV
29 October 2024

7dbab937-8268-4c38-8831-e7c54533ca50R01